English Decoration in the 18th Century

English Decoration in the 18th Century

John Fowler and John Cornforth

THE PYNE PRESS PRINCETON

The authors would like to express their thanks to owners and institutions for permission to reproduce subjects in the following plates (colour indicated by Roman numerals, monochrome by italic):

By Gracious Permission of Her Majesty the Queen XI, *56, 69, 161*; Lady Teresa Agnew *23*; Sir Richard Anstruther-Gough-Calthorpe *84*; Art Institute of Chicago *80*; Boston Museum of Fine Arts *195*; British Museum *52, 53, 93*; Cooper Hewitt Museum, New York *127*; Sir William Gladstone *204*; Goodwood Collection *155*; Mr Lawrence Impey *58*; Mr Francis Johnson and Mr Edward Ingram *98*; Keats-Shelley Memorial Association, Rome *54*; London Museum *27*; Mr W. S. Lewis *160*; The Marquis of Linlithgow *72*; Metropolitan Museum of Art, New York (Gift of Samuel H. Kress Foundation *1958*) *22*; Mr and Mrs Paul Mellon *118, 159*; National Gallery of Ireland, Dublin *85*; National Library of Ireland, Dublin *13, 196*; National Monuments Record *1, 55, 70, 171, 203, 217, 233*; National Trust *19, 209, 222, 234*; Philadelphia Museum of Art *95*; Private Collection *37, 147, 194*; Redburn Gallery *152*; Rijksmuseum, Amsterdam *119, 120, 121*; Royal Institute of British Architects, London, I, XXIX, *11, 12*; Mr Reresby Sitwell XVI; Society of Antiquaries *168*; Tate Gallery *87, 97*; Trustees of the Chatsworth Settlement VI;

Victoria and Albert Museum *8, 10, 18, 20, 26, 32, 34, 36, 46, 47, 50, 60, 63, 64, 65, 66, 67, 71, 81, 82, 89, 96, 100, 103, 104, 107, 128, 133, 138, 145, 146, 148, 150, 151, 153, 156, 158, 164, 185, 189, 198, 199, 213, 223, 226,* XXIII; The Duke of Westminster XVIII; The Marquis of Zetland XV, *88, 113*.

In addition they would like to thank photographers and publications for the following:

The Connoisseur 57; *Country Life* XXV, XXVI, XXXIII, *2, 3, 4, 5, 6, 7, 9, 14, 15, 16, 17, 21, 24, 25, 28, 29, 30, 31, 33, 35, 38, 39, 40, 41, 42, 43, 44, 45, 48, 49, 51, 59, 61, 62, 68, 73, 74, 75, 76, 77, 78, 79, 83, 86, 90, 91, 92, 94, 99, 101, 102, 105, 106, 108, 109, 110, 111, 112, 114, 115, 122, 124, 125, 126, 129, 130, 131, 132, 134, 135, 136, 137, 139, 140, 141, 142, 143, 144, 149, 154, 157, 162, 165, 166, 167, 169, 170, 172, 173, 174, 175, 176, 177, 178, 179, 180, 181, 182, 183, 184, 186, 187, 188, 190, 191, 192, 193, 197, 201, 202, 205, 206, 207, 208, 210, 211, 212, 214, 215, 216, 218, 219, 220, 221, 224, 227, 229, 230, 231, 232*; John R. Freeman *26, 32, 36, 46, 47, 89, 96, 100, 103, 107, 128, 150, 156, 158, 189, 213, 223, 226*. Angelo Hornak II, III, IV, V, VII, VIII, IX, X, XII, XIII, XIV, XVII, XIX, XX, XXI, XXII, XXIV, XXVII, XXVIII, XXIX, XXX, XXXI, XXXII, XXXIV, XXXV, XXXVI, XXXVII, XXXVIII, XL, *116, 117, 225*; *House and Garden 228*; Edwin Smith *123*;

SBN 87861-075-8

Library of Congress Catalog Card Number 74-81180

First published 1974 by
Barrie & Jenkins, London

Manufactured in Great Britain

Contents

Introduction   7

Acknowledgments   · 9

List of Illustrations   10

1 The concept of the decorator   15

2 The quicksands of style and fashion   31

3 The uses of houses and their arrangement   56

4 The practice of the upholsterer   82

5 Colour and the painter's craft   174

6 The treatment of floors   210

7 Lighting and heating   220

8 Attitudes to pictures and picture hanging   231

9 Ladies' amusements   248

10 Care and housekeeping   254

11 A matter of balance   259

Selected bibliography   267

References   271

Index   284

Introduction

The aim of this book is to relate fashions and practices in English decoration in the classical period to contemporary documents and to show how many of them grew out of social attitudes and changing patterns of behaviour. Consequently the book is not a technical manual, although it contains a certain amount of material of a practical nature, but rather it is intended as a guide to sources of ideas and information: it is as much about "why" as "how".

In recent years there has been a great deal of research on the development of architectural style in the years 1660 to 1830, on furniture and furniture-makers, on decorative painting and plasterwork, and both authors would wish to acknowledge their debt to Sir John Summerson's *Architecture in Britain 1530-1830*, H. M. Colvin's *Biographical Dictionary of English Architects 1660-1840*, Percy Macquoid and Ralph Edwards' *Dictionary of English Furniture*, Edward Croft-Murray's *Decorative Painting in England 1537-1837* and Geoffrey Beard's *Georgian Craftsmen*. But whereas these standard works deal with more permanent elements of the English house, the emphasis here is on the more transitory aspects of decoration, on the uses of colour, style in upholstery and the arrangement of rooms. As to dates we have interpreted the 18th century rather freely so as to include references to work done both in the late 17th and early 19th century as being part of the classical period: in this we have been influenced by the dates covered by the standard works.

Both authors are concerned about the problems of preservation, restoration and presentation of country houses and indeed that is why they began to work on the book. So it has been encouraging to notice a growing interest in the subject during the course of the last four or five years; but at the same time it has become more and more apparent how much fundamental research is needed in this field. Consequently the authors hope not only that the book will be of help to those who have to look after and restore important interiors but that it will stimulate others to undertake research.

Acknowledgements

When we began work on this book, neither of us knew quite where it would lead us, and, while its deficiencies are our responsibility, we are greatly indebted to many friends and colleagues for advice, information and suggestions of inestimable value. Members of the Department of Furniture and Woodwork at the Victoria and Albert Museum have been particularly generous in telling us of original and comparative material. Peter Thornton was kind enough to read and comment on the manuscript, as did Gervase Jackson-Stops.

The many owners of the houses where we have worked in our different ways over the years also deserve our thanks, for what they have shown us in their houses and their papers has been the basis of the book.

We hope that the authors of books and articles from which we have quoted will regard the notes and bibliography as sufficient acknowledgment, but we would particularly like to express our debt not only to the generations who have contributed country house articles to *Country Life* but to the rising band who contribute to *Furniture History*. It is the researches of Geoffrey Beard, Anthony Coleridge, Christopher Gilbert, Nicholas Goodison and Ivan Hall as well as Peter Thornton, Desmond Fitz-Gerald and John Hardy who have started to make this subject possible.

A book of this kind is made by its illustrations, and here we would like to acknowledge our indebtedness to owners who have permitted photography in the past or consented to yet more intrusions for this book. In particular the Dowager Marchioness of Cholmondeley deserves our thanks in allowing us to include so many details from Houghton. All the new colour photographs and some of the black and white were specially taken for us by Angelo Hornak; a few colour transparencies were originally taken for *Country Life* by Alex Starkey, and Alex Starkey and Jonathan Gibson took many of the photographs provided by *Country Life*, while others were originally taken by their predecessors. To them too we express our thanks.

In the course of the last three years we have tried many people with our project, but Anne Hills has patiently coped with all the original manuscripts and turned them into typescript.

And Michael Hodson has suffered more than an Editor should in pulling all the strands together.

List of illustrations

Colour Plates

I   A sectional design by Sir William Chambers for York House, Pall Mall, London.

II   An unused piece of early 18th century embroidered yellow satin at Ham House, Surrey.

III, IV, V   Details of the boudoir at Attingham Park, Shropshire.

VI   A watercolour of the saloon at Devonshire House, London, in 1820.

VII, VIII   The late 17th century canopy from a state bed in the Long Gallery at Hardwick Hall, Derbyshire.

IX   A section of the base valance of the Spangle Bed at Knole, Kent.

X   The state bed at Dyrham Park, Gloucestershire.

XI   An unused fragment of cut velvet made for Queen Anne's Bed.

XII, XIII, XIV   The Green Velvet Bed at Houghton Hall, Norfolk.

XV   *Sir Lawrence Dundas and his grandson in the Library at 19 Arlington Street, London* by Zoffany.

XVI   *The Sitwell Children* by Copley.

XVII   A curtain valance in the White Drawing Room at Houghton, about 1797.

XVIII   Buckler's watercolour of the drawing room at Eaton Hall, Cheshire, in 1826.

XIX   The Reynolds Room at Knole.

XX   The Blue Drawing Room at Ham House.

XXI   Crimson flock paper at Clandon Park, Surrey, about 1730.

XXII   Flock paper by Reveillon at Clandon, about 1780.

XXIII   A section of a panel of Lyons silk, about 1785.

XXIV   The White Drawing Room at Houghton.

XXV, XXVI   Modern examples of traditional trimmings, fringes, gimps and tassels.

XXVII   The saloon at Clandon.

XXVIII   A drawing of a panelled room marked out for painting.

XXIX, XXX   Enriched entablatures at Clandon.

XXXI, XXXII   The Marble Parlour at Houghton.

XXXIII   Part of a painted doorcase at West Wycombe Park, Buckinghamshire.

XXXIV, XXXV, XXXVI   Details of gilding in the state bedroom at Blickling Hall, Norfolk.

XXXVII, XXXVIII   The Balcony Room at Dyrham.

XXXIX   Malton's view of the Great Room at Portman House, London.

XL   A detail of a carved and painted bed at Alnwick Castle, Northumberland.

Monochrome Figures

1   The saloon at Wimborne House, Arlington Street, London, about 1890.
2   The saloon at Beningbrough Hall, Yorkshire, in 1927.
3, 4   Bedrooms at Kelmarsh Hall, Northamptonshire, about 1933.
5   The Double Cube Room at Wilton House, Wiltshire, about 1900.
6, 7, 8   The gallery at Osterley Park, Middlesex, 1910-1970.
9   The drawing room at Chirk Castle, Denbighshire.
10   A design by James Stuart for decoration at Kedleston Hall, Derbyshire.
11   A sectional drawing of a house by Edward Stevens, 1763.
12   A sectional drawing of a house by Thomas Hardwick.
13   A design for an interior by James Wyatt.
14   The Lower Library at Chatsworth, Derbyshire.
15   The Great Hall at Drayton House, Northamptonshire.
16   The saloon at Audley End, Essex.
17   The Queen's Closet at Ham House, Surrey.
18   An early 18th century chair upholstered in yellow satin at Ham House.
19   *View down the corridor* by Samuel Hoogstraeten, 1662.
20   A design for a state bedroom by Daniel Marot.
21   The ante-room at Chesterfield House, London.
22   The Tapestry Room, formerly at Croome Court, Worcestershire.
23   *Lady Holland* by Allan Ramsay.
24   The Painted Room at Spencer House, London.
25   The Boudoir at Attingham Park, Shropshire.
26, 27   The Saloon at Devonshire House, London, in 1811, and about 1915.
28   Pyne's view of the Crimson Drawing Room at Carlton House, London.
29, 30   William Playfair's design for the Egyptian billiard room at Cairness, Aberdeenshire, and a detail of the decoration in sanded wood.
31   The Library at Barnsley Park, Gloucestershire.
32   The Dining Room at Levens Hall, Westmorland.
33   The Elizabeth Saloon at Belvoir Castle, Leicestershire.
34   The title page to Weale's edition of Chippendale's designs, about 1830.
35   The State Dining Room at Chatsworth.
36   An engraving of the High Great Chamber at Hardwick, Derbyshire in 1835.
37   *The Family of the Earl of Arundel* by Fruytiers.
38   The State Drawing Room at Chatsworth.
39   A plan of the principal floor at Blenheim Palace, Oxfordshire.
40   A plan of the piano nobile at Houghton Hall, Norfolk.

41	A plan of the piano nobile at Holkham Hall, Norfolk.
42	A plan of the piano nobile at Kedleston, Derbyshire.
43	The elevation of Wolterton Hall, Norfolk.
44, 45	Turner's watercolour of the dining room at Farnley Hall, Yorkshire, and the room in recent years.
46, 47	Pyne's views of the Gothick Dining Room at Carlton House and the dining room at Frogmore.
48	The Saloon at Houghton.
49	A settee from the Gallery at Corsham Court, Wiltshire.
50	A chair from the Gallery at Osterley.
51	Repton's sectional drawing of Sheringham Hall, Norfolk.
52, 53	Plates from Repton's *Fragments*.
54	A watercolour of the drawing room at Field Place, Sussex, about 1816.
55	The ante-room at Spencer House, about 1890.
56	*Queen Charlotte in her dressing room, Buckingham Palace* by Zoffany.
57	The Countess of Ashburnham's dressing room, a silhouette.
58	*Lady Impey in her dressing room in India.*
59	A sofa bed at Belvoir.
60	Christopher Gibson's trade card.
61	The state bedroom at Powis Castle, Montgomeryshire.
62	The late 17th century state bed at Drayton House.
63, 64	Designs for beds by Marot.
65, 66, 67	The Earl of Melville's bed at the Victoria and Albert Museum.
68	A curtain valance at Beningbrough, about 1700.
69	Queen Anne's bed at Hampton Court Palace.
70	The state bedroom at Holkham.
71	The state bed at Osterley designed by Adam.
72	The state bed at Hopetoun House, West Lothian.
73	An early 19th century bed at Chatsworth.
74	A polonaise bed at Drumlanrig Castle, Dumfriesshire, about 1790.
75	The state bed at Castlecoole, Co. Fermanagh, about 1820.
76, 77	The former Crimson State Bedroom at Ashburnham Place, Sussex.
78	A bedroom at Ashburnham Place as it was in 1956.
79	An early 19th century bed formerly at Haseley Court, Oxfordshire.
80	*The Blue Curtain* by Adriaen van der Spelt.
81, 82	Designs by Marot for an interior and upholstery.
83	A modern festoon curtain at Clandon Park, Surrey.
84	*The Gough Family* by Verelst.
85	*Mrs Congreve and her Daughters in their London Drawing Room* by Reinagle.
86	Detail of a shutter case at Clandon.
87	*Paul Sandby* by Francis Cotes.
88	A reefed curtain. A detail of Plate XV.
89	A canopy bed designed by Chippendale.
90	An early 18th century curtain valance at Erthig, Denbighshire.
91, 92	Early festoon curtains at Dyrham Park, Gloucestershire.
93	*Marriage à la Mode* by William Hogarth.
94	Carved pelmet cornices and valances at Harewood House, Yorkshire.
95	*The Wanstead Assembly* by Hogarth.
96	The Prince of Wales's Chinese Drawing Room, Carlton House.
97	*The Last Day in the Old Home* by Martineau.
98	Alternative treatments for windows at Grimston Garth, Yorkshire, about 1786.
99	A draped valance in the state bedroom at Burghley House, Northamptonshire.
100	A continued drapery and window curtains. Illustration from George Smith's *Collection of Designs for Household Furniture*.
101	Curtains in the drawing room at Southill Park, Bedfordshire.
102	A continued drapery in the Drawing Room at Sezincote, Gloucestershire.
103, 104	Three alternative treatments of curtains and a continued drapery proposed by Gillows.
105	A draped curtain formerly in the state dressing room at Castlecoole.
106	A draped valance in the Speakers' Parlour at Clandon.
107	Chippendale's proposed treatment of a Venetian window.
108	The state bedroom at Clandon stripped down.
109	The gallery at Longford Castle, Wiltshire.

110	The Crimson Drawing Room at Hopetoun.
111, 112	The Red Velvet Drawing Room at Saltram, Devon.
113	The use of fillets. A detail from Plate XV.
114	Late 17th century hangings at Penshurst Place, Kent.
115	Chinoiserie leather panels in a closet at Honington Hall, Warwickshire.
116	Bizarre silk used for the upholstery of a settee at Knole, Kent.
117	The Taffeta Bedroom at Houghton
118	*A Tea Party at Lord Harrington's House* by Charles Philips.
119, 120, 121	A room from Kops's house in Haarlem.
122	The Chinese Room at Ombersley Court, Worcestershire.
123	The drawing room at Moccas Court, Herefordshire.
124	Mrs Whitbread's Room, Southill.
125	The boudoir at Shugborough, Staffordshire.
126	Detail of a wallpaper at Townley Hall, Co. Louth.
127	A design for a tented alcove by Crace & Co.
128	A design for a room with ruched hangings and tented ceiling by Gillows.
129	The Tent Room at Shrublands, Suffolk.
130	The Tent Room at Cranbury Park, Hampshire.
131	A mahogany chair from the Treasury, London.
132	A chair from the state bedroom at Holkham.
133	A mid 18th century armchair from Ham House.
134	An armchair from Southill.
135	A chair from Nostell Priory, Yorkshire.
136	A chair formerly at Brocket Hall, Hertfordshire.
137	A chair formerly at Langley Park, Norfolk.
138	A Chippendale chair.
139, 140, 141	A mid 18th century chair upholstered in original wool damask.
142, 143	A chair and an armchair en suite with the state bed at Clandon.
144	A late 17th century chair at Lyme Park, Cheshire.
145	An English carved and gilt chair at the Victoria and Albert Museum.
146	The chair as it was when acquired by the Museum.
147	*Portrait of Mrs Draper* by Richard Cosway.
148	A chair from the library at Osterley.
149	A chair from the gallery at Corsham.
150	An engraved design for a chair by Kent.
151	A gilt gesso chair, about 1720.
152	A chair formerly at Cusworth Hall, Yorkshire.
153	A satinwood armchair at Osterley.
154	A continental chair at Clandon.
155	A mid 18th century French bergère at Goodwood House, Sussex.
156	A "Burjair" from Ince and Mayhew's *Universal System*.
157	The sofa bed from the state bedroom at Holkham.
158	A couch from Ince and Mayhew's *Universal System*.
159	*Sergeant-At-Arms Bonfoy, his son, and John Clementson* by Mortimer.
160	A watercolour of the Great Parlour, Strawberry Hill, Middlesex.
161	*The Young Princes at Buckingham House* by Zoffany.
162	The Small Drawing Room, Kimbolton Castle, Huntingdon, about 1910.
163	A detail of a settee from the Hornby Castle suite.
164	A carved and gilt chair, about 1695.
165	A chair formerly at Rushbrooke Hall.
166	A chair from the Venetian Ambassador's Bedroom at Knole.
167	A mid 18th century bed at Uppark, Sussex.
168	Decorations for the lying-in-state of the 1st Duke of Albermarle, 1670.
169	The Saloon at Forde Abbey, Dorset.
170, 171	The chimneypiece and overmantel in the Queen's Room, Sudbury Hall, Derbyshire, before and after restoration.
172	The Cupola Room at Kensington Palace, London.
173	A Chippendale chair made for Sir Lawrence Dundas.
174, 175	Marbling in the Painted Room at Hill Court, Herefordshire.
176	Painted decoration at Great Hundridge Manor, Buckinghamshire.
177	Graining and marbling at Stanton Harcourt Parsonage, Oxfordshire.
178	Painted decoration at Swangrove, Badminton, Gloucestershire.
179	Chinoiserie decoration at Old Battersea House, London.
180, 181	Graining in the library, Belmont, Kent, about 1795.
182	Marbling in the hall at Attingham.

13

183	Graining in the Music Room at Pencarrow, Cornwall, about 1830.
184	An engraving of the Indian Room in Thomas Hope's London house.
185	The inlaid landing from 22 Hanover Square, London.
186	The staircase at Claydon House, Buckinghamshire.
187, 188	Details of inlaid floors at Ballyfin, Co. Leix.
189	Gillows' carpet plan for Eaton Hall, Cheshire.
190	The carpet in the White Drawing Room at Houghton.
191	An Axminster bed carpet at Blickling Hall, Norfolk.
192	A painted floor at Crowcombe Court, Somerset.
193	A painted floor at Belton House, Lincolnshire.
194	*Two Girls Decorating a Kitten* by Joseph Wright.
195	*The Tea Party* by Henry Sargent.
196	James Wyatt's design for the dining room, Slane Castle, Co. Meath.
197	A stove and lamp at Pencarrow.
198	The Etruscan Room at Osterley.
199	A chimney board made for Audley End.
200	*Lord Granard Having His Wig Powdered* by Herbert Pugh.
201, 202	The Gallery at Corsham.
203	The Great Room, Spencer House, about 1890.
204, 205	The saloon, Stourhead, Wiltshire, about 1820 and before the fire of 1902.
206, 207	The gallery at Stourhead about 1900 and today.
208, 209	The Cabinet at Felbrigg Hall, Norfolk, and a drawing of the proposed hanging of the pictures.
210	Part of the dining room at Farnborough Hall, Warwickshire.
211	The breakfast room at Saltram.
212	The Chinese Room at Erthig.
213	Pyne's view of the Blue Drawing Room at Carlton House.
214, 215	Turner's watercolour of the drawing room at Farnley Hall, Yorkshire, and the same room in 1946.
216	The library at Chesterfield House.
217	The gallery at Bridgewater House, London, about 1900.
218	The gallery at Adare Manor, Co. Limerick, in the mid 19th century.
219	The drawing room at À La Ronde, Devon.
220	The gallery to the Octagonal Hall at À La Ronde.
221	Felt pictures by Helena, Countess of Mount Cashel.
222	A pagoda at Erthig.
223	Pyne's view of the Japan Room at Frogmore.
224	The saloon at Castlecoole.
225	Leather covers on globes at Ham House.
226	Pyne's engraving of Queen Mary's Bed, Hampton Court Palace, showing case curtains.
227	The state bedroom at Inveraray Castle, Argyllshire.
228	Mrs Lancaster's London drawing room.
229, 230	The drawing room, Haseley Court, as it was in 1960.
231, 232	The Palladio Room, Clandon, stripped down and restored.
233	The Queen's Room at Sudbury.
234	The saloon at Sudbury.

Chapter 1
The concept of the decorator

This chapter is concerned with the development of the modern concept of the interior decorator and how the restoration of interiors is affected by changing attitudes to the past and styles. Reference is also made to the differences between the role of the decorator to-day and that of the 18th century architect, upholsterer, cabinet-maker and paper-stainer.

It may seem perverse to start a book concentrating on 18th century English decoration in New York in the 1890s, but a good case can be made for arguing that interior decoration as we understand it to-day started with Edith Wharton, who in collaboration with Ogden Codman wrote *The Decoration of Houses*. She claimed that the book, which was published in 1897, was the first study of house decoration as a branch of architecture to be published for 50 years, and in her autobiography, *A Backward Glance*,[1] she explained how she drifted into doing it, adding that "it became fashionable to use our volume as a touchstone of taste." If Miss Wharton wrote the first book, Elsie de Wolfe claimed to be "America's first woman decorator", with her first big commission at the Colony Club in New York in 1905. Although, according to Miss de Wolfe's autobiography *After All*, the ladies were not friends, their two books reveal that their interest in the treatment of their houses dated back to the '80s or '90s and to a fusion of their European experiences with their American background. The same fusion probably influenced two other Americans, Lady Randolph Churchill and her sister Mrs Moreton Frewen, for in *Left Hand, Right Hand* Sir Osbert Sitwell described 25 Chesham Place, London, which his parents rented from Mrs Frewen in 1900: "It was 'done-up' in the height of fashion of the moment, for interior decoration had only just started as a mode and on its own professional basis, and Lady Randolph had been almost the first person to interest herself in it and may perhaps have had a hand in the colour schemes. Before 1900, the aesthetes alone had shown an interest in the rooms in which they beautifully existed . . . [ordinary rich people] had not hitherto felt a conscious need for self dramatisation . . ."[2]

It is to the ladies rather than to the designs of William Morris, the laments of Sir Charles Eastlake and the experiments of James McNeill Whistler that we should look, for, quite apart from the merits of their work (and they were considerable), they made it a socially acceptable field. Again Sir Osbert explains this, for he says of the well-to-do, "with the turn of the late nineties into 1900, their confidence all of a sudden wilted. Thus I believe that the rage for interior decoration can be related to the enormous social changes that were only hidden from the still shadowy outline of the new century." Here Sir Osbert opens the door for a long and fascinating digression that we cannot make at this point, but the whole problem of style, fashion and social change is discussed in the next chapter.

One aspect of this change was the emancipation of women, for which there was growing pressure in the opening years of this century. Interior decoration whether on an amateur or semi-professional basis was one outlet for this, and both in Elsie de Wolfe's *The House in Good Taste*, which appeared in 1913, and her autobiography, the combination of practical advice with a feminist point of view comes out strongly. Two short quotations must serve to give the direction of her thought. "I know of nothing more significant," she wrote in her first chapter, "than the awakening of men and women throughout our country to the desire to improve their houses . . ." and then ". . . we take it for granted that this American house is always the woman's home: a man may build and decorate a beautiful house, but it remains for a woman to make a home of it for him."

Both she and Edith Wharton, as well as Eastlake and Frederick Litchfield, the author of an *Illustrated History of Furniture* published in 1892, denounced the taste of their contemporaries and of upholsterers, but in the long term their most valuable ally was the newly invented process engraving. This revolutionised book illustration and made cheap magazines illustrated with half-tone blocks possible. The importance of this was quickly realised. Magazines gave both designers and potential customers a much greater range of ideas than was ever possible before and drew to public attention the work of new designers, thus accelerating the pace of change in fashionable taste.

As yet no one has written a complete history of interior decoration in this century, although brief accounts of the 1920s and '30s have been written by Martin Battersby and the work of the 1930s has been surveyed by Madge Garland,[3] but a change of scale and approach can be detected even before the 1914–18 war. In London there are still a number of opulent interiors that are evocative of the years round about 1900, although none are now in private occupation and so have lost their original furnishings: at 66–71 Brook Street, now the Savile Club, there are rooms done by the Paris firm of Bouwens for Mrs Burns, the sister of Pierpont Morgan; at Derby House, Stratford Place, now the Oriental Club, there are rooms in a variety of styles mostly done by W. H. Romaine-Walker for the 7th Earl of Derby; and at 37 Charles Street, now the English Speaking Union, are rooms fitted up by W. Turner Lord for Lord Revelstoke. In the country there are equivalent interiors by Mewès and Davis at Luton Hoo, Bedfordshire, and Polesden Lacey, Surrey.

However these were exceptions, and the atmosphere of 25 Chesham Place as opposed to that of Wimborne House (Fig. 1) is captured by V. Sackville-West's descriptions of the contrast between Sylvia's house and those of Lord Roehampton's sisters in *The Edwardians:* "The very rooms in which they dwelt differed from Sylvia's rooms or the rooms of her friends. There, a certain fashion of expensive simplicity was beginning to make itself felt; a certain taste was arising which tended to eliminate unnecessary objects. Here, the overcrowded rooms preserved the unhappy confusion of an earlier day . . . Yes, certainly the room was overcrowded. There were too many chairs, too many hassocks, too many small tables, too much pampas grass in crane-necked vases, too many blinds and curtains looped and festooned about the windows. The whole effect was fusty, musty, and dusty. It needed destruction, it needed air . . ."[4]

After the 1914–18 war expensive simplicity became more fashionable, and was apparent in the work of such well known firms as Lenygon and Morant, Thornton Smith, Keeble and White Allom, which were all rather different in character from one another. Of these Lenygons were both the grandest and, from a historical point of view, the most interesting, for they did excellent period work and had one of the most handsome early 18th century houses in London, 31 Old Burlington Street, which they stocked with English furniture of the finest quality made at the end of the 17th and in the first half of the 18th century. They had considerable historical knowledge of both architectural

Section of York House November 1759

I. A SECTIONAL DESIGN BY SIR
WILLIAM CHAMBERS FOR YORK HOUSE,
PALL MALL, LONDON, ABOUT 1759.
One of the earliest English
drawings to show a complete
scheme of decoration.

I. THE SALOON AT WIMBORNE HOUSE, ARLINGTON STREET, LONDON, ABOUT 1890. This old photograph shows the kind of rooms described by V. Sackville-West in *The Edwardians* as inhabited by Lord Roehampton's sisters.

decoration and furniture and from about 1910 were advised by Margaret Jourdain, who wrote two books under the name of Francis Lenygon that were published by Batsfords. Few of their works survive now, but their approach, even if not certainly their hand, is apparent in old photographs of rooms like the Saloon at Beningbrough Hall, Yorkshire, which appeared in *Country Life* in 1927. (Fig. 2).

Thornton Smith was a bigger business and from 1915 to 1937 operated from three exquisite houses, including 32 Soho Square, which contained interiors possibly by Sir Robert Taylor. They worked in period styles, but concentrated on dramatic effects rather than authentic detail, producing in their studios a great deal of Japanned work, hand painted wallpapers in the Chinese taste, and copies of flower paintings and *veduti* pictures. Much of this was exported to America.

From 1899 to 1936 Keebles occupied another fine house nearby, Carlisle House, Carlisle Street, alas destroyed in the last war. Most of their work was in a safe period style, and they did a number of elaborate country house interiors, including rooms at Brechin Castle, Angus, with carefully copied historic detail, and at Grimsthorpe Castle about 1924. White Allom, another big firm, is now remembered for the work they did for Queen Mary at Buckingham Palace, but they were not in the forefront of fashionable taste.

Besides these well-established businesses, after the first war a number of smaller firms of a rather different character started and of these the one with the most influence on what might be called country house taste was Mrs Guy Bethell's highly personal shop in Duke Street, Mayfair, which she called Elden, a combination of letters from her name and that of her partner Mrs Dryden of Canons Ashby in Northamptonshire. Mrs Bethell and her two sisters, Lady Gilbey and Miss Coutts Fowlie, were gifted people, and very soon after starting the business she attracted the attention of the leaders of fashionable taste headed by Lady Essex, Lady Islington and Mrs Ronald Tree. Mrs Bethell had sound period knowledge as well as admirable taste, and although she was strongly influenced by the contemporary fashion for a so-called Italian style—Mr. Osbert Lancaster's Curzon Street Baroque—her rooms were usually understated and were never vulgar and flashy.

It was this that attracted Mrs Tree, who asked her to help her to decorate Kelmarsh in Northamptonshire, which she and her husband leased in 1923.

II. AN UNUSED PIECE OF THE YELLOW SATIN MATCHING THAT USED ON A SET OF EARLY 18TH CENTURY CHAIRS, SHOWING THE BRILLIANCE OF ITS COLOUR AND THE CONTRAST WITH THE RED CORDED SILK EMBROIDERY. On view at Ham House. For a complete chair see Figure 18.

2. THE SALOON AT BENINGBROUGH
HALL, YORKSHIRE, AS IT WAS ABOUT
1925. An early 18th century room
containing furniture and pictures
from Holme Lacy, Herefordshire,
as decorated and arranged in 1927,
probably by Lenygons.

3. A BEDROOM AT KELMARSH HALL,
NORTHAMPTONSHIRE. An example
of understatement photographed
in 1933.

4. THE EXHIBITION ROOM AT
KELMARSH. Designed by Mrs
Bethell in 1925.

When one looks again at photographs of the interiors taken by *Country Life*
for an article published in 1933 (February 25), it is hard to believe that they are
of rooms arranged and decorated over 40 years ago, or conversely, it is hard to
see why they were so novel at that time. The walls of Mrs Tree's room (Fig. 3)
were hung with ivory coloured silk and the bed was hung with cloth of silver
trimmed with 18th century silver galloon and fringe probably found in Italy.
Much of the painted or Japanned furniture was also Italian, and it is only the
tiger skin rug before the fire and the rather bare walls that give away the date of
the room. The so-called Exhibition Room (Fig. 4) was also Mrs Bethell's
work, but was not originally done for Mrs Tree but for an exhibition at
Olympia in 1925 that really counts as the first Antique Dealers' Fair. Mrs Tree,
or Mrs Lancaster as she is now, although never a professional like Mrs Bethell,
Syrie Maugham or Lady Colefax, should be mentioned in their company as
one of the key people in the development of English taste in decoration (as
opposed to modern design) during the last two generations. An American, like
Lady Randolph Churchill, she came to England as a young widow at the
suggestion of her aunt, Lady Astor, and since then has lived in three houses,
Kelmarsh in Northamptonshire, and Ditchley and Haseley Court, both in
Oxfordshire (Figs. 229, 230).

Syrie Maugham did not have Mrs Bethell's sense of period, but she had a
great feeling for luxury and for chic in upholstery that was admirably suited to
London interiors. Her colour sense was rather limited and to-day she is remembered for her white rooms, stripped panelling and pickled wood.

Lady Colefax, who lived at Argyll House in the King's Road, was a neighbour
of Mrs Somerset Maugham and a leading hostess in London in the 1920s. Her
husband Sir Arthur, who was a barrister, and knighted for his work as a patent
agent, was always rather overshadowed by her forceful and magnetic person-

ality, and when he lost the greater part of his money in the crash of 1929-30, she was determined not to abandon her role as a hostess. So she decided to turn her wide contacts to financial advantage, and first collaborated with antique dealers at 24 Bruton Street, the house formerly occupied by Lord and Lady Islington. This proved successful, and, as she had a flair for decorating, she decided to take the first floor of 24, where she started her own business about 1933. She chose as her partner the young Countess Munster, the former Miss Peggy Ward, and it was through the latter that John Fowler, one of the authors of this book, joined the partnership in 1938.

Mrs Bethell, Mrs Lancaster, Mrs Maugham and Lady Colefax, of course, do not complete the circle, for there were many other talented people including Mrs Mann and Mr Ronald Fleming who made a considerable contribution, but as we are concerned with the period before 1830 and the attitudes of the 1920s and 30s rather than with the dominant figures of recent years, we cannot do justice to their work here.

Moreover this is also not the place to trace the development of taste and fashion nearer to the present day, except to say that the outbreak of war in 1939 brought about a complete halt and no decoration of any real importance was done for 11 or 12 years. The length of the break makes it more difficult than it would otherwise have been to see the originality of the work done by Mrs Bethell and her contemporaries, and now so little survives that it is virtually impossible to judge it for ourselves.

When the rooms she decorated are compared with those of the Regency period or with those by the firms mentioned earlier in the chapter, their outstanding character is their apparently effortless ease and freedom. She rejected the hard lines and patterns and the mechanical effects that had been introduced in the early 19th century and tried to recapture the painterly aspect of decoration that is found in the finest houses of the late 17th century and early Palladian period, using faded muted colours, old materials, and effects that defy easy description. She did not have a strict view of what was "period" but liked to mix styles and dates to give a sense of unruffled continuity. It was a style that was both sophisticated and romantic, for it was based on an appreciation of pleasing decay, a quality already familiar to a limited number of artistic people, but one that was new to the fashionable world. Although Mrs Bethell and her clients would not have thought of it in such terms, it was a taste that probably owed a considerable amount to the influence of William Morris and to the Arts and Crafts Movement, but was transformed by contact with old country houses that had not been spoilt during the course of the previous 50 or 60 years. Here and on the continent there was not only an apparently unending supply of furniture, but of old materials as well, velvets, damasks and brocades, put away in the cupboards of churches and houses. Making use of these Mrs Bethell, and those who admired her work, were able to develop a new country house style that has not only been widely imitated in the course of the last 50 years but it has in its turn had a considerable bearing on the way we now look at country houses.

At the same time the whole concept of preserving country houses has developed, and it is at least arguable that both are manifestations of a similar romanticism, of reaction against 19th century philistinism and of a strong nostalgia for Augustan order.

However in its apparent simplicity Mrs Bethell's style was misleading: like most simple things, it was a style that was difficult to handle successfully and it was also not a cheap one. Nor did it mean a rejection of the grand style or of bold colours and patterns. Unfortunately it is all too easy for the soft, mellow, understated look to become the washed-out look, which is a totally different one; and, equally unfortunately, there are now many people who think of 18th century rooms in terms of feeble colours and weak indeterminate patterns and are shocked when large Early Georgian rooms are handled with boldness.

These remarks may seem irrelevant to the study of historic decoration, but if the aim is to try to develop an objective approach to decoration and restoration, it is necessary to try to understand how and why we look at the past in the way we do and to be aware of what influences there have been on country houses in the course of this century. Very few have been completely untouched, and many have been rearranged more than once in accordance with an increasing regard for the 18th century, so that often what one is led to believe is an original scheme or at least one of considerable antiquity is in fact a re-interpretation of the '20s or '30s. Indeed, on going through the various sets of *Country Life* anthologies of country houses starting with the first volume of *In English Homes* produced in 1904, not only is the increasing self-consciousness apparent, but also the degree of change.

Many examples could be cited, including Wilton (Fig. 5), Sudbury, Ragley and Osterley, but in some ways the last is perhaps the most revealing, for it is possible to follow the appearance of the Gallery through from before the First World War (Fig. 6), when it might be a room in *The Edwardians*, to its rearrangement in the 1920s (Fig. 7), and then on to the recent re-arrangement of the furniture by the Victoria and Albert Museum in 1970 (Fig. 8).

This lack of absolute standards and involvement with changing taste and fashion both make restoration of interiors singularly difficult. Indeed, we believe that there may be no such thing as an absolute restoration, putting the

5. THE DOUBLE CUBE ROOM AT WILTON HOUSE, WILTSHIRE, AS IT WAS ABOUT 1900. A state room before the impact of 20th century taste.

6. THE GALLERY AT OSTERLEY PARK, MIDDLESEX, AS IT APPEARED ABOUT 1910.

7. THE GALLERY IN THE 1920S.

8. THE GALLERY AS REARRANGED IN 1970. The pictures were destroyed in the war and the tapestries are on loan, but the re-arrangement of the furniture by the Victoria and Albert Museum is a reconstruction of Adam's intention.

clock back to 1680, 1715 or 1750, when the house was built or the room was formed: all restorations are to some degree re-interpretations and are influenced by the times in which they are carried out. Of course one can be taken in, and one is frequently puzzled as to when work was done, but usually after a period of years the date of the restoration becomes apparent and indeed with time may be seen to be important for its own sake. Charlecote in Warwickshire,[5] for instance, is an Elizabethan house done up in the Old English style of the 1830s, and now the restoration seems of much greater interest than what remains of the original work. Similarly it is fascinating to find that at Chirk Castle, Denbighshire, some of the 18th century rooms including the drawing-room (Fig. 9), were done up by Pugin.[6] At Stourhead, in Wiltshire, taste has not yet come full circle so that the house still seems defeatingly Edwardian: after the Palladian villa was burnt in 1902, it was carefully re-constructed, but all the detail and so the feeling of the house is distressingly un-Palladian. Thus anyone attempting to reconstruct a period interior needs to think not only about the relevant historical style but also about the fashions of their own time in architecture, furniture arrangement and way of living, for they condition his approach.

Of course this does not matter if authenticity is not the object, but just as decoration has developed in this century because people have become more self-conscious, it has developed because people have become more worried by history and a desire for accuracy. And this in its turn has caused a division, albeit perhaps ill-defined, between decoration and restoration. In England there has been no tradition of serious interior restoration, and although structures are carefully handled by the Ancient Monuments division of the

22

9. THE DINING ROOM AT CHIRK
CASTLE, DENBIGHSHIRE. An
Adamesque room repainted under
Pugin's direction in the 1840s.

Department of the Environment, the same sensitivity is seldom seen within buildings in public ownership and there is very grave suspicion of the concept of interior decoration. Most of the time this suspicion is entirely justified, but while it lasts, and no attempt is made to resolve it, or to to research on the problems involved, there is no hope of working out a better balance between a highly academic approach and a loosely artistic one. Americans who specialise in the former are frequently shocked by the *ad hoc* approach that exists in England, but then they in turn are shocked when it is pointed out to them that their academic restorations can be totally lifeless and be dated as well.

It is easy enough to push the blame for this situation on to the decorator and say that he has not proved himself equal to the task that faces him; but if this line is taken, it fails to recognise changes in the attitudes and understanding of patrons and clients. As we hope to show, developments in decoration have always been closely related to changing fashions in living, and in the past the sense of order and suitability in a house reflected that of Society as a whole. Today Society does not have that secure and confident position—indeed it is arguable that Society does not exist at all—and although some people have a great deal of money to spend, they are not able to have that long term attitude to life that flourished in the 18th and 19th centuries. Nor is that attitude understood. Consequently even if the forms of decoration in the past are observed with a fair degree of accuracy, the ideas behind them are not appreciated, and thus the finished work often fails to be convincing.

Consequently there is something to be said for at least considering the patron before the decorator in the 18th century, for although a great deal has been written on Augustan patronage, the positive aspects of a patron's role are still hard to grasp, and we find it hard to see what Boffrand meant when he said "It is the client who, so to speak, gives the key to the architect."[7]

However frequently one finds an architect's table or drawing instruments in

24

a country house, the Duke of Chandos's enquiry about such instruments in 1714 still comes as a surprise. He wrote to his cousin about a set saying "As I am upon making alterations here, I frequently have to draw lines."[8] It is remarks like this that help to get behind the mask of detachment cultivated by such figures as Lord Chesterfield. Writing in 1744 to his son of developing a taste in painting and sculpture, he warned him not to descend "into those *minuties*, which our modern virtuosi most affectedly dwell upon . . . All these sorts of things I would have you know, to a certain degree; but remember, that they must only be the amusements, and not the business, of a man of parts."[9] And yet the previous year he could write to Solomon Dayrolles soon after moving into Chesterfield House "The rest of the day is employed in riding, and fitting up my house; which, I assure you, takes a good deal of time, now that we are come to the minute parts of finishing and furnishing."[10] For Lord Chesterfield, as for so many patrons, decorating, like building and gardening, was a source of pleasure and a form of occupation. He would not have admitted this directly, but a slightly younger contemporary, Lady Louisa Conolly, makes the point in a disarming way. In a letter dated July 16, 1761, she writes of her new dairy at Castletown, Co. Kildare: "Its so pleasant I think to have some work going on, that one looks over oneself."[11] Even Lord Chatham thought in these terms, as can be seen in a letter he wrote to Sir John Griffin in 1765: "As you are at Audley End I imagine you are deeply engaged in the amusing cares of building, planting, decorating etc."[12] And it was much the same with George IV in his later years, as Mrs Arbuthnot records in 1827: "The King has the greatest contempt for the Ministers, but thinks of nothing but *upholstery* and his *buildings*."[13]

Lord Chesterfield, Horace Walpole, William Wyndham of Felbrigg, and Thomas Jefferson, to name the outstanding American example, were passionately concerned with the details of their houses, pestering their friends, their architects, their stewards as well as the craftsmen, and there was no standard way of completing a house. Sometimes a patron left it to his architect; sometimes the architect designed the furniture; and sometimes the patron's wife made significant contributions. There are many graphic illustrations of how people solved their problems, not the least interesting being those in the *London Tradesman* of 1747. "The Upholder is chief Agent in this Case: He is the Man upon whose Judgement I rely in the Choice of Goods, . . . This Tradesman's Genius must be universal in every Branch of Furniture . . . He was originally a Species of the Taylor; but, by degrees, has crept over his Head, and set up as a Connoisseur in every Article that belongs to a House."[14] Thus when Ralph Milbanke wrote to Judith Noel he told her: "I shall stay here till Tuesday, for I have appointed Mr. Davies with papers and borders and chairs and tables and all the materials that compose an upholsterer's shop to meet me in Edward Street that day."[15] And by that time a fashionable upholsterer was sufficiently established to be able to dictate to an uncertain client. Thus when Lady Cust went to London in 1743, she wrote home: "I have been at a great upholsterer's today, he says he has not made any furniture [in its 18th century sense of referring to the work of the upholsterer rather than of the cabinet-maker] of Mohair this year, so I believe I shall be afrayed to bye it but when my horses come I will go more about."[16]

In France there was a much clearer distinction between the *ébenistes* who were cabinet-makers, the *menusiers* who made seat furniture, and the *tapissiers* who were responsible for upholstery, and overall control lay to a very considerable extent in the hands of the *marchand merciers* who were dealers and entrepreneurs. However from the records of English houses it seems that ultimate control did not lie with one single trade. Sometimes it was with the upholsterer because his was usually the most expensive part of fitting up a room. When the coronation chair was made for Queen Anne in 1702, the frame by Thomas Roberts cost £17, but Anthony Ryland charged £72 for the uphol-

25

stery.[17] Towards the end of the century, when the Prince of Wales was decorating the Chinese Drawing Room at Carlton House (Fig. 96), the proportion of costs of the seat furniture was: woodwork, 27%, gilding 10%, upholstery and tassels 63%.[18] Naturally this situation favoured the upholsterer, particularly if he had sufficient capital to provide the materials used as well; but it seems that the situation at Woburn in the 1750s was not unusual. There the 4th Duke of Bedford employed Henry Flitcroft as architect, G. B. Borra as interior designer, and Samuel Norman of the Royal Tapestry Manufactory to do the fitting up; Norman painted and gilded the woodwork, made and put up the blinds and curtains and hung the walls and supplied the seat furniture: but the Duke provided the damask, which he had brought from a mercer called Robert Swann.[19] Norman would probably come within the modern concept of an interior decorator, and his firm was one of a number capable of undertaking such a range of work.

Perhaps the most famous cabinet-maker who worked as a decorator as we understand the term was Thomas Chippendale, whose book *The Gentleman and Cabinet-Maker's Director* came out in 1754. From the records of Nostell Priory, Harewood House and Mersham-le-Hatch it is clear that he not only supplied furniture but wallpapers and borders, curtains and blinds, bedclothes and carpets and all manner of household equipment. It must have been a very large concern, but as yet very little is known about how he organised all these activities and what arrangements he had with subcontractors. However it is interesting that the *London Tradesman* says "A Master Cabinet-maker is a very profitable trade; especially if he works for and serves the Quality himself; but if he must serve them through the channel of the upholder his profits are not very considerable."[20]

Thomas Bromwich is less well known because he never seems to have supplied furniture, but he too should be counted as a decorator although he was principally known as a producer of wallpaper. According to his trade card he "Makes and Sells all manner of Screens/Window-Blinds and Covers for Tables/Rooms, Cabins, Staircases etc. Hung with Guilt Leather, or India Pictures, Chints's, Callicoes, Cottons, Needlework & Damasks, /Matched in Paper, to the utmost exactness, at Reasonable Rates."[21] His name occurs frequently in the accounts of famous houses in the third quarter of the 18th century, and, judging by Mrs Lybbe Powys's enthusiastic descriptions of his work at Fawley Court, he obviously had a high reputation.[22]

Paperhanging was an important trade, but, like upholstery, paper tends to have a limited life, and so it is difficult to judge the role of the leading firms. Certainly in 1808 George Smith wrote: "The business of Decoration being generally entrusted to the vendor of paperhangings, it is perhaps too much to expect any like arrangement or rule;" but from this it is hard to separate disgust from exaggeration and jealousy.[23]

To what extent the architect concerned himself with the details of decoration is impossible to generalise. Both William Kent and Robert Adam were deeply interested in the whole process of completing a house, but each commission was different, and with Chippendale, for instance, it is obvious that Adam did not always dictate to him in detail.

One clue lies in the kinds of drawings that architects made, and it is significant that coloured designs are a great rarity in England before the 1760s. Indeed the earliest designs that show the arrangement of furniture and some indication of colours are those by James Stuart for Kedleston in 1757 (Fig. 10). So far nothing of a similar kind by Kent has come to light, and even John Talman's unresolved drawing of an interior appears completely isolated.[24] No comparable drawings for English commissions by Daniel Marot have been identified, although there are drawings by him in Holland that show variation in tones and details of gilding.[25]

Stuart's Kedleston designs are not exhibition drawings, but within two years,

William Chambers doubtless inspired by what he had seen on the continent, produced a sectional drawing of York House that shows colour schemes (Plate I). The idea was taken up four years later in a set of drawings by his pupil Edward Stevens: dated 1763 they show a markedly Chambersian interior, but no furniture or pictures are indicated (Fig. 11). And a similar approach is to be seen in a contemporary scheme by Thomas Hardwick, another of his pupils (Fig. 12). Chambers was evidently very concerned about colours as we know from two letters, one to him from the Duchess of Queensberry in 1772 and one from him to Lord Melbourne in 1772. The former wrote "Sir William knows that the assemblage & blending of couleurs are Great Principles of his own masterful supreme taste,." To Melbourne Chambers wrote in 1773: "Chippendale called upon me yesterday with some Designs for furnishings the rooms wch upon the whole seem very well but I wish to be a little consulted about these as I am really a very pretty connoisseur in furniture . . ."[26]

Adam's use of coloured drawings and drawings showing furniture are well known, but it is interesting to see how his method of presentation was anticipated by Stuart. James Wyatt, on the other hand, still remains a more shadowy figure and his whole approach to decoration needs much more investigation. Some of his ceiling designs are most carefully worked out in tone and a few large-scale drawings for painted furniture survive, but there are few like that shown in Fig. 13.

Thus in our present state of knowledge all that can be said with safety is that during the first half of the 18th century architects became much more aware of the possibilities of decoration and of the contribution it could make to the successful conclusion of their designs. To some extent these possibilities were new, or at least greater, than they had been, for the furniture trade had developed considerably in the last quarter of the 17th century and the range of pieces made was much wider than it had been in the early days of the Restoration.

10. A DESIGN BY JAMES STUART FOR THE DECORATION OF THE DINING ROOM AT KEDLESTON HALL, DERBYSHIRE, 1757. Apparently the earliest recorded English design to show the arrangement of furniture and some indication of colours.

27

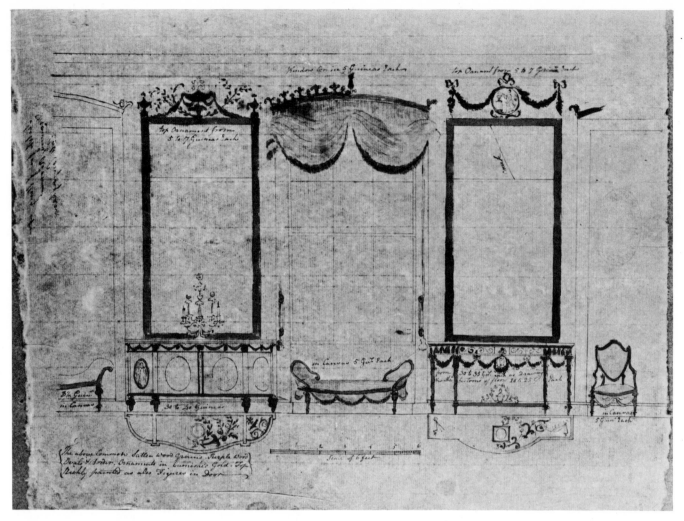

Both Marot and the younger Talman were well aware of this, but it is undoubtedly William Kent who must count as the first great English decorator. Returning to England from Italy in 1719, he soon proved he was not the English Raphael, but he had developed a broad approach to architecture, decoration and furniture design and was able to impose a total look on a room, or an apartment in a house. This particular talent was soon exploited, and in 1721 he began to work in royal circles. Six years later he was appointed to Houghton, Sir Robert Walpole's house in Norfolk, over the heads of both Colen Campbell and Thomas Ripley, and it is surely no accident that the special use of the word "decorate" in connection with his approach was coined about that time.[27]

However at the very end of the 18th century it seems that architects tended to relax their degree of control, and as all aspects of decoration became more important and complex, as we shall see, a new degree of dominance was developed by the leading firms of upholsterers. This change in attitude was apparent in Sir Jeffry Wyatville's work at Windsor Castle, for he made it clear that he regarded "internal decorations as something of a comparitively temporary nature, liable to change with the fluctuations of taste, or new doctrines of convenience . . ." And in 1830 he spoke of the "internal decoration and gilding . . . forming a part of the building" and so his responsibility, but "the finishing of such parts of the walls of the room as do not form any part that appertains to the building, such as the framing to the silk-work and glasses, belongs to the furniture, and not to the building."[28]

The vast amount of work involved in such large and costly schemes tended to encourage the firms to expand and so become less personal in style, and it seems that Morell and Hughes, Crace & Co. and Morant's were evidently in a very much bigger way of business than, let us say, Norman, Chippendale or

13. A DESIGN FOR AN INTERIOR BY JAMES WYATT. A detailed drawing showing the relationship of the furniture and upholstery to the architectural design.

11. A SECTIONAL DRAWING OF A HOUSE BY EDWARD STEVENS, 1763.

12. A SECTIONAL DRAWING OF A HOUSE BY THOMAS HARDWICK. Both Hardwick and Stevens were pupils of Chambers and these schemes were influenced by his approach and style.

Bromwich. A satirical impression of one, Mr Soho, is given by Maria Edgeworth in *The Absentee*: "This first architectural upholsterer of the age, as he styled himself, and was universally admitted by all the world of fashion, then, with full powers given him, spoke *en maitre*. The whole face of things must be changed—there must be new hangings, new draperies, new cornices, new candelabras, new everything![29]

> The upholsterer's eye, in a fine frenzy rolling,
> Glances from ceiling to floor, from floor to ceiling;
> And, as imagination bodies forth
> The form of things unknown, the upholsterer's pencil
> Turns to shape and gives to airy nothing
> A local habitation and a NAME."

The other point of view is put by the 6th Duke of Devonshire, an inveterate builder, improver and decorator. After 30 years of constantly altering his many houses, he wrote in his *Handbook*: "He who has to furnish a great house is embarked in a sea of trouble and nothing but experience can teach what ought to be done—except Mr John Crace who, I have lately found, can teach it still better."[30] Today we might not fully share the Duke's enthusiasm for Mr Crace (Fig. 14), but, equally, we might regret the reaction against his influence and that of other decorators that set in about 1850. A few great schemes continued to be done like the refitting of Alnwick Castle by a team of Italians, but this was the exception. Members of many of the older families whose ancestors had been patrons of the leading architects and designers in the 18th century were no longer interested in such things and retreated into an attitude that considered a concern for them bad form.

14. THE LOWER LIBRARY AT CHATSWORTH, DERBYSHIRE. Decorated for the 6th Duke of Devonshire by John Crace, about 1840.

Chapter 2
The quicksand of style and fashion

This chapter is concerned with a brief analysis of fashion and with a chronology of influences and changes in taste from 1660 to 1830.

The basic element in the development of fashion is imitation and the need of the leaders "to keep ahead of the Joneses". This affects all aspects of life—clothes, manners and talk, as well as architecture and decoration—and, when communication is poor, changes take place slowly, because the opportunities to imitate are only limited. But as communications improve, people adopt new ideas more quickly, and all too soon those who have carefully hedged themselves with a degree of what they take to be exclusive find they need to develop new defences against outsiders. Thus what is smart one moment becomes commonplace the next and *démodé* the third.

Although this was well understood from the late 17th century and is one element in the comedies of manners, the first Englishman to apply this to business and to leave a written record of his thoughts was apparently Josiah Wedgwood. In his letters to his partner Thomas Bentley there are two particularly vivid illustrations. In 1767 he wrote: "The reasons you have given against my fixing upon an Auction Room . . . are solid, ingenious, and more than sufficient, and there is another nearly as strong as any of them. At present the Nobility and Gentry recommend one another to my rooms . . . but everybody would be apt to stroll into an Auction Room . . . and that would be the most effectual method I could take to keep my present sett of customers out of it. For you well know they will not mix with the rest of the World any farther than their amusements, or conveniencys, make it necessary to do so."[1]

Five years later he wrote: "The Great People have had these Vases in their Palaces long enough for them to be seen and admired by the *Middling Class* of People, which Class we know are vastly, I had almost said, infinitely superior, in number to the Great, and though a *great price* was, I believe, at first necessary to make the Vases esteemed *ornament for Palaces*, that reason no longer exists. Their character is established, and the middling people would probably buy quantities of them at a reduced price . . ."[2]

Some 40 years later William Porden was concerned with the same kind of problem when working for Lord Grosvenor at Eaton Hall (Plate 18) and in London. On different occasions he wrote to his patron: "It would not be pleasant to make the beauties of Eaton common before it is finished, nor to permit another to reap the benefit of your Lordship's experiments which have cost so much expense and study;" "the chairs are very good, but they want some improvement in their form and embellishments and after all they are any-bodies chairs—they were made for the Marquis of Abercorn and Sir

Thomas Somebody—I would have them made for Lord Grosvenor;" and "I am anxious that your Lordship should be superior to everyone else, and that you should be followed, not follow any man in matters of taste."[3]

Wedgwood's and Porden's remarks are of cardinal importance in understanding the nature of fashion and how and why it changes, but at the same time it is extremely difficult to catch all the inflexions that indicate alterations in fashion and taste a century or two ago, and when one reads of work being done, either in letters or documents, it is often impossible to know how up to date the patron and his craftsmen were.

Closely related to this concern for the exclusive is a desire for novelty, and so for novelty bound up with technical advances, improvements in methods of manufacture and inventions of new products. Indeed one history of decoration in England could be written solely from this point of view, and although some individual developments will be referred to later, it seemed right to make the general point at this stage. The fashion for wallpaper from the late 1730s was directly related to improvements in flocking and colour printing. Equally the lightness and gaiety of the Rococo found admirable expression in printed linens and cottons, the production of which was mastered in England towards the middle of the century.

Sometimes a successful fashion was related to the introduction of a cheaper way of achieving an effect. Part of the point of flock paper was that it was an economical alternative to cut velvet or damask hangings. So it was with papier maché a few years later: ornaments made of it proved an acceptable alternative to stucco work while it could be made into fillets for wallhangings and paper that were much cheaper than carved wood. Adam had a particular penchant for patent materials, casting ornaments in lead and pewter for doors and chimney pieces, ordering grates in a new alloy called tutenag or plakton, and so on.

But of course fashionable taste could be as misled then as now by the novelty of a product, and not all were successful. Boulton, who was a man of great curiosity and inventive capacity, found this to his cost, and some of his schemes were failures, even though, as in the case of mechanical painting, they might win the support of such a formidable figure as Mrs Montagu, who used this invention in her house in Portman Square.[4]

But fashion was not the only consideration that influenced a patron's decisions about the decoration of his house. The old idea of port lingered a long time, and a country house was not just an expression of personal likes and dislikes; it was a symbol of a family's position, and a grand house was seen as part of the national heritage. As Vanbrugh wrote, Blenheim "was to be calculat'd for, and Adapted to, a private Habitation, yet it ought at ye same time, to be consider'd as both a Royall and a National Monument, . . ."[5] from the beginning. Such a view affected its treatment, as can be seen in Perceval's letters to Bishop Berkeley about Castletown, Co. Kildare, the grandest early 18th century house in Ireland. "I am glad for the honour of my country," he wrote, "that Mr. Conolly has undertaken so magnificent a pile of building, and your advice has been taken upon it." And he urged the use of Irish marble "for since this house will be the finest Ireland ever saw, and by your description fit for a Prince, I would have it as it were the epitome of the Kingdom, and all the natural varieties she afford should have a place there."[6]

The honour of a family was invariably bound up with its antiquity, or its claim to antiquity, and also this often had a bearing on the way a house was treated. On occasion it led to sets of portraits being made up to decorate a room, as happened in the halls of two Northamptonshire houses, Drayton and Boughton at the end of the 17th or beginning of the 18th centuries. In both houses the antiquarian spirit was strong: at Drayton the 2nd Earl of Peterborough had portraits painted of the royal benefactors of the Mordaunt family, Henry V, Henry VII, Henry VIII, and Charles I (Fig. 15); and at Boughton there were

III. A DETAIL OF THE BOUDOIR AT
ATTINGHAM PARK, SHROPSHIRE,
SHOWING THE GILDING OF ONE OF
THE CAPITALS AND THE COMBINATION
OF GILDING AND COLOUR. An
alternative method of gilding
columns is shown in Plate XXXV.

IV. DETAIL OF THE CHIMNEYPIECE
WALL IN THE BOUDOIR, ATTINGHAM
PARK. A rare example of untouched
late 18th century painting that
shows the use of different tones.
(See also Plate V.)

portraits of late medieval and Tudor Montagus ordered either by the 1st or 2nd Duke of Montagu.[7] And at Aston Hall, Birmingham, there are 18th century portraits of Elizabethan Holtes. The same spirit is expressed in Daniel Garrett's corrected Jacobean facade of Northumberland House, London, restored and improved about 1750 to express the ancestry of the Percys and the Seymours. Much later, in Porden's retention of the Charles II ceiling in the saloon at Eaton Hall, a bridge was made between the 19th century Grosvenors and Hugh Lupus. The 18th century history of Audley End illustrates this on a more substantial scale: it starts with Vanbrugh's screen in the Great Hall, continues with Lord Howard de Walden's redecoration of the saloon between 1763 and 1785 (Fig. 16) and ends with the 2nd and 3rd Lord Braybrooke's Jacobean-style decorations of the early 1830s. At each stage the owner was moved by contemporary ideas and fashions, but the concept of the continuity of the family and of traditional values was always the vital element. As a contributor to *Common Sense* wrote in 1739: "There was something respectable in those old hospitable Gothic halls, hung round with helmets, breast-plates, and swords of our ancestory; I entered them with a constitutional sort of reverence, and looked upon those arms with gratitude as the tenor of former ministers and the check of Kings . . . and when I see them thrown by to make way for some tawdry gilding and carving, I can't help considering such alterations as ominous even to our constitution."[8]

Such conservatism is strongly tinged with sentiment, and sentiment is a force never to be discounted in the history of decoration, for it has always acted as a stop against change and concessions to fashion in family houses. Uppark, in Sussex, is, or perhaps regrettably one now has to say 'was', an example of the conservative effects of longevity and loyalty: Sir Harry Featherstonhaugh, Emma Hamilton's early lover, inherited from his father in 1774 at the age of 20 and at the age of 70 he married Mary Ann Bullock, said to have been at one time

15. THE GREAT HALL, DRAYTON HOUSE, NORTHAMPTONSHIRE. Portraits of earlier royal benefactors of the Mordaunt family painted about 1700 apparently as part of Talman's refitting of the Great Hall.

V. PART OF A PAINTED DOOR IN THE BOUDOIR, ATTINGHAM PARK.

33

16. THE SALOON AT AUDLEY END,
ESSEX. The decoration of the walls
was executed between 1763 and
1785 to marry up with the original
Jacobean ceiling, chimneypiece
and overmantel. The series of
portraits includes versions of earlier
ones painted by Biagio Rebecca
for the room.

the diary-maid; his widow succeeded in 1847 and, on her death in 1877, she left Uppark to her sister, Miss Bullock-Featherstonhaugh, who maintained it exactly "as Sir 'Arry 'ad it" until her death in 1895. This is an exceptional record and one of the fascinating things about it is that during the sisters' ownership interest in decoration in houses of Uppark's type and quality became regarded as bad form. A gentleman did not notice his own surroundings or the possessions in the houses of his friends, but accepted them as part of his birthright, and thought it in bad taste if anyone else mentioned them either. It was this attitude that the American ladies like the Jerome sisters undermined.

These underlying and constantly changing concepts of fashion and good taste, and vulgarity and bad form crop up again and again as one reads about attitudes to decoration; but as in so many aspects of English artistic life, there was some sense of inferiority as well, a feeling that went with a sense of being cut off from the main stream of European ideas and achievement. This was particularly marked in decoration, because the French laid such stress on all the refinements of living. It is a combination of this uncertainty with a desire to show that imported goods could be afforded that underlies the complex history of French influence on English decoration and attitudes. It is a subject so crucial to the English style that it seemed worth considering the chronological development of the English style primarily in terms of French influence.

However, before embarking on this inevitably compressed bird's-eye view we would suggest that decoration should also be considered in relation to fashion in dress as well as the development of architectural style. This is particularly important in the 18th century because of the great significance attached to dress and also because of the relationship of pattern and cut in the

34

development of fashion. To start with, prominent people spent much more of their income on dress than would be usual today, and proportionately they spent more on dress than on the fitting up of their houses. But whereas we regard changes in fashion in dress consisting primarily in alterations in line and cut, they considered pattern and colour as the principal sources of novelty. And as a result of this they probably placed more emphasis on the patterns used in decoration, particularly in the first four decades of the 18th century. In addition the patterns themselves were affected by two different forces. During the 1730s and 40s the hooped overskirt and petticoat got bigger and bigger, while at the same time the general development of late Baroque and Rococo ornament design favoured a less formal and more relaxed style.

The history of costume is more complicated than the history of decoration, because it is even more ephemeral and subject to constant, albeit minor, alterations. It seizes on a new idea earlier, develops it more rapidly and discards it more quickly.

Gradually during the 18th century the balance between pattern and cut in fashion altered, but at the same time there was an increasing emphasis on informality and comfort in dress, both male and female. The adoption, for instance, of the frock with its flat turned-down collar as informal dress for men in London and everyday dress in the country in the 1730s reflects a fundamental change in social habits and attitudes to sporting country life. Equally robes and sacks were inconvenient, as Lady Hertford wrote to Lady Pomfret in 1741: "I am myself so awkward as to be yet unable to use myself to that dress [robes or saques], unless for visits of ceremony; since I do not feel at home, in my own house, without an apron; nor can endure a hoop, that would overturn all the chairs and stools in my closet."[9] It is remarks like these that show how dangerous it is to look at the changes in decoration in the middle decades of the 18th century purely in terms of architectural style.

Later in the century publishing began to play a more important role in changes in fashion in dress and decoration. Not only were coloured fashion plates and fashion magazines introduced, but books and sets of engravings on the Orders, architectural design and planning and furniture were joined by others that provided guidance on the complete decoration of rooms. Moreau's *Monument de Costume* appeared in 1775, and in the early '80s the first fashion magazines were published in France. In London the earliest, Heideloff's *Gallery of Fashion*, appeared in 1794. Thus there were new possibilities of annual fashion in costume, and line became a more important element, a development that it is tempting to see reflected in the linear style of engraving of Percier and Fontaine and so the whole Regency movement. This linear style encouraged a more close-fitting style of dress, and this too probably had a bearing on the way rooms came to be arranged, as we shall see later in this chapter.

However carefully one analyses fashion and what contributes to change, one always comes back to the inconsistency of human nature and fluctuations in enthusiasm, to that element which Lady Holland (Fig. 23) saw in herself when she wrote in 1764: "I am rather changeable to be sure in those things [the decoration of her house]; but tho' whims and fripperies may have a run, one always returns to what is really handsome and noble and plain."[10] And a desire for novelty was not just a purely feminine trait, for when Lady Sarah Spencer went to Carlton House in May, 1810, she said that it "is so magnificent just now . . . He [the Prince] changes the furniture so very often, that one can scarcely find time to catch a glimpse at each transient arrangement before it is all turned off for some other."

This is a particularly valuable observation for it is a warning against placing too much emphasis on the hard and fast rules of what seems to us "period style". Carlton House, like all other houses, was always changing: pictures were moved, furniture was altered, colours were changed, failures were discarded and old favourites hung on to. And so in all aspects of the history of decoration one is dealing with the quicksands of taste. But provided such limitations and qualifications on any definitions that may seem convincing are born in mind, it is not too dangerous to set out on a brief chronology.

There has always been a strong love-hate element in all aspects of Anglo-French relations that makes it difficult to separate influences and imitations from a morass of jealousies, criticisms and patriotic fervour, for both countries have usually been unwilling to admit the extent of their borrowings. As far as English decoration is concerned, the influence of France has been the most important single force, but this influence has not been consistent, and to understand it, it may be helpful to think of the development of the English style between 1660 and 1830 in four main periods. These periods do not correspond with architectural styles and also they cannot be defined too precisely because of overlapping.

The first phase covers the reign of Charles II, with a case to be made for pushing the *terminus ante-quem* back to the arrival of his mother Queen Henrietta Maria as the bride of Charles I in 1625; and if for convenience it needs a label, the Years of Experiment might be used.

In the same way the second might be called the Age of Parade, for it not only embraces the Baroque but the Palladian period as well. Again it cannot be defined too precisely, for many of the ideas associated with the Baroque in England only gradually won acceptance; and during the Palladian period, fundamental changes started to take place that are not adequately covered by the term Rococo.

The Rococo was but one element in the third phase, which starts rather tentively in the 1720s and continues until the mid 1770s. It is marked by a new degree of sophistication that involved a sense of relaxation in Society, the establishment of the villa as the dominant type of house, and a new freedom for ladies of intelligence and spirit; and it is the period in which the concept of interior decoration became established in England, even if the term itself was seldom used.

The fourth period opens with the years of Holland's best work and then is marked by a decline in taste in the early 19th century. Fashion became more regimented as the markets expanded, work became coarser and insensitive, and upholsterers became the dictators of decoration.

Evelyn and his contemporaries attributed all the signs of extravagance at Charles II's court to the influence of France, and it was typical of the time that the author of *England's Interest and Improvement* should write in 1663 that it was the French who "had introduced new modes and new tastes and set us all agog and having increased among us considerable trades, witness the vast multitude of broad and narrow silk weavers, makers of looking glasses, paper, fringes and gilded leather".

To a large extent this was true, for during the first 70 years of the century the French court, having finally given up its peripatetic life, had developed a settled pattern and formal etiquette that demanded a much more elaborate kind of setting. And to this end the French kings, starting with Henri IV and later encouraged by Richelieu and Mazarin patronised the luxury arts as an act of policy. Slowly the emphasis switched from an attitude to furniture and decoration based on a mobile life with hangings and covers as the most costly items, to an architectural view that saw furniture and all aspects of decoration as subservient to a general controlled design for a single room or a whole apartment. With this change came a demand for a greater variety of types of furniture as well as for new standards of decoration and enrichment, and to meet this Henri IV and his successors encouraged skilled foreign craftsmen to settle in Paris.

To what extent these developments influenced the furnishing of the palaces of Charles I and the houses of his inner court circle is now difficult to judge, for very few pieces of court furniture survive and there are no beds or hangings. All we have are the fascinating inventories of the Royal Palaces made after Charles I's execution.[11] Apart from these the main evidence is provided by the early tapestries woven at Mortlake, including the Acts of the Apostles, for the weaving of which Charles I acquired the Raphael cartoons.

The outbreak of the Civil War brought all that kind of patronage to an end, but the habit of house building was resumed in the late 1640s and 1650s, and judging by Webb's work at Wilton and elsewhere the tradition of rich furnishing was unlikely to have been given up. But for evidence we have to rely on inventories like that of the Countess of Warwick in 1659. The costly fabrics used for beds, curtains and upholstery that are listed have a character that we tend to regard as an innovation of the 1660s, and, although the Restoration undoubtedly provided new opportunities as well as closer ties with France, it would probably be wise to treat Evelyn's remarks with at least a degree of caution.

It was a fortunate chance that the Restoration in England coincided with important developments in France. By August, 1661, Fouquet's chateau of Vaux-le-Vicomte was virtually complete after four years' work, and this achieved a new degree of splendour through the unity of design, decoration and furnishing. It made a deep impression on the young Louis XIV, who came of age that year, and it inspired Colbert's establishment in 1663 of the Manufacture Royale des Meubles de la Couronne at Gobelins under the direction of Le Brun. As Directeur du Bâtiments and Premier Peintre du Roi as well as the head of Gobelins, Le Brun was a new kind of artistic dictator, but as he did not regard his status as an artist as incompatible with that of a decorative designer, he harnessed all the arts together for the glory of Louis XIV and the prosperity of France.

The principal task which faced him from the late 60s until the early 80s was the creation of Versailles, which was sufficiently complete for the court to become established there in 1682. That vast palace, with its elaborately painted and gilded ceilings, its panelling of coloured marbles and its silver furniture, chandeliers, chairs and benches, and even silver tubs for orange trees, was the envy of the kings and princes of Europe. But its first and grandest phase was short, for in 1692 virtually all the silver furniture had to be melted down to pay for the King's wars.

In Restoration England there was no Gobelins and no Le Brun, and it took some time for the style associated with Hugh May and Roger Pratt to establish itself, for like Inigo Jones in the 1620s and '30s, they were hampered by a shortage of skilled craftsmen. Not only skill in execution was lacking, but skill in design as well: draughtsmanship and engraving were generally of a low standard, and all fine books and prints had to be imported. Pricke's *The Ornaments of Architecture* (1674) and *The Architect's Storehouse* (1674) are both crudely illustrated with copies of French prints, some at least 30 years old.[12]

This situation is apparent at Ham House, where there are great differences in quality between the different aspects of the Duke and Duchess of Lauderdale's decorations. The woodwork, the carving and the plasterwork is not particularly accomplished, nor is the painting, graining and marbling that still survives in many rooms. But in contrast the fragments of parquety flooring in the original state bedroom and the Queen's Closet (Fig. 17) and the scagliola used for the window sills and fire-place in the Closet are both fine work and in keeping with the ebonised and veneered furniture with silver mounts, the silver-mounted chimney furniture and the use of rich stuffs. Great care was lavished on upholstery, not only on the materials but on the way they were worked up and enriched.

Today Ham has a faded mellow quality that is obviously quite different from

17. THE QUEEN'S CLOSET AT HAM HOUSE, SURREY, ABOUT 1670. The richness of the crimson and gold upholstery of the sleeping chairs in the alcove, which also matches the wall hangings, complements the parquetry floor and the use of scagliola for the fireplace.

the overpowering and highly coloured impression it must originally have made, as can be seen if the upholstery of one of a set of early 18th century chairs done in yellow satin with a panel design embroidered in red corded silk (Fig. 18) is compared with an original but unused, and so unfaded, piece that has been discovered recently (Plate II). The rooms must have been showy and opulent in a vigorous way, and even rather crude by mid and late 18th century standards.

But the approach of a contemporary of Charles II to visual matters was quite different from that of a contemporary of George III: it was the age of the virtuoso and, as Walter Houghton[13] has shown, a virtuoso's curiosity was scientific, or at least pseudo-scientific, rather than aesthetic: he was fascinated by oddities, exotics, deceits, objects that displayed ingenuity and involved a great deal of detail, and this is reflected in the fashion for the imports from the East, for carved and gaily painted figures of blackamoors, for closely observed naturalistic carving, still life painting and trompe l'oeil. There are many contemporary remarks that bear this out, particularly in the diaries of Pepys, Evelyn and Celia Fiennes. It was very typical of the age that Pepys should have been so fascinated with Samuel Hoogstraeten's perspective that hung in Thomas Povey's house and is now at Dyrham Park in Gloucestershire (Fig. 19), and that Celia Fiennes's highest form of praise was that something was so well

18. AN EARLY 18TH CENTURY
CHAIR FROM A SET AT HAM HOUSE.
The yellow satin upholstery is
original. An unused piece is
shown in Plate II.

done that it looked like something else. When she went to Burghley she described the figures on the blue velvet bed as "so finely wrought in Satten stitch it
looks like painting," and at Chatsworth she admired the ceiling of the gallery
because "round the top was raile and barristers so naturally drawn just round
the cornish that you would take it for a railed walke round the top to looke
down into the gallery."[14]

Architecturally the early Charles II style continued in vogue for several
decades as the style of the richer gentry, but it was not sufficiently monumental
for the King or his richer courtiers, and fairly soon they looked again to France.

In the mid 1670s, just after the Lauderdales had redecorated Ham and
before the French court had moved to Versailles, Charles II began to remodel
the state rooms at Windsor Castle in accordance with the designs of Hugh May,
and with Verrio as chief painter and Gibbons as chief carver. Even from the
parts of this scheme that remain and from Pyne's views its novelty is apparent:
there is a new sense of scale and grandeur combined with a marvellous sense of
detail, and the total impression is of decoration for parade. Henceforth for the

39

19. *VIEW DOWN THE CORRIDOR*
BY SAMUEL HOOGSTRAETEN, 1662.
It epitomizes the Restoration taste
for detail, ingenuity and deceit in
decoration.

next seventy years virtually all great building schemes, whether royal or aristocratic, had a similar quasi-public character and were bound up with political success or ambition.

Charles II was undoubtedly inspired by Louis XIV's building schemes when he was considering improvements at Windsor, and it was inevitable that these, in their turn, should have influenced his more prominent courtiers. But few went as far as Ralph Montagu and the Duke of Somerset in building markedly French looking houses in London, and at Boughton and Petworth. However, the French concept of an *appartement* was taken up, and even the term itself was adopted in the royal palaces and at great houses like Chatsworth, Burghley and Boughton. The details of this type of arrangement will be discussed in the next chapter, but here attention must be drawn to the extraordinary emphasis placed on the state bed. It was much the most important and costly piece of furniture in such a house and was the climax to it. All the rooms that were passed through on the way to it were part of a processional route and dominated by a sense of parade.

Indeed the state beds found in English houses at the very end of the 17th century were much taller and more elaborate than anything recorded in France, and evidently the layout of the rooms and the etiquette attached to them was more elaborate and formal.[15]

Partly this elaboration of the beds (Figs. 20, 63, 64) was due to Daniel Marcot who worked in England from 1694 to 1696 and maintained his contacts in the following years. Born in 1663, the son of Jean Marot, the author of *L'Archit-ecture Francaise*, he was brought up in close contact with the formulators of the Louis XIV style, but in 1685 he fled from France to become the chief designer to William and Mary in Holland. Unfortunately the details of his English commissions and connections are still obscure, but it is important to realise that his influence here antedates the publication of his designs in 1702. They were no longer a novelty in France at that date, and by 1712, when a second edition appeared, a reaction against his Baroque exuberance was already starting in England.

20. A DESIGN FOR A STATE BEDROOM BY DANIEL MAROT, 1702. The hangings of the *lit à la duchesse* match the wall hangings and are *en suite* with the chairs placed round the edge of the room; the door to the right of the bed is partly masked by portières.

Marot was not the only Huguenot to come to England, and undoubtedly the influence of France on England was greatly increased by Louis XIV's policy of persecution that culminated in the revocation of the Edict of Nantes. in 1685. A great number of skilled craftsmen came over, particularly those trained in the luxury crafts and trades, and recent research has produced an imposing list of painters, gilders, carvers, silversmiths and upholsterers who carried out much of the finest work done in England in the last quarter of the 17th century. Many of them evidently sought help from Ralph Montagu, and through his control of the Royal Wardrobe, which was responsible for the furnishing of the royal houses, his own patronage and introductions to other grandees, English houses achieved an unparalleled richness. But whereas evidence of the talent of painters, gilders and carvers still survives, we have only the most tantalisingly vague idea of the skill of an upholsterer like Lapierre (Plates VII, VIII).

The eclipse of Le Brun after 1683, the cut-back in France in the 1690s and the relative poverty of the last decades of Louis XIV's reign combined with the years of war between the two countries coincided with increasingly close contacts not only between England and Holland but with Italy as well, and particularly Venice. The early Caroline tradition of collecting, established by the Earl of Arundel, had been revived to some degree in the 1680s by, among others, Lord Exeter and Sir Thomas Isham, but Lord Manchester's embassy to Venice in 1707 marked the opening of a period of closer and more fruitful relations between the two countries. The Grand Tour became a much more positive and organised concept, and English patrons even had hopes of discovering a native genius for history painting. This was the reason for William Kent's visit to Italy, and if on his return he showed his failure in that direction, he soon proved himself to be a decorator of a type that had hitherto not existed in England.

Not a radical by nature, he provided the equally conservative and well-established Whig aristocracy with a modified version of the Baroque style that had been in fashion for 50 years: he accepted the concept of parade and gave it a Palladian dress, fusing architecture, decoration, furniture and works of art into a single splendid whole, a fusion rather different from the proto-Rococo worked out by designers during the Régence in France, but possessing strong elements of its richness and grandeur.

Just as there was a divide in the mid 1670s and 1680s between the domestic style established in the early years of Charles II's reign and the Baroque that was partly a matter of scale and social purpose, there was another that developed slowly in the 1720s and 30s. What Sir John Summerson[16] has defined as the great house remained the dominant one, but from the early 1720s a few patrons and architects began to experiment with the villa, a much smaller and more compact type of house in which privacy, convenience and elegance were to be more important than parade and magnificence. However it took nearly 30 years for the villa to become fashionable, and it was not until the 1750s that in the hands of Isaac Ware, Robert Taylor and William Chambers it became the dominant type.

It was a development of fundamental importance and cannot be adequately studied just in terms of architecture, but needs to be seen in the context of changes in costume, styles of portraiture, gardening and the role of women. It was part of a change about which A. L. Rowse has written in connection with the family of the 3rd Duke of Marlborough, who died in 1758: "At the same time we observe a marked change in the tone and temper of the family. Though this is chiefly a matter of heredity and personal characteristics, it also reflects a change in the temper of the time, in society. People were becoming more relaxed, or at any rate less hard, less rough and dangerous. We note a decided improvement in the manners and way of life between the earlier and later eighteenth century ... Life had been very hard for [the 1st Duke and Duchess] though it was not altogether easy for their great grandchildren they could afford to take it more lightly, give themselves up to enjoyment, amuse themselves. Their position had been made for them. They could afford to be nice. And in fact they were: there is noticeable in this generation an extreme degree of refinement and sensibility, a delicacy that became almost Chinese and certainly decadent in the case of the fourth Duke."[17]

As life became easier, tastes became more sophisticated and skills more specialised. The role of the architect in house design became more dominant and the trades of the upholsterer, cabinet maker and paper hanger more complex as we have seen. There was more emphasis on change and fashion particularly in the set of artists and designers who frequented Slaughter's Coffee House and to whom the earliest phases of the Rococo in England are now credited.

In France the first stirrings of the Rococo have been traced back to the 1680s, to Bérain's development of the arabesque and to the work of Pierre le Pautre and Lassurance in the *Bâtiments* under J. H. Mansart in the last 15 years of the century; but it only became fashionable after Louis XIV's death, when the Duc d'Orleans took the court back to Paris from Versailles and the leadership of fashion passed into the hands of the *haute-bourgeoisie*. In that circle behaviour became less formal and a strong desire developed both for comfort and intimacy in houses; and, most important, talented intellectual ladies were able to make a new role for themselves. It was to meet the needs of this new life that new types of furniture were designed, and the art of chairmaking, for instance, took on its highly specialised character as can be seen from the bewildering variety of new forms and names introduced in the 1720s.

Although there were many anti-French blasts and laments in England in the 1730s like that in the *London Magazine* of 1738 which says "The ridiculous imitation of the French is now become the epidemical distemper of this Kingdom, poor England produces nothing fit to eat or drink or wear,"[18] the influence was constructive for the Slaughter's Coffee House circle who began to meet about that time.[19] The circle involved Gravelot, the engraver, who had arrived from France in 1730, Hogarth, Hayman, Gainsborough, Roubiliac, Ware and Paine, but they did not become a recognisable anti-Burlington force until the early 1740s when Frederick Prince of Wales came of age. In his circle moved Thomas Lyttleton of Hagley, Lord Chesterfield and Lord Baltimore, all builders in the 1740s of houses that combined elements inspired by French design with a more orthodox Palladianism.

The best known of these French style decorations were undoubtedly those designed by Ware at Chesterfield House (Fig. 21) and characteristically illustrated in his *Complete Body of Architecture* of 1756 with plenty of anti-Gallican remarks no doubt inspired by the Seven Years War. And there were, or are, others at Woodcote Park, Woburn Abbey, Stratfield Saye, Petworth and Norfolk House, London.[20] Recently the Woburn and Stratfield Saye interiors and the Norfolk House Music Room have been linked with Borra and the Franco-Italian traditions of Turin, but what is revealing is the difference in proportion between English and French rooms that Walpole pointed out to Ann Pitt in the 1760s.[21] The English working from engravings copied French ornament, but they never adopted French proportions and generally found the combination of white and gold *boiserie* with sheets of looking-glass monotonous.

In the 1760s the resumption of close connections with France led to a rather different group of rooms, the tapestry rooms designed for various clients by Robert Adam.[22] After the Treaty of Paris of 1763 that concluded the Seven Years War many English went to Paris and either ordered furniture or acquired ideas as to how to alter their houses. Among them was Lord Coventry, who saw the prospectus for a new type of Gobelin tapestry and thereupon ordered a set in 1764, asking Adam to design a room at Croome Court to take it (Fig. 22). Of the nine sets woven between that year and 1789, no less than six found their

43

44

way to England, being ordered by William Weddell of Newby, Sir Henry Bridgeman of Weston, by the Duke of Richmond in 1765 when he was Ambassador, by Sir Lawrence Dundas for Moor Park, by Robert Child for Osterley and by the Duke of Portland. The success of these sets with the English may seem a little surprising, but perhaps it was because tapestry and tapestry rooms had never gone entirely out of favour. It had been used in state bedrooms and dressing rooms at Houghton and Holkham, and rooms with arabesque tapestries had been arranged at Hagley, Normanton and Squerries; and at West Wycombe the tapestry room was done with a set based on designs by Teniers.

Not only were French designs and artefacts admired, but so was the French way of life. When Lady Holland, who is seen sitting in a French-style chair in her portrait by Ramsey painted in 1763–66 (Fig. 23), went to France in 1765 to visit her brother, the Duke of Richmond, who was then ambassador, she wrote home: "Their houses are in general excellent; no people ever studied so much or succeeded so well in enjoying all the conveniences of life as the French do."[23]

Robert Adam would have agreed with her, and, indeed, part of the reason for his success was his appreciation of the French approach and control of detail as can be seen in his handling of the Croome Court Tapestry Room. In a sense both Chambers and Stuart were more original, for Chambers had moved in the most advanced neo-classical circles in Paris and Rome since about 1750 and had produced a revolutionary neo-classical design for a mausoleum for the Prince of Wales as early as 1751, and Stuart's designs for Kedleston in 1757 and for the Painted Room at Spencer House in 1759 (Fig. 24) have strong claim to be considered among the first neo-classical interiors in Europe; but neither had the temperament or the application for the kind of fashionable success that Adam so ardently desired and set out to achieve.

Some of his grandest commissions like that at Syon were in a sense old

21. THE ANTE-ROOM AT CHESTERFIELD HOUSE, LONDON, BY ISAAC WARE. Now demolished, it was the best known of the French style interiors executed in England in the 1740s.

22. THE TAPESTRY ROOM FROM CROOME COURT, WORCESTERSHIRE. A room by Robert Adam decorated to take the Gobelin tapestry ordered in 1764 (now in the Metropolitan Museum, New York).

23. LADY HOLLAND BY ALLAN RAMSAY, 1763-66. The former Lady Caroline Lennox, a daughter of the 2nd Duke of Richmond, she was a great admirer of French fashions.

Caroline Lady Holland.

24. THE PAINTED ROOM AT SPENCER HOUSE, LONDON, 1759. Decorated by James Stuart, it is one of the earliest complete neo-classical interiors in Europe.

fashioned, for the Duke and Duchess of Northumberland's way of life was closer in spirit to the Baroque age than to the 1760s, but it was dressed up with all the latest fashions as befitted an extravagant heiress.

"No Fashion is meant to last longer than a lover"—Horace Walpole on France, 1766

The increasing sophistication of taste in the third quarter of the 18th century brought with it a tendency to become bored. As early as 1750 Mrs Montagu was talking of being "Sick of Grecian elegance and symmetry, or Gothic grandeur and magnificence," and all having to "seek the barbarous gout of the Chinese."[24] And in 1766 Walpole said of France "No fashion is meant to last longer than a lover." Twenty-five years later when Lady Sarah Bunbury was arranging a house on the outskirts of Dublin for her sister, the Duchess of Leinster, she wrote: "But then you may grow tired of a fancy finishing; so be very sure you will like it for ten or fifteen years at least: for by that time it will be dirty and old fashioned."[25] And by the early 1770s Horace Walpole was clearly tired of the Adam style, for within nine years of first employing him himself, he described the Syon gateway as "all lace and embroidery, and as *croquant* as his frames for tables . . . From Kent's mahogany we are dwindled to Adam's filigree."[26]

By then the pace of change in all aspects of fashionable decoration, stucco and chimneypiece design, furniture, upholstery and colour, was getting faster, and this helps to explain why new themes and ideas were taken up with such wholehearted enthusiasm. Here the coming of age of the Prince of Wales in 1783 was a landmark for he immediately commissioned Henry Holland to remodel Carlton House. At that time neither the Prince nor his architect had been to France, but the Prince had become a friend of the Duc de Chartres, who became Duc d'Orleans in 1785, and the latter undoubtedly encouraged his Francophilia just as the Prince encouraged the Duc's Anglomania. This Francophilia encouraged a move towards the simpler lines of the Louis Seize style (a simplicity that was at least in certain aspects of furniture design the result of English influence) and it was taken up with enthusiasm by Holland as a result of his visit to Paris in 1785. However even before that he had taken on a French draughtsman called Trécourt.

About the same time it seems that at least two firms working for Holland decided to take on skilled French craftsmen, but sadly we know little more about them than what is recorded by J. B. Papworth and J. G. Crace.[27] According to Papworth, Sheringham's of Great Marlborough Street started in business in 1786 and employed Delabrière, Boileau, Dumont le Romain and Boulanger; according to Crace they employed two Italians, Rosetti and Louis. Papworth describes how the firm became a training ground: "he was used to spend some time in the study of Internal Decoration (and Fresco work) as then practised, it having been lately introduced from France by Mr. Sheringham of Great Marlborough Street, and was making its way into general use;" and he also records meeting there in 1793 George Morant, one of the best known decorators of the next generation.

The other important firm was that of the Eckhardt's, which also started in 1786. They specialised in elaborate wallpapers, and, according to Crace, employed among others Boileau, Feuglet, Joinot and Jones. There is a conflict of evidence as to who worked where, but it is apparent that both were influenced by current French fashions, and together with the French *marchand mercier*, Daguerre, who also opened a shop in London the same year, they were probably responsible for most of the Louis Seize decoration done in England in the late 1780s and 1790s. Little of it survives, but one of the most elegant interiors is the circular boudoir at Attingham Park, Shropshire, possibly painted by Delabrière in the late 1780s. (Fig. 25. Plates III, IV, V).

When Horace Walpole was so struck by Carlton House in 1785, it was not finished, and there was probably less sign of Louis Seize influence than it showed in later years. By the late 80s it must have had the most elegant interiors ever achieved in England, and it is a matter of lasting regret that there is no record of them in their prime. And to judge the quality of Holland's work one must go to Althorp, Woburn and Southill (Fig. 124) As in the 1750s it was not possible to create rooms with French proportions, but Holland got closer to it by reducing the height of the chimney piece and the dado and by using narrow pier glasses, usually with over-panels containing trophies between windows and over chimneypieces, thus creating a strong vertical emphasis.

However a French character was also imparted by much richer treatment of surfaces than one might expect to-day. It was probably under Holland's influence that the festoon curtain (Fig. 83) was largely replaced by the French draw curtain and draped valance (Fig. 96); and walls were panelled and hung with elaborately bordered fabrics. This kind of work offered scope to upholsterers and their work became increasingly complex and expensive, involving yards of velvet and satin and deep fringes, as can be seen in Pyne's views of Carlton House in his *Royal Residences* (Fig. 26): at the same time it gave upholsterers the chance to develop a much more dominating position in the field of interior decoration, a position they were to enjoy for about 100 years. Perhaps the best illustration of this is the history of the Saloon at Devonshire House in the lifetime of the 6th Duke, for by chance there is a drawing that shows it at the time of his succession in 1811 (Fig. 27) and then there is another of it after he had refurnished it about 1820 (Plate XXXIX); and its final state is recorded in *Country Life* photographs taken in about 1915 (Fig. 28).

It was not only the upholsterers who benefited, but painters and gilders and

47

25. THE BOUDOIR AT ATTINGHAM
PARK, SHROPSHIRE. Designed by
George Stewart and painted in the
late 1780s, perhaps by Delabrière,
it is one of the best preserved
English interiors influenced by
the Louis XVI style.

a host of other specialists. Graining (Fig. 180) and marbling both came back into fashion after a lapse of some 70 years, and there was a great demand for scagliola (Plate 39). Also huge sums were spent on gilding.

But it was a style that could easily degenerate into vulgarity as certainly happened at Carlton House after Holland's death. However there were fundamental reasons for this. The Baroque style and the Palladian were both essentially aristocratic, but the villa and all subsequent developments in decoration as in dress were marked by a gradual breaking down of barriers; what was smart, new and exclusive was increasingly dependant on money, and money itself was becoming more plentiful. Wedgwood and Boulton both understood this, and Boulton's rejection of a proposal from the Eckhardts in 1796 illustrates this new situation admirably for his reasons would have been inconceivable thirty years before: "He knows from his own repeated Experience that such branches as depend upon the Fashion of the Day, the Whim, the Tast, Caprice and Fancy of Nobility and persons of Fashion are never profitable in the end and often Ruinous to the Undertaker: and after 50 years Experience in various Manufactorys Matthew Boulton is convinced that it is much better to work for

48

VI. THE SALOON AT DEVONSHIRE
HOUSE, LONDON, ABOUT 1820.
William Hunt's watercolour shows
the room after the 6th Duke of
Devonshire's first alterations.

VII. THE CANOPY IN THE LONG
GALLERY AT HARDWICK HALL,
DERBYSHIRE. Originally part of the
angel bed made by Lapierre for
Chatsworth at the order of the 1st
Duke of Devonshire, it is perhaps
the finest example of late 17th
century upholstery.

VIII. A DETAIL OF THE CANOPY
AT HARDWICK.

IX. A SECTION OF THE BASE VALANCE
OF THE 17TH CENTURY SPANGLE
BED AT KNOLE, KENT. As this is
covered, it is less faded than the
bed. The crimson silk is
ornamented with a strap design
of buff silk embroidered and
bordered with gold and silver
thread, and it is trimmed with
deep trellis fringe.

26. THE SALOON AT DEVONSHIRE
HOUSE, LONDON. This drawing done
in 1811 shows Kent's interior
before it was first enriched by the
6th Duke of Devonshire. A later
view is shown in Plate VI.

27. THE SALOON AT DEVONSHIRE
HOUSE AS IT WAS ABOUT 1915.
Photographed a few years before
its demolition, this shows the effect
of the 6th Duke's later alterations,
about 1840.

Crimson Drawing Room.
CARLTON HOUSE.

28. THE CRIMSON DRAWING ROOM
AT CARLTON HOUSE, LONDON.
Pyne's plate, published in 1819,
shows elaborate continued draperies
right round the room, and two
patterns of chair drawn forward
from the walls in two facing rows,
evidence of a taste that had moved
a long way from that of Holland
who had designed the ceiling.

the Gross Mass of the people of the world, than for the Lords and Princes of it . . ."[28] The first architectural books published in England had been intended for the aristocracy, and it was not until the mid 1740s that writers began to think of a wider public.

In furniture it took rather longer, and decoration came in later still, only just squeezing into Hepplewhite's and Sheraton's books. The style popularised by the Prince of Wales and Holland needed books to explain it, and, inspired by Percier and Fontaine, Thomas Hope wanted to improve public taste with his *Household Furniture and Internal Decorations* of 1805 (Fig. 184).

George Smith was much less high-minded and his three books, *A Collection of Designs for Household Furniture and Interior Decoration* (1808), *A Collection of Ornamental Designs* (1812) and *The Cabinet-Maker & Upholsterer's Guide* (1826) were intended for a prosperous but not well informed public. To-day we find him a useful source of documented ideas, but in fact he was a great vulgarian and one of the people responsible for the decay of taste and standards in the early 19th century. In his 1812 book he produced designs for Borders "capable of being executed in carpetting, paper, or silk; they might also be cast and finished in ormulu or bronze." When one encounters such loose thinking, it is not surprising why so much work of that time lacks any life.

Apart from Percier and Fontaine's *Recueil de décorations intérieures* first published in 1801 and reissued in 1812, little is known in England about the later 18th and early 19th century French books of designs that are the equivalent of the early fashion plates and magazines, and so it is not easy to relate precisely the relationship of the French Empire style to the English Regency.

However in one aspect of it, the Egyptian style, it is possible to see how the influences worked and the fashion developed. Leaving aside such pre-1790 manifestations and use of Egyptian detail as occur in Piranesi, or in the chimney-piece of the Lansdowne House Gallery and Muntz's design for an Egyptian Room for Lord Charlemont, the English were as up to date as the French in their adoption of Egyptian motifs in the last years of the century. Indeed the billiard room at Cairness[29] by William Playfair (Figs. 29, 30) and the drawings sent from Rome by C. H. Tatham, Holland's former assistant, antedate the French fashion, which was stimulated by Napoleon's Egyptian campaign from 1798 to 1801. If patriotism and a love of the historical and exotic acted as a stimulus to it, the actual vocabulary of ideas and motifs was provided by Denon's *Voyages dans la Basse et la Haute Egypte*, first published in London in 1802 and in Paris two years later. In England the ideas caught on very quickly, and during the next 10–15 years not only were chimneypieces made with Egyptian detail as in the Drawing Room at Southill (1800), the Gallery at Attingham (1807) and at Bayfordbury (1812), but Egyptian motifs appear in furniture as in the Library at Stourhead (1802), and whole schemes of decoration were designed. Most of the elaborate ones have disappeared, among them the dining room at Goodwood, which according to Mason's guide, "was suggested from the drawings of Denon . . ."[30] and the Egyptian Hall under the North Portico at Stowe, which was described in the 1817 guidebook as "fitted up from Denon's designs of remains in the interior of one of the small temples of Tintyra." The Library at Barnsley Park (Fig. 31) is much less extreme an essay in the Egyptian taste, but it shows how quickly the motifs were absorbed into the vocabulary of decorators.

The Egyptian was but one of several revivals, for among the most significant strains running through the period was a growing desire for variety.

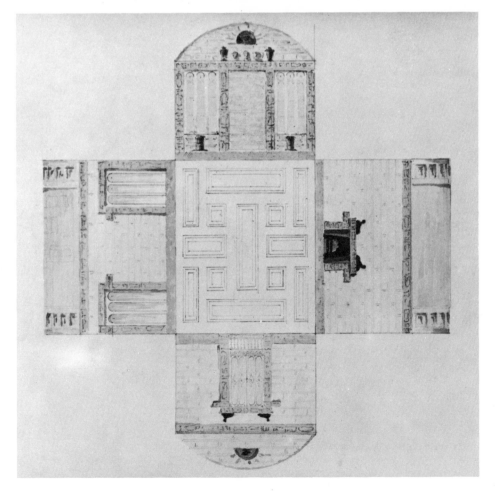

29. WILLIAM PLAYFAIR'S DESIGN FOR THE EGYPTIAN BILLIARD ROOM AT CAIRNESS, ABERDEENSHIRE, ABOUT 1790.

51

30. EGYPTIAN DECORATION IN SANDED WOOD IN THE BILLIARD ROOM AT CAIRNESS.

31. EGYPTIAN MOTIFS IN THE LIBRARY AT BARNSLEY PARK, GLOUCESTERSHIRE, ABOUT 1806-10.

Also the habit of collecting furniture, as opposed to ordering what was currently fashionable from a leading maker, was increasing. A few people like Horace Walpole had collected furniture and bric-à-brac for its historical associations and he was always interested to see early furniture surviving in houses he visited, but the concept of antique furniture does not seem to have become fashionable until the last quarter of the 18th century. Not a great deal is known about early dealing, but it was probably influenced by French interest in Louis XIV furniture in the 1770s and 80s and also by the Prince of Wales's admiration for it.[31]

Important as was the taste for French furniture in the development of the antique trade, as is known from Beckford's collection at Fonthill, it did not completely dominate it. And so it is interesting to come on Lady Wharncliffe's description of Levens in 1809. "It is in its original state," she wrote, "& they have had the good taste in fitting it up to preserve its character, & furnish it in the old style. Nothing can be better done . . ."[32] Its appearance a few years later was recorded in Nash's *Mansions of England in Olden Time*, (Fig. 32) and although from the figures it might be presumed that the interiors are romanticised, it is clear that they do show the rooms as they were, for the original watercolour for the plate of the dining room, but without the figures, is preserved at Levens. Another house that still preserves that kind of spirit is Cothele in Cornwall, and there it is apparent from contemporary illustrations that a definite attempt was made to play up the character of the Old English manor house for the benefit of the numerous visitors who went to see it.

In the 1820s the art of the *ancien régime* became fashionable in both countries and for those who could afford it, rooms in the French taste were considered very smart. In England their introduction is usually credited to Elizabeth, Duchess of Rutland, the wife of the 5th Duke, who had been to Paris in 1814 and brought back among other things a set of Gobelins tapestries now in the Gallery at Belvoir Castle. However her main essay there, the Elizabeth Saloon (Fig. 33), was only finished after her death in 1825. From 1815 to 1824 Lord Stuart de Rothesay was Ambassador in Paris and he collected *boiseries* and

32. THE DINING ROOM AT LEVENS HALL, WESTMORLAND. The lithograph from Nash's *Mansions of England in Olden Time* shows an early 19th century interpretation of a room in the Old English style.

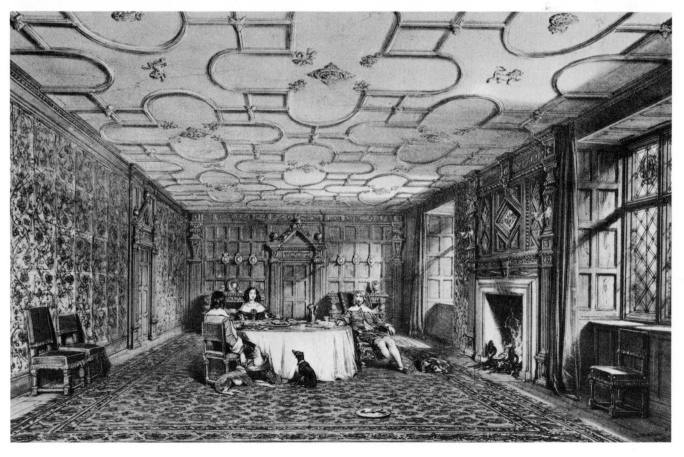

33. THE ELIZABETH SALOON AT
BELVOIR CASTLE, LEICESTERSHIRE.
One of the most elaborate Louis
revival rooms of the 1820s
and 30s.

fittings as well as French furniture, which he installed at Highclere Castle.
And in the 1830s the 2nd Earl de Grey rebuilt Wrest as a careful recreation of
a mid 18th century *château*. There was even sufficient demand for a reissue of
Chippendale designs by Weale in 1830 which includes copies of French rococo
engravings (Fig. 34). French furniture was obviously plentiful, but suitable
boiseries and chimneypieces were hard to find, and, as carving had become
expensive, B. D. Wyatt developed a way of casting Louis XIV and Louis XV
ornaments in composition and sinking them into plaster panels, a process he
used with great effect at Stafford House in the late 1820s and 1830s. Few
designers or patrons seem to have been as careful in their selection of sources
as Lord de Grey, and the results are generally just Louis rather than Quatorze
or Quinze, but the main point was that the style should look "in no way
answerable to the dwellings of persons of small fortune."[33]

The Louis revival is a particular element in the history of taste, but it was
important in the long run because it was probably largely responsible for the
alliance between antique dealers and decorators that still remains strong today.

The final aspect of this period that should be mentioned here, and which
will be discussed at greater length in the next chapter, is the first signs of break-
down in the formal arrangement of rooms that had been characteristic throughout the 18th century.

54

34. FRENCH INFLUENCE IN 1830:
THE TITLE PAGE TO WEALE'S EDITION
OF CHIPPENDALE'S DESIGNS.
Reprints of French Rococo
engravings are also included.

To the promoters of the Louis revival one of the points of the style was that it could not be readily imitated, but to older families who could not afford to be fashionable, it was flashy and vulgar. This can be sensed in Miss Elizabeth George's description of Stowe in 1845[34] and in old Mrs Charlton's views recorded in *The Recollections of a Northumbrian Lady* (1815–1866). Remembering how well she and her husband were received in Brussels in 1842, she thought of London where "the whole dignity of a family seemed to be concentrated in the style and standard of the furniture. Any *nouveau riche*, any scallywag of the present day who can produce, not quarterings, but yard on yard of smart upholstery is on a social footing with the aristocracy and, in a manner of speaking, give the latter their position in society."[35] If this reaction is related to Sir Osbert Sitwell's observations, much of the history of English taste in the second half of the 19th century becomes clear.

Chapter 3
The uses of houses and their arrangement

The separation of style from use and arrangement is essentially an artificial one, but it is almost inevitable because of the way art history has developed in this century. There has been a concentration on the former to the virtual exclusion of the latter, and it seems that few questions about the relevance of social practice in relation to architecture are ever asked. However recent changes in the arrangement of rooms at Ham House, Surrey, and Osterley Park,[1] Middlesex (Fig. 8), seem to signal a new approach, but it is still too early for this account to be more than a preliminary patchwork made up of a selection of quotations and a discussion of some aspects of planning.

The idea of state rooms or rooms of parade in a country house is no longer intelligible, the traditional concept for the apartment has dropped out, and we are not clear about the difference in the 18th century between a saloon and a drawing room. And to add to our difficulties, it is unlikely that two generations of any family ever lived in a house in exactly the same way. However at least most of the largest houses built or refitted in the last quarter of the 17th century had one feature in common, a Great Apartment, and that provides a logical point to begin our account.

At Chatsworth, Burghley, Boughton and Warwick Castle, to name but four places, it is the Great Apartment—the phrase comes from contemporary Boughton inventories—that provides the key to the interior. Although they are differently placed in relation to entrances and staircases, they all consist of a state bedroom, a Chamber of State as it was called in some places, preceded by one, two or even three rooms that served as a Presence Chamber, a Drawing Room and an Ante-Room and followed by a dressing room and closet. This was not an entirely novel form in the 1670s and 80s, for Bess of Hardwick had arranged the second floor at Hardwick on somewhat similar lines in the late 16th century; but what was new was the stronger emphasis on an enfilade and on the processional character of the sequence of rooms, even if none of them possessed the same drama as Hardwick.

The tightening up and elaboration of the apartment was not a specifically English phenomenon, but was influenced by French developments during the 17th century, as indicated by the French origin of the names used. The tendency in France was for the *chambre* to become a more private room, and for its public aspect to be taken over by the ante-chamber and the *grande salle*, the former often being used for meals. A dining room long remained the exception in a French house, but gradually the *grande salle* began to be replaced by two rooms, a *grand salon* and a *salon de compagnie*, the equivalent of the saloon and the drawing room in the larger 18th century English country houses. The *cabinet* or dressing room was the most intimate of the rooms and usually had one or more closets opening off it.[2]

The apartments in the four houses mentioned represent this kind of planning on its grandest scale in England, and it is surely no accident that work on them was in progress in the reign of Louis XIV's rival, William III. At Chatsworth, Burghley and Boughton it was fairly easy to copy the arrangement of the King's apartment in the up-to-date royal palaces, that is to say providing a grand staircase leading to the ante-room and the sequence of rooms that followed on.

At Hampton Court Palace the ante-room is arranged as a guard-room with trophies of arms on the panelling, and at Chatsworth and Boughton the walls are wainscotted. At Boughton the first room was called the Great Chamber; later at Chatsworth its counterpart (Fig. 35) was quite wrongly called the State Dining Room, and by Walpole's day the Heaven Room at Burghley had become the Great Room.[3] Whereas the Boughton designation harks back to Elizabethan and Jacobean practice, the later names at the other two houses were concessions to 18th century ideas on what was thought appropriate in a large house.

In these houses there is a strong emphasis on tradition even if they all did not have a Presence Chamber and chairs of state with canopies. Recently there has been considerable interest in the layout and purposes of state rooms, but our knowledge of the use of canopies is still far from complete. Originally a medieval symbol of kingship, they were not confined to royal houses but were also a privilege of great noblemen, and considerable importance was attached to them in the late 16th and early 17th century. To what extent they were used in the late 17th century houses is not known nor have we encountered any references to them in contemporary accounts, but earlier ones were sometimes left *in situ*. Indeed at Hardwick one remained in the High Great Chamber until

35. THE FIRST OF THE STATE ROOMS AT CHATSWORTH. Now called the State Dining Room, it was intended as the ante-room.

37. A CANOPY IN USE. Fruytiers's *Family of the Earl of Arundel*, 1643, is thought to record Van Dyck's design for a large state group.

38. THE DRAWING ROOM OF THE STATE APARTMENT AT CHATSWORTH. In contrast to the ante-room, it was always hung with tapestry.

early in this century. Its earlier appearance is recorded by P. Robinson in his additional *Vitruvius Britannicus* volume of 1835 (Fig. 36) and it is interesting to compare this view with Fruytiers's *Family of the Earl of Arundel* painted in 1643 (Fig. 37). In the painting the chairs are not visible because they are in use, but both at Knole and Hardwick there are 17th century chairs of state and the stools that went with them. And at Knole "a canopy of state of crimson silk damask wrought & fringed with gold" together with a chair, three stools and a dais was to be seen in the Cartoon Gallery as late as 1799. Probably the last one to disappear from a private house was the one at Hamilton Palace, which apparently remained until the house was demolished in the 1920s. However that may have been a royal perquisite like several state beds apparently made out of canopies, and now it is only at Hampton Court Palace that the original kind of arrangement can be seen. From the point of view of planning and decoration in the period under consideration here, they were an archaism, but no other single object emphasises so clearly the pre-18th century sense of hierarchy and the processional character of a great house.

Both at Chatsworth (Fig. 38) and at Boughton the second room is the Drawing Room and in both houses it has always been hung with tapestries. Then at Chatsworth follows another room now called the Music Room, again a concession to 18th century fashion, but originally the Presence Chamber and presumably intended to be provided with a chair of estate and a canopy. Next comes the State Bedroom, which would have been the chief room of the apartment and had a bed that was the most costly object in the house (and of which the canopy survives in the long gallery at Hardwick (Plate VII)). Beyond lies the Dressing Room which was originally decorated with cut lacquer panels, for it was usual to treat it as extravagently as the bedroom and often with more fantasy.

In other houses where the owner might not be so concerned with his own dignity and ability to house his sovereign with sufficient grandeur, the apart-

36. A CANOPY IN POSITION IN THE HIGH GREAT CHAMBER AT HARDWICK HALL, DERBYSHIRE. A plate from Robinson's *Vitruvius Britannicus* (1835).

ment would remain the key to the plan with fewer rooms appropriated to daily activities than was to become the custom later. At Ham, for instance, the Marble Dining Room on the ground floor of the garden front was flanked by the Duke and Duchess of Lauderdale's own apartments, which alternated in a delightfully intimate way. Over them lay the Great Apartment of three rooms preceded by the Gallery and two rooms in the north front that must have formed a spectacular approach when all the materials were so brilliant that they could distract the eye from the relative modesty of the architectural decoration. At Ham rather than at Chatsworth one is still strongly aware of the house being arranged in apartments, and the same is true of Dyrham, where despite some disturbance, it is still possible to follow John Povey's meaning in 1700 when he wrote to his father: "The Main Building containing not more than six or seven Apartments more for State than use except upon Extraordinary occasion."[4]

The basic idea of the apartment was a comfortable one and still survives as the most luxurious way of staying in a hotel, but just as a hotel needs public rooms adapted to specific purposes so did a large country house. Not only a dining room and a drawing room, but a gallery for pictures or sculpture, a library and even a music room seemed essential.

Naturally the change did not come over-night, but one sign of it is the process of fossilization that went on at Chatsworth and Boughton, and the half-hearted attempt to bring rooms up to date by giving them modern names. If the original usage now seems difficult to understand, it is comforting to find that in less than 70 years Georgians were evidently out of sympathy with it: when Philip Yorke went to Chatsworth in 1763, he found the arrangement of the state apartment inconvenient and the rooms "of little use but to be walked through."[5] Horace Walpole's reaction was somewhat similar, but he dwelt on how sad and old fashioned they were.[6] Use and taste had both changed profoundly.

Signs of change start to become apparent in the late 1770s. Vanbrugh had contributed little that was novel as far as planning was concerned: Blenheim, for instance, was a restatement of the Vaux-le-Vicomte idea of two apartments flanking a central *grande salle* (Fig. 39). However it is hard to judge this now as the beds have been removed and the atmosphere is of a series of Beaux Arts drawing-rooms.

As far as great houses are concerned, the key appears to be Houghton, and Kent's taking over the commission about 1727. As originally planned the piano nobile (Fig. 40) was divided by the hall and saloon, with two apartments to the north and the family rooms to the south. It is not know what modifications if any Kent made in the disposition of the south rooms, but it is surely significant that he arranged the Marble Parlour and a Cabinet for Sir Robert Walpole in what had been intended to be the ante-room and bed chamber of the east apartment.

Here for the first time one starts to notice the balance changing and more attention given to rooms for entertaining a company of people. At Holkham (Fig. 41) the process is taken two stages farther; a more or less self-contained family house was provided in one wing and the whole of the *piano nobile* of the main block was devoted to entertaining, to rooms for company and works of art and to the traditional rooms for an illustrious guest.

As the villa became a more fashionable and sophisticated type of house with an increasing emphasis on elegance and comfort, the traditional idea of a state apartment tended to look old fashioned, and it was only demanded by those who were either very grand or wished to be thought so. Here Kedleston and Osterley provide an interesting comparison. At Kedleston there is a spectacular state bed as the climax to an apartment, consisting altogether of four rooms, the other rooms on the *piano nobile* being a hall, saloon, dining room, music room, drawing room and library (Fig. 42). Kedleston, in fact, has everything that

39. THE PLAN OF THE PRINCIPAL FLOOR AT BLENHEIM PALACE, OXFORDSHIRE. The original arrangement was of two apartments flanking the central saloon.

40. THE PLAN OF THE PIANO NOBILE AT HOUGHTON HALL, NORFOLK. Kent altered the north-east apartment to provide a dining room with a cabinet for pictures beyond.

60

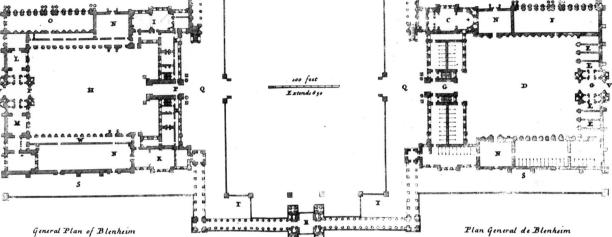

A The Body of the house
B Great Court
C The Chappel
D The Stable Court
E Coach houses
F A Greenhouse
G The Gates
H The Kitchin Court
I The Kitchin
K The Common Hall
L The Bakehouse
M The Landry

N Back Courts
O A Greenhouse
P The Gates
Q Terrasses
R The Great Gate
S Terrasses
T The Colonade upon ỹ great Terrasse
V Water Cistern
W Little Porticos
X Passages
Y The Principall Approach & way by
    the great Bridge

100 feet
Extends 650

General Plan of Blenheim

Plan General de Blenheim

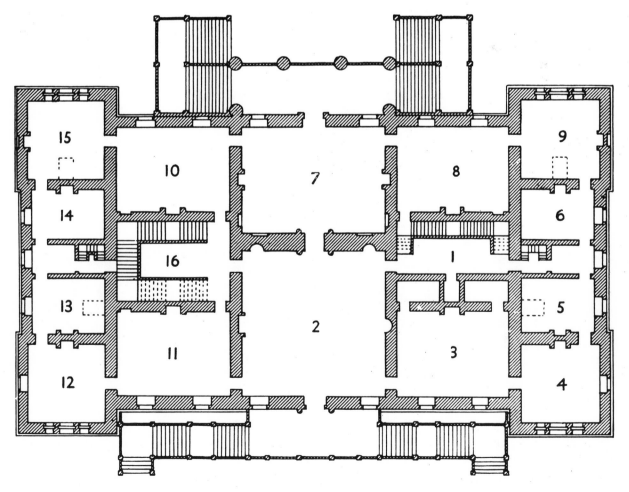

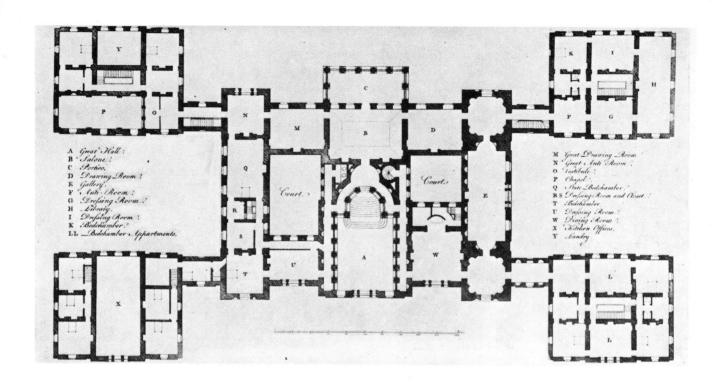

A Great Hall.
B Salone.
C Portico.
D Drawing Room.
E Gallery.
F Anti Room.
G Dressing Room.
H Library.
I Dressing Room.
K Bedchamber.
LL Bedchamber Apartments.

M Great Drawing Room.
N Great Anti Room.
O Vestibule.
P Chapel.
Q State Bedchamber.
RS Dressing Room and Closet.
T Bedchamber.
U Dressing Room.
W Dining Room.
X Kitchen Offices.
Y Laundry.

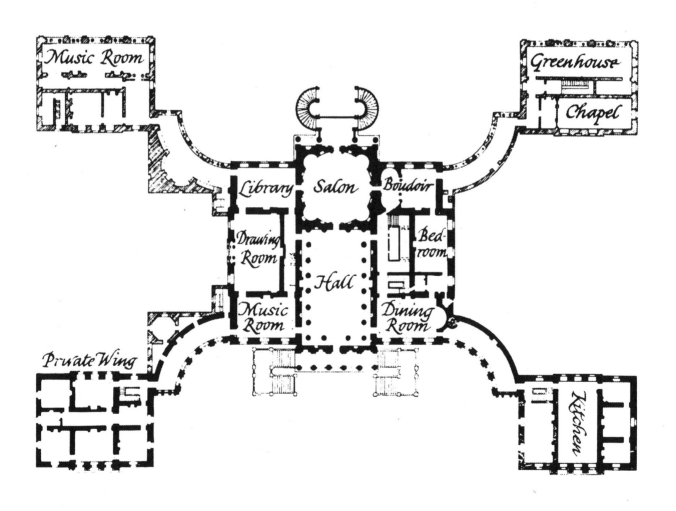

Music Room

Greenhouse

Chapel

Library   Salon   Boudoir

Drawing Room   Bedroom

Hall

Music Room   Dining Room

Private Wing

Kitchen

0   20   40   60   80   100 Feet

Adam wings not built

62

could be expected in a great house, but then, as Sir John Summerson has said, Kedleston was the last of the great houses.[7]

Adam's remodelling of Osterley was planned for a banker whose wealth was matched by his pretension and who was evidently prepared to be dictated to by his architect. To an age that was very aware of the niceties of rank Osterley was obviously an ostentatious house. However after 200 years this is not so obvious, and we are soothed by the lack of grandeur in its planning: beyond the hall lies the gallery, possibly by Chambers; to the right in the wing lie the rooms in daily use, the dining room, library and breakfast room; to the left lies a full state apartment based on late 17th century precedent, drawing room, tapestry room, state bedroom and Etruscan room or dressing room. There is conscious variety in their decoration, but even so it is hard to believe that the drawing and tapestry room were used regularly like the drawing room at Kedleston, and one is left with a permanent sense of unease about the conception.

To-day it is difficult to understand the way of life that state rooms implied and what they represented to contemporaries, and, just because the concept was accepted, there seem to be remarkably few comments on them. However Mrs Delany comes to our aid; writing of Lord Guildford's prospective visit to Bulstrode, where she says the great apartment consisted of no less than eight rooms and three closets, she suspected "that the good Earl would find himself more comfortable if he was not honoured with the great apartment."[8] And when Mrs Boscawen went to Holkham in 1774, she was obviously surprised to find that "all the rooms in the house are every day and all day open, not one uninhabited chamber or closet shut up."[9] The situation at Belvoir in 1834 was probably more usual: Lady Salisbury was there for the Duke's birthday and while she found that nothing could have been more magnificent or better *monté* it was the only occasion in the year when the Elizabeth Saloon (Fig. 33) was used.[10]

This may have been a slight exaggeration, as is known from the account of the 1st Lady Wharncliffe's visit three years before; but even so it obviously struck her as worth noting the occasions when the big rooms were used. "Yesterday we dined and sat in the small rooms which were nothing remarkable —today I believe we are to occupy the large ones;" and she goes on to record dining in the great dining room.[11]

In view of our uncertainty about country house etiquette, Philip Yorke's description of Wolterton in Norfolk in 1754[12] is particularly valuable, because it gives a remarkably complete picture of a large but fairly typical 18th century house (Fig. 43). Built between 1726 and 1740 by Horatio, Lord Walpole, the brother of the Prime Minister, it was originally a three storey house of seven bays without wings,[13] and was regarded by Horace Walpole, the builder's nephew, as "one of the best houses of the size in England." Philip Yorke describes how the family lived " in the rustic (the ground floor) where are 4 good plain rooms, the dining parlour, the drawing room, the study (which has an arcade before it) and the breakfast room. The rest are for servants. On the first floor are 8 rooms, a hall, saloon, drawing room, dining parlour and 2 apartments consisting of a bedchamber and dressing-room . . . The attic consists wholly of lodging rooms, which are very good ones" and the servants were put in the garrets.

The use of the rustic was obviously widespread even when entertaining, but it seems to have surprised the young Lady Shelburne when she went to Fonthill in 1769: "It surprised me," she noted in her diary "that with so fine an appartment we shou'd always breakfast dine and sup in the Rustick story. We slept in the Atticks which are very handsomely furnished."[14]

The first floor was clearly "a floor of taste, expense, state and parade," as Lord Hervey wrote of the *piano nobile* at Houghton,[15] and with it went a desire for formal decoration that would last with proper care for a long time

41. THE PLAN OF THE PIANO NOBILE AT HOLKHAM HALL, NORFOLK. The family apartments are placed in a wing rather than in the main block, and more space is devoted to rooms for entertaining and displaying works of art.

42. THE PLAN OF THE PIANO NOBILE AT KEDLESTON. The last of the great houses, it is also one of the last houses to have a complete Baroque-Palladian layout of rooms of parade.

63

43. WOLTERTON HALL, NORFOLK.
Built between 1726 and 1730, it
was regarded by Horace Walpole,
the builder's nephew, as "one of
the best houses of its size in
England", and a contemporary
description gives a good idea of
how it and the other similar houses
were used.

to come. The *piano nobile* was not a place for flights of fancy but for rich,
patterned materials, marble and stucco, gilding and tapestry. And such was
the state of family finances that usually the generation who inherited a new
suite of great rooms could not afford to alter them, and soon they emerged
more or less unscathed from the position of being *démodé* to become a symbol of
the family's long establishment. Thus within half a century there was a strong
prejudice against touching them, and when restoration did become necessary,
often the tendency was to embellish and improve rather than alter them.
Certainly this was in the 6th Duke of Devonshire's mind when he did so much
at Chatsworth in the 1820s and 1830s and apparently also in the 4th Earl of
Radnor's when he called in Salvin to complete Longford Castle in the 1870s.

The concept of the villa has already been briefly mentioned, as have the
changes in habit in France during the Régence and early Rococo periods, and
both were part of a much more fundamental alteration in the pattern of upper
class life. The new taste for intimacy and informality was only part of this:
portraiture, costume design, types of fabric and their patterns, forms of furniture, musical instruments and concepts of comfort were all affected, and even
the choice of words that was used to describe the fads and fashions was new.
The letters of Lady de Grey in the 1740s and the Lennox sisters (Caroline,
Lady Holland, Emily, later Countess of Kildare and 1st Duchess of Leinster,
Louisa, who married Tom Conolly, and Sarah, who married Sir Charles
Bunbury and afterwards Colonel Napier) written in the late 1750s onwards
are particularly revealing over this. In 1743 Lady de Grey was writing ". . . in
the prettiest closet in the world, ornamented so elegantly and looking so neat
and cheerful,"[16] and two years later about evenings in the library ". . . you
can't imagine anything more cheerful than that room, nor more comfortable
than reading there the rest of the evening." Lady Kildare's letters are full of

references to houses being "sprucish", "smart" and "pretty",[17] and it is hard to believe that such descriptions could have been used by an older woman, like Isabella Finch, Kent's patron at 44 Berkeley Square, who died in 1771. Hers is a marvellous house, imaginative and splendid but essentially formal like Holkham or Houghton. But that was not at all Lady Louisa's style, nor judging by the comments of some of her contemporaries on other Palladian houses was it their's either. When Mrs Powys went to Houghton in 1756, she found "the fitting up and furniture very superb; and the cornishes and mouldings of all the apartments being gilt, it makes the whole what I call magnificently glaring, more especially as the rooms are, instead of white, painted dark green olive; but this most likely will be soon altered."[18]

Lady Louisa says less about comfort than one might expect, and before 1740 there are few references to it, or indeed to discomfort either, but from then on they increase. Needless to say Mrs Delany and Horace Walpole were well aware of the possibilities: Mrs Delany mentions the seats of her drawing room chairs as being "low and easy as you love,"[19] and Walpole, describing the breakfast room at Strawberry Hill, says it had "a thousand plump chairs, couches, and luxourious settees"[20] covered with a linen that matched the wall paper. If it was the English who really developed a sense of comfort in the home, again this was under French influence, for it was the French who developed the highly specialised art of chair making and upholstery. Low chairs of the kind described by Mrs Delany are now a great rarity, but the English debt to France is made abundantly clear by François de Troy's *Lecture de Molière* painted about 1728.[21]

These new concerns and priorities involved a concept of decoration quite different from that current in Kent's early days. When Lady Louisa Conolly's sister, Lady Kildare, wrote to her husband in 1757: "I shall wish to have our house look *sprucish*. Every mortal's house here (in London) is so pretty and smart, and well furnish'd, that I do long to have ours so too a little,"[22] one can sense a new direction, a turning away from cut velvets for the saloon to pretty taffetas (for hangings but not upholstery) and cottons for dressing rooms and bedrooms, materials that were much cheaper, more modish and not boringly long lasting; a new, essentially impermanent, style of decoration for rooms that were lived in all the time.

Allied to this was the use of more rooms for special purposes in a house when the household was large, a habit that surprised French visitors. How this worked in practice is admirably illustrated in Miss Sandford's description of life at Carton in 1779, in the time of the 2nd Duke of Leinster. "The house was crowded—a thousand comes and goes," she wrote. "We breakfast between ten and eleven, though it is called half-past nine. We have an immense table— chocolate—honey—hot bread—cold bread—brown bread—white bread—green bread—and all coloured breads and cakes. After breakfast Mr Scott (the Duke's chaplain) reads a few short prayers, and we then go as we like—a back room for reading, a billiard room, a print room (ante-room), a drawing room and whole suites of rooms, not forgetting the music room (hall). We dine at half-past four or five . . . courses upon courses, which I believe takes up two full hours. It is pretty late when we leave the parlour (saloon) we then go to tea, so to cards about nine . . . play till supper-time—'tis pretty late by the time we go to bed. I forgot to tell you the part you would like best—French horns playing at breakfast and dinner . . . There are all sorts of amusements; the gentlemen are out hunting and shooting all the morning."[23]

As a contrast to this the Reverend Thomas Talbot's letters to his wife from Saltram in 1811 give an equally vivid picture of life *en famille:* "As to the mode of existence here in the absence of Company it is the most remote from show or even elegance that can be conceived, the whole lower part of the house is abandoned, the library excepted . . . the living room is upstairs over the right hand ante-room on the Saloon side." Little silver was used in the dining

XI. AN UNUSED FRAGMENT OF THE CUT VELVET MADE FOR QUEEN ANNE'S BED. See Figure 69 for the bed at Hampton Court Palace. The velvet is thought to be Spitalfields. (On loan from H.M. the Queen to the Victoria and Albert Museum.)

room, and the servants waited outside the door, only coming in when called. The parson obviously felt that his sister was not living like a countess, but the quiet life she led helps to explain why the house has survived in the way it has.[24]

If the plan of a house is taken apart and each room is examined in turn, the relationship between use, decoration, and, indeed, the survival of historic decoration into the present century becomes even more apparent. The hall is the natural place to begin and, according to Ware, its purpose in London and the country was different. In town he held that it need not be magnificent or elegant because it was "a place of reception for servants;" whereas in the country "where there are other ways into the house, the hall may be an elegant room, and it is there we propose its being made large and noble . . . It serves as a summer-room for dining; it is an anti-chamber in which people of business, or of the second rank, wait and amuse themselves; and it is a good apartment for the reception of large companies at public feasts."[25] What Ware says about the variety of use is confirmed by Mrs Delany: writing about the hall at Dangan in 1733 she says that it is so large "that very often breakfast, battledore and shuttlecock and the harpsicord, go on at *the same time* without molesting one another."[26] Its use by people of business, or the second rank, is reflected in the special character of the seats, which were usually not upholstered but bore the family crest or arms. But Adam's comments on his plan for Syon as recorded in his *Works* probably did not apply in all great houses. Whereas he says that "the hall both in our houses and those in France, is a spacious apartment, intended as the room of access where servants in livery wait"[27] and those out of livery and tradesmen wait in the flanking ante-rooms. Prince Puckler-Muskau writing 50 years later about Penrhyn records that "the servants never wait in the ante-room,—here called the hall,—which, like the overture of an opera, is designed to express the character of the whole: it is generally decorated with statues or pictures and like the elegant staircase and the various apartments, is appropriated to the use of the family and guests, who have the good taste rather to wait on themselves than have an attendant spirit always at their heels."[28]

In addition to these practical considerations the hall in certain houses has a more overtly classical character. At Holkham, for instance, the Baroque and Palladian tradition of a stone hall is taken a stage further, for the plan was derived from Palladio's design for a basilica after Vitruvius, an allusion that was doubtless intended to be understood by visitors. A generation later, at West Wycombe and Kedleston the halls are conceived as classical *atria*, and at West Wycombe the antique character is expressed not only in the busts but in the heating system inspired by a hypocaust discovered in a Roman villa at Lincoln.

Changes in eating habits are particularly important, and although, as we have seen, the concept of the dining room was developed in France about 1630, there continued to be uncertainty about its use in both countries well into the 18th century. Even as late as 1755 Mrs Delany seems to have been doubtful either about the propriety of having one or about how to describe it, for she writes "of my 'dining-room' vulgarly so called;"[29] but she did not need to use inverted commas much longer for Johnson's *Dictionary* published that year includes the term dining room.

Sometimes the term appears in plans of the Restoration period, but judging by a particularly ambitious plan for Hamstead Marshall,[30] Lord Craven's household were expected to eat in four places: adjoining the hall was the Little Parlour or Ordinary Roome to eate in, and next to that was the Withdrawing Room or Roome for the Lord to eat in; on the other side of the hall were two other rooms for meals, one for the Gentlemen and one for the Servants. At that time the favourite form of table was an oval, and all but the most important people sat on stools. When the Grand Duke Cosimo dined at Althorp and

66

Wilton on his visit to England in 1669, he made a great play with not sitting in an armchair but on a stool, and he found an oval table contributed to a spirit of conviviality.[31] And in a large house there might well be more than one table in a room; at Belton, for instance, the 1688 inventory lists two oval tables in the dining room.[32]

Where there was a dining room, it seems that it was only used for dinner. At Narford in 1728 Sir Matthew Decker saw "a fine dining room, painted white and gilt" and "a little room either for dining or supper" and he found a similar arrangement at Raynham.[33] At Houghton, as we have seen, Walpole altered one of the main apartments to provide the Marble Parlour (Plate XXXI), but this was probably only used on fairly formal occasions: before it was finished he dined in the Hunting Room on the ground floor and had breakfast and supper in two other rooms. Much the same arrangment existed at Wanstead in 1769, where "under the hall is a very noble arcade; out of which is a common dining parlour forty feet by thirty-five; a breakfast room, thirty by thirty-five, exceedingly elegant."[34] Rochefoucauld obviously found this extravagance of rooms most surprising, for when he visited Heveningham in 1784, he listed not only the dining room, but the breakfast room, "which was never dined in,"[35] and the print room where Sir Gerard Vanneck dined when he was on his own. Even as late as the early 19th century there was no set pattern in some houses. At Saltram, for instance, it was only on fairly special occasions that the Adam dining room was used, and sometimes the family may even have dined upstairs.[36]

Probably the only survivor of this practice nowadays is the use of two tables, one big and one small, in the dining rooms of some country houses, but then it has to be remembered that the pattern of meals in Walpole's day and Rochfoucauld's was different from what is usual to-day. Generally speaking the hour of dinner got later and later during the 18th and early 19th century. Old Mrs Conolly of Castletown, for instance, who died in 1752, dined at 3 o'clock, and tea and coffee were brought in at 5.30 pm.[37] At Bulstrode in 1740 dinner was at 2.00, tea at 8.00 and supper at 10.00. But under the influence of London fashion the hour got set back so that it differed in town and country. Horace Walpole describes with evident amusement Mrs Boscawen coming up to London in 1776, having had dinner to find people wandering about in the streets: in her youth people had dined at 2.00 in London and the country, but by then the fashionable hour in London was 4.30 or 5.00.[38] At Marchmont in 1772 dinner was still at 3.00,[39] and Lady de Grey, who recorded that, warned a prospective visitor to Newby in 1793 that "you must consent to dine before 4 every day."[40] However in the shooting season dinner tended to be later: at Court of Hill in 1771, Mrs Powys records "never met at dinner till after four . . . tho in the shooting season seldom before five." By the early 19th century the hour had gone back even further: when Farington dined with the Angersteins in 1806, he was asked for 6 and they ate at 6.30 pm and he dined at 7.00 with Sir Abraham Hume.[41]

However as Mrs Boscawen had found 30 years before, this was later than was sometimes the custom in the country. At Deepdene, Maria Edgeworth was late, because she "had taken it for granted that the Hopes dine at the same hour in Town and Country. But instead of 7 they dine at 6 in the country."[42]

Dinner was the central feature of the day, but again there was evidently a difference between French and English attitudes on which Adam comments in his *Works:* whereas the French rarely had their eating rooms as part of the great apartment and did not devote great attention to their decoration, because they left promptly after meals, in England they "are considered as the apartments of conversation, in which we are to pass a great part of our time. This renders it desirable to have them fitted up with elegance and splendour, but in a style different from that of the apartments. Instead of being hung with damask, tapestry etc, they are always finished with stucco, and adorned with statues and paintings, that they may not retain the smell of the victuals."[43]

He might have added that dining rooms particularly in country houses should generally be fairly light in tone because they were likely to be used most in summer and so be seen in the afternoon light. The use of dark tones is surely related to changes in the hour of eating in the early 19th century.

The tradition of medium sized tables and folding tables that could be moved about at will lasted until the last quarter of the 18th century. The great table made for Walpole at Houghton in four sections and expanding to over 16 feet is quite exceptional. People at that time still preferred company in smaller groups. At Cannons, for instance, the Duke of Chandos had four tables in the dining room, one at which he sat, another called the chaplain's, a third for the Gentlemen of the Horse, and a last one for the officers of his household.[44] Old Mrs Conolly of Castletown "generally had two tables of eight or ten people each."[45]

Sets of dining tables, as the big tables were called, only became fashionable about 1780 and they changed the character of the dining room. Their introduction was probably due to the desire to entertain more people, because, according to Madame de la Tour du Pin writing of customs in France in the late 1770s and early 1780s, "it was not the custom to give great dinner parties, for people dined early . . . By dinner-time, the ladies would sometimes have had their hair dressed, but they would still be in deshabille."[46] Once introduced, the big tables inevitably made meals more formal and the dining room useless for any other purpose. They may also have had a decisive effect on the way the room was arranged between meals. The usual 18th century practice was to place the chairs round the edge of the room when not in use, an arrangement recently restored at Osterley where there was no table permanently in the room; but early 19th century views (Fig. 44) of Farnley Hall, Yorkshire, and Carlton House show the chairs up to the table when it was laid. On the other hand in Pyne's view of the dining room at Frogmore, when the table is not laid, the chairs are shown against the wall (Figs. 46, 47). These drawings suggest the fashion probably changed constantly, and it would be dangerous to be too dogmatic about correct practice. Robert Kerr writing an architectural bible for the *nouveau-riche* in the 1860s says: "One feature which has always a substantial and hospitable aspect in this apartment is the unbroken line of chairs at the wall," but he goes on to say: "In superior rooms it is sometimes the practice to place the chairs, when not in use, not against the wall, but around the table."[47]

Supper on the other hand was an informal meal and frequently it was brought into the room in which the family were sitting. However at Bulstrode in 1783 Miss Hamilton "went to supper about $\frac{1}{2}$ past 10, and conversed (as we have dumb waiters and *no servants to wait* at supper) abt ye King and Windsor Castle."[48] One of the earliest references to a dumb waiter is in Lord Bristol's accounts for 1727,[49] but as in other fashions the French took it much further than the English and produced very elaborate pieces of furniture so that the rich could eat both elegantly and intimately.

Tea in the afternoon might be thought to be the descendant of the tea and coffee that old Mrs Conolly provided at half past five, after dinner, or the tea and bread and butter at seven observed by Sophie von la Roche in 1786, but it seems to have been a much later innovation judging by Fanny Kemble's account of a visit to Belvoir in 1842,[50] an account that incidentally throws an interesting light on the life of guests in a large country house. Her introduction "took place during this visit to Belvoir, when I received on several occasions private and rather mysterious invitations to the Duchess of Bedford's room, and found her with a 'small and select' circle of female guests of the castle, busily employed in brewing and drinking tea, with her grace's own private tea-kettle. I do not believe that now universally honoured and observed institution of 'five o clock' tea dates further back in the annals of English civilisation than this

44. THE DINING ROOM AT FARNLEY HALL, YORKSHIRE. Turner's water colour shows the chairs drawn up to the table.

45. THE DINING ROOM IN RECENT YEARS. Designed by John Carr in 1786 and decorated with grisailles by Theodore de Bruyn.

70

very private, and, I think, rather shamefaced practice of it."

The provision of a saloon in addition to a drawing room was naturally dependent on the means and ambitions of a family, but it was evidently not just a matter of prestige. There was a tendency in the second quarter of the 18th century to entertain people in larger numbers. Not only does Lady Hertford write in 1741: "Assemblies are now so much in fashion that most persons fancy themselves under a necessity of inviting all their acquaintances three of four times to their houses, not in small parties . . .;"[51] but Ware, writing in 1756, says: "We see an addition of a great room now to almost every house of consequence."[52] Sometimes, as at Kenwood, it also served as a library, and at other houses including Crichel it later became a dining room, but both were primarily rooms for company and usually as formal as Ware's definition of a saloon "a great room intended for state, or for the reception of paintings."[53]

Where a room was only intended for formal use, the centre of the floor was generally kept clear of furniture and may not always have been carpeted. At Clandon, for instance, the saloon floor (Plate XXVII) is of white marble like the hall, and as a result the room is impossibly cold for most of the year. At Kedleston most of the light in the Saloon comes from an oculus in the dome. Both these are extreme examples of formality, but they underline the intention. At Holkham and Houghton on the other hand, there is none of this literal chill, and in both houses the saloon forms a splendid contrast to the hall, tones of white giving way to tones of crimson with plenty of gilding. At Houghton the saloon furniture (Fig. 48) designed by Kent is conceived as part of the architecture and was made originally to go round the edge of the room, the arrangement reflecting French custom and the design Italian inspiration. A saloon and a drawing room were not interchangeable names for the same room as is usually assumed to-day, even if they were arranged on similar lines at least until the end of the 18th century. And it is interesting to observe how the difference was expressed in the hangings. At Houghton and at Holkham, the hangings of the Saloon are much bolder than those used in the drawing room; at the former, a crimson cut velvet originally gave way to plain green velvet, and at the latter, crimson cut wool velvet gives way to crimson silk velvet. And at Erthig the 1726 inventory bears this out: a bold crimson and yellow caffoy gave way to a flowered crimson velvet.

Recently the Victoria and Albert Museum has rearranged the furniture at Osterley and has started to rearrange Ham as well, and both exercises have been stimulating and instructive in that they have made one aware of the disordered arrangement that reigns in many country houses under a false guise of being historic and traditional. In particular they show how sets of seat furniture should be placed in order to enhance the architecture, with pairs of sophas flanking the chimneypiece, window seats set in the window embrasures, torchères in the corners and so on. And in rooms like the galleries at Corsham and Osterley there is a great gain, for one now appreciates such details as that of the nailing of the damask matching the nailing on the seat furniture in the former (Fig. 49), and in the latter that the carved pattern of the dado rail is repeated in the seat rail of the settees and chairs (Fig. 50). But at Osterley there has been another result that is surely unexpected: Adam's sense of design has been restored and so has the air of parade, but at the same time the rooms give a sense of an architect imposing his will on uncertain clients; the total effect is extraordinarily *nouveau* and seems as unconvincing as manners learned from an etiquette book or the advice given in Robert Kerr's much later book on the *Gentleman's House*. The rooms may have looked as they do today when the family were away or not entertaining except that everything would have been covered up; but if the Childs were actually using the rooms, a certain amount of moving of chairs and tables must have gone on. This is known from Mrs Delany's account of the visit to Bulstrode of Princess

46. THE GOTHICK DINING ROOM AT CARLTON HOUSE. This, and the following plate, from Pyne's *Royal Residences* show the chairs against the wall when the table was not laid for a meal and up to the table when laid.

47. THE DINING ROOM AT FROGMORE, NEAR WINDSOR.

71

48. THE SALOON AT HOUGHTON. "A great room intended for state", hung with crimson cut velvet and with furniture designed by Kent as an integral part of the room. The emphasis on unity extends to the table tops being of the same marble as the fireplace.

Amelia, one of the daughters of George III; a great deal of tidying up had to be done, "all the comfortable sophas and great chairs, all the piramids of books (adorning *almost every chair*), all the tables and *even the spinning* wheel were banish'd for that day, and the blue damask chairs set in prim form around the room, only one arm'd chair placed in the middle for Her Royal Highness . . ."[54] When the Duchess of Portland and Mrs Delany visited the Queen at Windsor two chairs were brought in for them "to sit in which were easier chairs than those belonging to the room."[55] Just as there was not the same elaborate etiquette in England over the use of *tabourets* as there was at the French court, there was not the same distinction made between the *chaise courante* and the *chaise meublante*, and Sheraton writes in his *Drawing Book* as if the French practice was unfamiliar: "In France, where their drawing rooms are fitted up in the most splendid manner, they use a sett of small and plainer chairs, reserving the others merely for ornament."[56]

From the accounts of Horace Walpole and Mrs Delany as well as from numerous portraits and conversation pictures, it is clear that there was a degree of informality and adaptability about English houses that may seem rather surprising now, and in the end this triumphed over the dictates of an architect like Adam. This particularly English contribution came gradually, depending

72

49. A SETTEE IN THE GALLERY AT
CORSHAM COURT, WILTSHIRE, 1762.
The style of architectural design
extends even to the two lines of
nailing on the settee that matches
the pattern of the fillet used for
the wallhangings. One of the chairs
is illustrated in Figure 149.

50. A CHAIR FROM A SET IN THE
GALLERY AT OSTERLEY. The design
of the seat rail of the chair matches
that of the dado rail. The room is
illustrated in Figures 6-8.

very much on the ages of generations in a house, and it would probably be wrong to attribute it definitely to one decade, say the 1770s or 1780s. Even as late as 1810 a French visitor, Louis Simond, was very surprised when he went to Osterley and found "the tables, sofas and chairs, were studiously *dérangés* about the fireplaces, and in the middle of the rooms, as if the family had left them although the house had not been inhabited for several years. Such is the modern fashion of placing furniture carried to an extreme, as fashions always are, that the apartments of a fashionable house looked like an upholsterer's or cabinet-maker's shop."[57]

French taste was always more formal than English, and it is interesting to be able to compare Simond's impression with that of an English visitor, Lady Sarah Spencer, a year before. "The drawing-room (Figs. 6, 7, 8) in which we were received, and in which they always sit, is 10 or 11 feet longer, and I think much broader than the gallery at Althorp. It is 130 feet long, and yet by means of two huge chimneypieces, a profusion of sofas, chairs and tables of all sizes, a billiard table, books, pictures, and a pianoforte, it looks as comfortable and as well-filled as a small room would. All the rest of the house is of a piece with this room—immense, magnificent, and very comfortable."[58]

It seems that a fairly crowded room was already quite usual by that date, for when Lady Wharncliffe went to Hornby Castle, Yorkshire, in 1807, it struck her as old fashioned: "This is a delightful *castle*-like looking house; very large and would be perfectly comfortable but that there is nothing in it but the old furniture, so that the rooms look *bare*, and like the drawing room at Ickworth in my poor dear Grandmama's time."[59]

One of the most interesting impressions of a very large house in the early 19th century is of Stowe in 1845 written by Elizabeth George, a young woman given permission to visit it after the visit of Queen Victoria and Prince Albert.[60] She was both independent and old fashioned in her views for she felt "the house was splendidly furnish'd before preparations were made for the Royal visit, and in my humble opinion all these costly additions are de trop and have so crowded the apartments as to give them the appearance of a large furniture warehouse—and no space being left vacant on the floors—you do not appreciate the noble proportions of the rooms . . . The middle of the rooms at that time were not crowded with furniture—one or two very curious or rich tables perhaps, with a few rich chairs stood ready for use, but the greater proportion of furniture was ranged out of the way along the walls—you walk'd freely about, at liberty to gaze on the valuable and rare paintings, sculpture etc. Now the furniture is arranged in the modern style viz—grouped—Marquetrie tables, each surrounded by seats of different kinds—sofas, ottomans and chairs."

By the 1860s the bareness of old fashioned rooms was already evocative of the 18th century, or at least that was the impression made on Lady Morgan by a house in Dublin where "the ponderous chairs and settees, as the sofas were called, were regimented against the wall."[61]

The introduction of the centre table may have been crucial. Again it is not known exactly when this came into fashion, and here English watercolours of interiors do not provide the answer for it seems that few were done before the end of the 18th century. Instead one has to rely on descriptions by people like Mrs Delany, and fortunately she describes one in use at the Queen's Lodge at Windsor where she was summoned with the Duchess of Portland in 1785: "I have been several evenings at the Queen's Lodge, with no other company but their own most lovely family. They sit round a large table, on which are books, work, pencils, and paper."[62] The same custom prevailed at Edgeworthstown for Maria Edgeworth describes how "If you look at the oblong table in the centre, you will see the rallying point of the family, who are usually around it, reading, writing or working." Both quotations bring to life the rooms shown in the Gillow drawings in the Victoria and Albert Museum.[63]

74

Here one finds the spirit, even if not the arrangement, of the living room as it would be recognised to-day. Again this starts earlier than might be expected in rooms like the gallery at Castletown after it was redecorated in the early 1770s. Lady Louisa Conolly describes life in it soon after she had finished her alterations: "I must leave off, supper being on the table. In the gallery where we live 'tis the most comfortable room you ever saw, and quite warm; supper at one end, the company at the other, and I am writing in one of the piers at a distance from all" and in another letter "Our gallery was in great vogue, and really is a charming room, for there are such variety of occupations in it, that people cannot be formal in it . . . I have seldom seen twenty people in a room so easily disposed of . . ."[64]

By the early 19th century the word living room was in use, for in 1816 Repton wrote: "The most recent modern custom is to use thé library as the general living-room; and that sort of state room formerly called the best parlour, and of late years the drawing-room, is now generally found a melancholy apartment, when entirely shut up and opened to give the visitors a formal cold reception."[65] He had provided one in his scheme for Armley Hall, Yorkshire, in 1810,[66] and when he designed Sheringham, he was instructed that the house should consist of a well-proportioned dining room and a room a little larger for books, music and pictures as a *general living room* and "no useless Drawing Room (Fig. 51)."[67] And to make the point in his *Fragments on the Theory and Practice of Landscape Gardening* (1816) he provided constrasting illustrations (Figs. 52, 53) with the accompanying verse: "No more the Cedar Parlour's formal gloom / With dulness chills, 'tis now the Living Room; / Where Guests, to whim, a taste, or fancy true, / Scatter'd in groups, their different plans to pursue."[68] At Easton Grey in Wiltshire in 1820 Maria Edgeworth found "the library drawing room with low sofas, plenty of movable tables, open bookcases, and all that speaks the habits and affords the means of agreeable occupation."[69]

The low sofas, which Miss Edgeworth mentions, could have been the so-called grecian couches that were specifically designed to be free standing in a room and seem to have been frequently placed at right angles to the fireplace. The movable tables might have been teapoys and what George Smith called quartetto tables (nests of tables) which were used "to prevent the company rising from the seats when taking refreshment."[70]

The break up of a room into different areas with groups of chairs as in the watercolour of the drawing room at Field Place in Sussex (Fig. 54) led to an effect that strikes us as typically Victorian in its atmosphere of chaos and claustrophobia. But the impression that old photographs give is not an entirely fair one, for they rarely show rooms actually in use, and so what is forgotten is the need to seat a large number of people in groups of a size that stimulated conversation or at least made it possible. Lady Louisa Conolly had obviously achieved that in that gallery at Castletown in the 1770s, and what the 19th

51. A SECTIONAL DRAWING OF SHERINGHAM HALL, NORFOLK. From Repton's *Fragments or the Theory and Practice of Landscape Gardening* (1816), it shows his solution to the instruction of providing a parlour, a dining room and a living room rather than a drawing room.

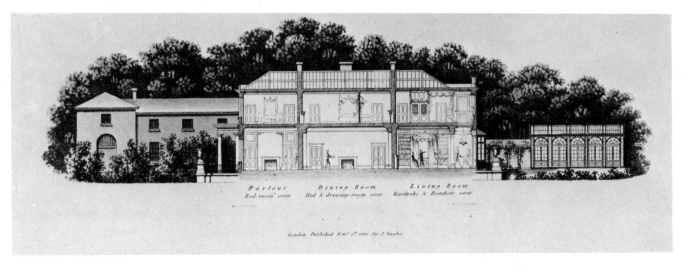

Parlour   Dining Room   Living Room
Bed room over   Bed & dressing room over   Wardrobe & Boudoir over

London Published Feb.y 1st 1816 by J. Taylor

century did was to formalize and regularise 18th century informality. And just as the early Victorians developed the use of chintz for permanent loose covers (Fig. 55), they gave up a way of arrangement that depended on servants coming in to tidy up the disarray. Not surprisingly there are very few references to this, but Maria Edgeworth provides one small clue. Writing of a visit to Lady Elizabeth Whitbread's house in 1822, she describes the drawing room: ". . . and everything in the room tell Honora exactly the same as the day we left it even to the angle at which the footstools stood before arm chairs when the room was dressed for dinner."[71] With the disappearance of servants in recent years obviously there is much less "dressing of rooms", but Miss Edgeworth's observation suggests that a great deal of moving furniture must have gone on in the 18th century, moving out into the room by the family and company and moving back to the wall by the servants. Indeed this probably explains why the Groom of the Chambers was such an important servant in a large house, but as fashions in living changed, his duties declined to such an extent that we find his role a largely incomprehensible one.

With the development of reception rooms as we understand them today the 17th century concept of the apartment lost some of its prominence and the bedroom became a private rather than a public room. However the bedroom accommodation continued to be laid out in sets of rooms, and in the largest

54. THE DRAWING ROOM AT FIELD
PLACE, SUSSEX, ABOUT 1816 (?)
The watercolour by Elizabeth
Shelley shows the room already
broken up into different areas by a
variety of tables and chairs. Most
of the seat furniture has striped
case covers unrelated to the colours
of the room.

55. THE VICTORIAN USE OF CHINTZ
COVERS: AN INFORMAL ARRANGE-
MENT IN THE ANTE-ROOM AT
SPENCER HOUSE, LONDON, ABOUT
1890.

houses these were of the greatest elaboration. At Audley End in 1768 the state apartment consisted of a bed-chamber, two dressing rooms, two powdering closets, an ante-chamber, and a servants room. At Luton Hoo there were no less than 5 apartments, each with 2 dressing rooms and with rooms for a man servant and a maid servant. Today when we look at the facade of a three storey house like Wolterton (Figure 43) we tend to presume and presume quite wrongly that the family lived on the first floor and the servants and the children were on the ground floor and the top storey, which we may refer to rather scathingly as the attics.

However in the 18th century the word attic did not have the rather pejorative meaning that is associated with it now; instead the word garret was used. At Houghton, for instance, Decker found the "attic story" almost entirely finished and clear and neatly furnished in 1728, "all the rooms are 14 feet high; here are twelve good handsome bed chambers, four of which are pretty large. To ten of the bed chambers is a little room for a servant which makes it all compleet commodious, besides many closets for woods and other necessaries."[72] A generation later, at Fonthill Splendens Lady Shelburne describes sleeping in "the Atticks, which are very handsomely furnished;" she had a large bedroom, two dressing rooms and a light closet.[73]

At Clandon traces of expensive flock wallpaper have been found on the top storey, part of which was occupied by the family as we know from the 1778 inventory, and at Ombersley two of the bedrooms on the top floor contain good late 18th century pictorial wall papers. And in a more modest house, Stretton in Staffordshire, which was the English house of the Conollys of Castletown, Lady Louisa said: "In the garret you may put almost anybody, it is so comfortably furnished."[74]

In a large country house there was invariably a degree of separation of the family from their guests. A whole wing might be set aside for the private rooms as at Holkham (Fig. 41) or Kedleston (Fig. 42) or one front as at Houghton (Fig. 40); or as at Nostell the division might be made by the placing of staircases. Pococke, who went to Nostell in 1750, found it "the most convenient house I have seen; there are two grand staircases, one leading to the apartments in the attick story for the family, the other for strangers, and back stairs communicating with one of the others, and leading up to the garrets for servants."[75] The state apartment on the piano nobile consisted of the State Bedroom, Dressing Room, 2 Closets and the Ante Room, which led into the Breakfast Room.

In the early 19th century when households became much larger, the Palladian idea of a family wing was revived by Barry. At Trentham he converted the 18th century house into rooms for entertaining and guests and adapted a side block for the Duke and Duchess of Sutherland; and this idea was copied by other families of comparable means including the Grosvenors at Eaton Hall, when they employed Waterhouse to remodel it for them in the 1870s. Fifty years earlier when Porden had remodelled the old Caroline house, he had written to Lord Grosvenor: "This plan seems to unite all the comforts of a small private House in the midst of magnificence and to keep the guests and the Family as much distinct as if they had separate dwellings."[76]

There are few references to how people slept in the 18th century, but when Lord and Lady Shelburne were contemplating a London House, their architectural mentor, General Clerk, wrote to them disapproving very strongly of the idea of them having bedrooms on the same floor;[77] and in the end they, like the owners of other large London houses, accepted the idea of the wife's rooms being placed over the husband's and linked by a private staircase. In a country house the custom seems to have been for the family bedroom to have two dressing rooms.

A woman's dressing room was the room in which she might spend a great part of the day and receive her more intimate friends. There are several contemporary illustrations of them in use, and of these Zoffany's picture of Queen Charlotte is the most famous (Fig. 56), but there is also a charming silhouette of the Countess of Ashburnham's Dressing Room (Fig. 57) and a watercolour showing Lady Impey's room in her house in India (Fig. 58).[78] They bring to life the descriptions of people like Mrs Delany and Lady Kildare. When Mrs Delany stayed with the Duchess of Portland at Bulstrode in 1751, she describes how "After dinner our Duchess and I hold a tête à tête in the dear dressing-room till five; then all hands to work till between six and seven, then tea, and we return to the dressing room, and I read whilst the rest work."[79] And at Carton in 1762 when Lady Kildare was there without her husband she told him how the children "play and romp in Lady Kildare's dressing-room, and I sit in the India paper drawing-room so I have them or not just as I like."[80]

This use of the dressing room explains the very fine furniture that was often made for it, pieces like the Longford chinoiserie dressing table now at Clandon and the dressing table formerly at Kimbolton. In addition in a large house there was often a sofa bed as well. One of these survives *in situ* in the King's dressing room at Belvoir (Fig. 59), and there used to be another in the state dressing room at Castlecoole (Fig. 105); but they were not confined to state rooms, for when Maria Edgeworth stayed at Bowood in 1818, she wrote that one of her rooms "is quite a sitting room dressing room with a canopy sofa bed."[81] A writing table was also very important, and it is interesting to find that when Miss Edgeworth stayed with the Strutts in 1813 she noticed that "in each

56. QUEEN CHARLOTTE IN HER DRESSING ROOM AT BUCKINGHAM HOUSE, BY ZOFFANY. Festoon curtains are shown in use; the dressing table is a good example of a toilette.

57. THE COUNTESS OF ASHBURNHAM'S DRESSING ROOM. A silhouette by John Joliffe, about 1765.

XII. THE GREEN VELVET BED AT HOUGHTON HALL, NORFOLK, DESIGNED BY KENT. The gold braid, now tarnished, is used like the gilding on an entablature to emphasise its architectural character.

58. LADY IMPEY IN HER DRESSING ROOM IN INDIA. This watercolour gives the sense of such a room being used by the mistress of the house. The curtains appear to be reefed, but as there are no cords shown, they may have been fixed draperies.

XIII. A DETAIL OF ONE OF THE
CURTAINS AT HOUGHTON, SHOWING
THE NOW TARNISHED GOLD
APPLIQUÉ.

XIV. THE TESTER OF THE GREEN
VELVET BED, HOUGHTON. It is
designed as a variation of a full
entablature and the embellishments
are emphasised by the appliqué
of ornaments as in carved, painted
or moulded work.

dressing room there was a writing desk and table with everything that could be wanted for writing—And in each bed chamber a dressing table so completely stored with all things necessary for the toilette . . ."[82]

Because they were used so much and were among the rooms most subject to changes in fashion, few 18th century ones survive, but at Attingham there is a beautiful circular room (Fig. 25, Plates III, IV, V) possibly painted by Delabrière, one of Henry Holland's team of French decorators who worked at Carlton House and Southill.

In London a dressing room was evidently used as an extra drawing room. Mrs Boscawen records in 1748: "This afternoon I saw company in my dressing room for the first time since it being finished . . ."[83] Twenty years later Lady Cowper "had a party at her home on the 1st inst. Two quadrille tables in the gilt-drawing room, and the dressing room lighted up for those that were désoeuvrés."[84] A lady's bedroom in a London house on the other hand was very private: "Visits are received only in a room on the ground floor" wrote Meister in Letters During Residence in England in 1799."[85] "The lady's bed-chamber is a sanctuary which no stranger is permitted to enter. It would be an act of the greatest possible indecorum to go into it, unless the visitor were upon a very familiar footing with the family . . ."

Chapter 4
The practice of the upholsterer

To the 18th century patron and tradesman the word "furniture" did not primarily mean the moveable work of the joiner, carver and cabinet maker as it does today, but rather the hangings and coverings that were used. Today we regard these as less permanent and so of secondary importance, but before about 1820 the reverse was the case, and in letters, inventories and bills "furniture" invariably means the work of the upholsterer. Many examples could be quoted, but one from Lady Shelburne's journal will suffice: writing in 1767 about the progress of work at Shelburne House, she recorded one day that Mr Adam dined, and "with the latter I consulted on the furniture of our painted Antichamber & determined that it should be pea-green satin spotted with white and trimmed with a pink and white fringe."[1] The woodwork is not mentioned at all.

It is this attitude that explains why the upholder, or upholsterer was, as R. Campbell said in the *London Tradesman*, the "Chief Agent" in the fitting up of a house: "his proper craft is to fit up Beds, Window Curtains, Hangings and to cover Chairs that have Stuffed Bottoms." But he was a contractor as well as a craftsman employing a variety of men skilled in different trades: "He employs journeymen to his own proper calling, Cabinet-Makers, Glass-Grinders, Look-Glass Frame-Carvers, Carvers for Chairs, Testers, and Posts of Bed, the Woolen-Draper, the Mercer, the Linen-Draper, several Species of Smiths, and a vast many Tradesmen of the other mechanic Branches."[2]

This dominance was based on the French development of upholstered seat furniture and beds in the 17th century, but the study of pre-1680 work in England must be almost entirely confined to documents for so few pieces have survived. Even some of the famous Knole furniture, which had always been thought to date from before the Civil War, now turns out to be more likely to date from after 1660,[3] and for an account of upholsterers' work at the court of Charles I one has to rely on the detailed inventory of the King's possessions taken before the sale in 1651.[4] The richness of the fabrics and the elaboration of their working is as staggering as the huge sums put on them. The great treasures of his collection like the Raphael Cartoons pale in comparison with the state beds, the Cartoons for instance being listed at £300, and one crimson velvet bed with its carpets and chairs at £500 and another of richly embroidered green satin at £1000.

It is tantalising that we have no contemporary objects to compare with the entries in the inventory, and there is little in France apart from the fine d'Effiat bed in the Louvre, which is thought to have been made about 1640.

However, from the beginning of the third quarter of the century there is a remarkable series of beds in England through which it is possible to trace the development of a great deal of upholstery design down to about 1730. As far

82

as we know no window or door curtains survive; and wall hangings other than tapestries are exceedingly rare, but fortunately elaborate examples exist at Ham House and Penshurst. But at Knole and in other houses there are splendid high backed chairs that still retain their original sumptuous coverings and trimmings that bring alive descriptions in inventories and letters. Undoubtedly the quality of this work was not only inspired by French fashion but achieved on numerous occasions with the aid of French workmen who came over in considerable numbers between 1670 and 1690. Indeed it is thought that 80,000 textile workers came over in the course of these two decades[5] as well as upholsterers like Lapierre, whose name occurs in the accounts of the Royal Wardrobe, the Duke of Devonshire, the Duchess of Buccleuch and Ralph Montagu.

Any discussion of style and fashion in the last decades of the 17th century must revolve round the contribution made by Marot, not only through his work in England from 1694 to 1696, about which little is known, but through his engravings first published in Amsterdam in 1702, and reissued in 1712.[6] By French standards his designs were rather old fashioned by the time he published them, but he is a figure of cardinal importance, because he was the first person to produce designs not only for architectural decoration but for furniture and upholstery as well. It would be wrong to claim that he was the first to give a room unity through the use of a single material for hangings, curtains and upholstery, but he was probably the first to give upholsterers' work outside the circle of the French court any real sophistication and fantasy. By nature an ornamentalist, he combined a carver's feeling for silhouette with an engraver's feeling for flat ornament that could be translated into patterns

60. CHRISTOPHER GIBSON'S TRADE CARD. This proof engraving gives an idea of the range of business of an 18th century upholsterer and cabinet-maker. Not only are there chairs and an angel bed on view, but rolls of materials and heraldic devices connected with funeral decorations.

83

of braid, a combination that is well illustrated in the Melville bed at the Victoria and Albert Museum.

Fashions in the Design of Beds

Social attitudes have changed so much in the course of the past 250 years that it is virtually impossible to understand the importance that was placed on state beds during the 17th and early 18th century. It was a kind of cult object symbolic of a family's standing and hospitality, but we know remarkably little about its use for there are few references to honoured guests being put into them.[7] One occasion that is recorded is the Duke of Lorraine sleeping in the Needlework bed at Houghton on his visit there at the end of 1731. State beds did not necessarily play any part in the ceremonies connected with a marriage or a death, and indeed there were special mourning beds whose use is described later in this section. However they seem to have been used at christenings, for Lady Shelburne describes Queen Charlotte being put in one at Buckingham House when the Princess Royal was christened in October 1766. Apparently the company waited in the Queen's Presence Chamber until the Queen was placed in the bed prepared for her in the Great Drawing Room. "At the upper end of it was a Crimson Velvet Bed fring'd with gold & lin'd with silver Tissue on the Top of it Plumes of White Feathers. The Queen sat up in it under a counterpane entirely of Point lace on crimson Velvet supported by three Satin Pillows trimmed with lace. She was dress'd in white & silver with a lace chapuchin & her hair curled without Powder."[8]

Evidently this was not a purely royal custom, for in the 1817 guide to Stowe the bed in the Chandos Bed Room is stated as being "the State bed used at the christening of the eldest daughter of James, the last Duke of Chandos, and Ann Eliza his wife, father & mother of the present Lady Buckingham."[9]

This special ceremonial character influenced not only its proper placing in a house, but made it an object on which it was considered appropriate to lay out a huge sum on materials and trimmings. The frame itself was usually a minor matter, and all the parts not seen might be very roughly finished off, but the greatest care was taken with the upholstery. One of the most famous examples is the bed that Lapierre made for the 1st Duke of Devonshire for Chatsworth in 1697 and of which the head and canopy can be seen in the Gallery at Hardwick (Plates VII, VIII): the woodwork cost £15 but the upholstery £470. William III spent £50 on a set of feathers for the canopy of a bed; and Sir Robert Walpole spent no less than £1200 in 1732 on the gold lace for the Green Velvet Bed at Houghton (Plates XII, XIII, XIV).[10]

Although some of the finest late 17th century beds in England were made by French craftsmen, it now seems that the form of the bed was an English development: French beds were never as tall and exaggerated as those produced in England particularly in the 1690s and early 1700s, the French proportion being close to that of the Boughton bed.[11] Also state beds in England and France were usually differently placed. In France the custom was to provide a *chambre de parade* with the bed set on a dais in an alcove and protected from the room by a balustrade; this continued until at least the 1730s, as can be seen at the Hotel Soubise in Paris. In England this arrangement was rare, but it is shown in Webb's design for the King's bedroom at Greenwich, and Celia Fiennes describes a state bed at Nottingham Castle "being rail'd in as the presence chamber used to be." At Ham House it has recently been realised that the parquet floor at the east end of the drawing room on the first floor is all that remains of the dais on which the state bed used to stand. Much later this idea was revived at Stowe: sometime between 1797 and 1827 the state bed designed by Borra about 1760 was placed on a dais and set behind a balustrade of polished brass, a typical piece of pretentiousness in the generation before the crash of 1848.[12] Today the only house where the state bed stands recessed and protected by a balustrade is in the late 17th century state bedroom at Powis Castle (Fig. 61).

Here we cannot go into the development of state bed design, for the list of outstanding examples surviving from the period 1670–1740 is a long one. There are beds at Knole, Hampton Court Palace, Dalemain, Hardwick, Burghley, Dyrham, Blair, Drayton, Belvoir, Warwick, Belton, Beningbrough (from Holme Lacy), Wingfield Castle, Clandon, Houghton and Holkham in addition to the Melville and Boughton beds at the Victoria and Albert Museum and the Erthig bed at present on loan there. Two that we have lost sight of are those from Glemham and Stoke Edith; the bed from Hampton Court, Herefordshire is in store in the Metropolitan Museum, New York. All are worthy of detailed consideration, but instead we have to be selective and consider them as illustrations of special points in upholstery.

Only fragments of upholstery from pre-1660 beds survive, but it is clear from descriptions of others, like that belonging to the Countess of Warwick, which was of crimson figured satin "trimmed with imbroidered buttons and loopes", that richly upholstered and decorated beds were found in English houses long before the Restoration. However probably the earliest one to survive is that at Dalemain in Cumberland, which is reputed to have been given by Lady Anne Clifford about 1670. The bed is not in its original condition, but at least the tester is complete: the cornice is carved and gilded like a Charles II picture frame, and the canopy is a combination of carved gilt wood and black embroidery on a white ground; little trimming is used, but originally the valances were probably richly fringed.[13]

It is interesting to compare this survivor with the three beds at Knole, all of the finest quality, two probably coming from royal palaces. The earliest of

61. THE 17TH CENTURY STATE BEDROOM AT POWIS CASTLE, MONTGOMERYSHIRE. The only surviving example in an English house of a state bed set in an alcove and railed off from the room.

85

the three is the Spangled Bed, which used to be dated about 1620, but is possibly 50 years later. Its silhouette is quite severe, its mouldings recalling those found on Charles II panelling, and it relies for its effect on the enrichment of its fabric, a crimson silk with a strap design of buff silk embroidered and bordered with gold and silver thread. The curtains are bordered with more of the spangled decoration, and the top valance is trimmed with a deep trellis fringe in gold thread. Much of the colour has gone now, but the base valance (Plate IX), which has always been covered up, gives an idea of the brilliant effect that was originally achieved.

The bed in the Venetian Ambassador's Room, which bears the monogram JR, was probably made about 1685–8 by Thomas Roberts for Whitehall Palace. This survives more or less intact with its carved and gilt cornice, and all its hangings of bluish-green cut velvet lavishly trimmed with pink tassel fringe. The curtains of this bed and of the King's Bed clear the ground, and this seems to have been usual: where they reach the floor it is likely that the bed has been cut down or the curtains altered in some way. The outer valances are formed of short festoons with the fringe used double to give a sense of weight to the design.

In the view of some, the bed in the King's Room is not only the finest of the three, but the finest in the country. Certainly it must have been the most costly, for the brocade is heavy with gold and silver thread, and it is trimmed with heavy gold fringe, but as a piece of upholstery it is less inventive than some others. However it is one of the few to retain its original complement of four draw curtains, with its cantonnieres (the curtains' hiding the joins at the corners) fixed. The Belvoir bed has a somewhat similar arrangement of shorter cantonnieres; and the Drayton bed has cantonnieres consisting of broad panels of embroidery.

As an alternative to using a single rich material, sometimes materials of contrasting texture were used in alternating panels. The Drayton bed is an illustration of this, for the panels of needlework are contrasted with widths of green velvet (Fig. 62). A variant of this was to panel one material with another, that is to say to use a deep border of one material round another. Sometimes this is found on bed curtains as on the Spangled Bed at Knole, but it is even more clearly seen in the Blue Drawing Room at Ham House (Plate XX).

The Spangled Bed at Knole and the Drayton bed have a sobriety of form that suggests a date before Marot's designs became influential. Inspired by his engravings (Figs. 63, 64) the silhouette of canopies tended to become more broken and the head boards to become much more *mouvementé* with scrolls and swirls in three dimensions. The outstanding examples of this kind of taste are the canopy now at Hardwick and the Melville bed at the Victoria and Albert Museum (Figs. 65, 67), which was made for the Earl of Melville, one of William III's courtiers and a man likely to have had direct contact with Marot. It is over 15 feet high, and great play is made with the contrast between the crimson velvet hangings and the oyster silk damask used to line the bed. No other surviving bed has such an extended cornice with such exaggerated projections, and weeks of embroiderers' time must have gone into applying the braid and fringe to emphasise the curves of the cresting and the convolutions of the head of the bed. The outer valance is an admirable example of box pleating, the use of festoons, tassels, bells and what are now usually called *choux*.

The term *choux* is typical of upholstery in being French, for it literally means cabbage, that is to say a puckering of material roughly roundish in shape, lightly stitched to hold it and mounted on buckram or other material before being attached to a valance. With lighter materials, such as taffeta, the *choux* may be lightly stuffed with lamb's wool.

A bell, or *campane* if one prefers the traditional French term, is a form of

62. THE LATE 17TH CENTURY STATE
BED AT DRAYTON HOUSE. Panels
of needlework alternate with widths
of green velvet.

63. A STATE BEDROOM BY MAROT.
The rod for the case curtains
round the bed is shown.

87

64. AN ANGEL BED BY MAROT.

box pleat, but instead of being repeated it is used as a single ornament, as can be seen on the valances of the Hardwick canopy.

The use of festoons is shown by Marot in his engravings of beds, valances and curtains, and although no curtains survive, good examples of festooning can be seen not only on the Melville bed and on the Hardwick canopy, but on the canopy of the Stoke Edith bed.

There is an element of vulgarity about the Melville bed that is not present in the canopy at Hardwick (Plates VII, VIII), which is perhaps the most brilliant example of late 17th century upholstery to have come down to us. Each side consists of a moulded cornice decorated with scrolls supporting a cartouche and garlands, and from this hang Marotesque valances that break into festoons. These are trimmed with galloon rather than fringe, and unity is given to the design by the deep bells that hang from the *choux* below the central cartouche and at each corner. The head is equally remarkable, for the design is picked out with butterfly fringe and two widths of galloon.

Quite apart from this, the Hardwick canopy is of interest, for it appears to be part of the earliest known angel bed or *lit à la duchesse* in England,[14] that

88

65. A BED MADE FOR THE EARL OF MELVILLE, ABOUT 1690. In this picture the bed appears too low because of the loss of the original mattresses: the pillow should come just below the decoration on the headboard; the cords round the curtains are 19th century.

is to say a bed with a canopy hung from the ceiling rather than supported by four posts. A number of slightly later ones survive, but as in the case of the Clandon bed they have usually had two posts added, probably when they were moved from their original position into rooms with higher ceilings where the ropes would be too obvious. Sometimes the canopy of an angel bed is shaped to fit the cornice of a room, so that the inner and outer corners are not identical.

Early in the 18th century elaborately draped and festooned valances went out of fashion, and, although the sections of the cornices of canopies tended to meet and end in complicated scrolls, the actual valances tended to become flatter and, although quite elaborately shaped, to be ornamented with patterns of galloon rather than tassel fringe. Perhaps the best example of this kind of work is to be seen on the window valances that match the valances on the state bed from Holme Lacy, now at Beningbrough (Fig. 68). The scrolls are particularly well done: they are formed by drawing on a running stitch sewn through what is intended to be the inside of the scroll.

The valances of the Dyrham bed (Plate X) made about 1710 also illustrate this type of decoration. The whole bed is rather coarse in conception, but it

89

is particularly interesting as it was made shortly before the elaborate broken silhouette and rich trimming both went out of fashion. The main fabric used is crimson velvet, but it is panelled in olive green, and the valances are enriched with yellow silk appliqués and scrolls of gold galloon.

Within four years there was a great change in taste as can be seen if this bed is compared with the one at Hampton Court Palace ordered for Windsor by Queen Anne in July, 1714 (Fig. 69). Gone are the elaborate silhouette, the patterns of galloon, and the lavish use of tassels and fringe, and the return to a sober silhouette seems to anticipate Palladian fashion. Instead the dominant feature is the rich fabric, a silk velvet with a cut and uncut pile on a satin ground in shades of crimson and gold on white. Fortunately one unused piece (Plate XI) is shown at the Victoria and Albert Museum (loan 978) and gives an idea of its original impact.

It is interesting to compare the Queen's bed with the Green Velvet Bed at Houghton, undoubtedly designed by Kent. The Houghton bed (Plates XII, XIII, XIV) is a splendid concept, the gold braid, now black with age, being used like the gilding on an entablature to emphasise its architectural character. The head of the bed is dominated by a great fluted shell, the spines again being picked out with braid. It seems that this feature became a favourite in Kent's circle, for it occurs in a modified form in a design for a state bed by Vardy in the Victoria and Albert Museum and on the splendid cut velvet bed at Hardwick now attributed to him on the strength of it.[15] At Holkham the original bed beneath the canopy in the state bedroom was a sofa-bed, the bed base folding up beneath the seat of the sofa. In the old photograph of Fig. 70, the sofa is shown at the foot of a later fixed bed: it still exists (Fig. 157) but is now placed facing the state bed. The only comparable piece of furniture is a sofa bed at Burghley, but there the canopy, if it ever existed, has now disappeared.

Although these beds survive for the most part in remarkable condition considering their age, they are seldom shown to advantage in one respect: the beds themselves are usually not made up to the right height, and so the balance of the design is destroyed. At Hampton Court Palace the original mattresses still exist on some of the beds, and it is possible to judge the effect of the feather bed on top of three or four mattresses. As in the story of the princess and the pea, there should be many layers starting with a straw palliasse on top of a laced canvas or a kind of duckboard; on to the palliasse went one or more hair, or wool and hair, mattresses, and then finally on top went the feather

66. A DETAIL OF THE HEAD OF THE MELVILLE BED.

67. A DETAIL OF THE CANOPY OF THE MELVILLE BED.

68. A CURTAIN VALANCE EN SUITE WITH THE HOLME LACY STATE BED NOW AT BENINGBROUGH, ABOUT 1705. One of the best examples of the ornamental use of galloon.

69. QUEEN ANNE'S BED AT HAMPTON
COURT PALACE. Ordered in 1714,
it shows a reaction against the
Baroque extravagance of the
Dyrham bed.

bed. When the Duchess of Marlborough was furnishing Blenheim, she wrote
"I shall want a vast number of Feather Beds and quilts. I would have some of
the Feather Beds swansdown, all good and sweet Feathers, even for the
servants." By the second quarter of the 19th century fashions were changing,
but when Miss George went to Stowe in 1845, she disapproved of the new
beds: "Then it was not the fashion for Great People to sleep on mattresses—
a full down or feather bed look'd much better and more comfortable than the
flat and untidy couches do now."[16]

From the point of view of upholstery beds made after the late 1740s tend
to be less interesting, largely because their design passed increasingly into the
control of the cabinet maker, carver, gilder and painter, and the upholsterers'
work became of secondary importance, except on rare occasions like Queen
Charlotte's needlework bed and the Osterley bed (Fig. 71). No one can dispute
Adam's ingenuity in his design for the latter, but there is little feeling for the
materials as such and Walpole's remark in 1778 "What would Vitruvius think
of a dome decorated by a milliner" seems very apt. Also it is disappointing
that several of the finest beds like the Chinese bed from Badminton now at
the Victoria and Albert Museum, Chambers's state bed at Blenheim, the Stowe
bed now at the Lady Lever Gallery, and the Nostell bed have lost their
original hangings; and one of the most fanciful of all, that made for Burghley

70. THE STATE BEDROOM AT HOLKHAM. This old photograph shows the original folding sofa bed, which was made to go under the canopy, placed at the foot of a later bed of conventional type.

71. THE STATE BED AT OSTERLEY DESIGNED BY ADAM. The original counterpane survives but is not shown here. The carpet round the bed is a special bed-carpet: it is only a strip and does not extend under the bed. Another bed carpet is illustrated in Figure 191.

in 1790, has been considerably altered.[17]

The best survivors from the 1750s, '60s and '70s tend to be less showy and, although fine, cannot really be compared with the late 17th and early 18th century examples in terms of imaginative conception. One of the best is the Hopetoun bed (Fig. 72) which is domed and has an elaborate carved and gilt cornice. The valances are flat, but decorated with applied ornaments and they are trimmed with a fine ornamented knotted fringe. The headboard and dome are finely worked, the pattern of the fabric being carefully cut to fit the design. In this it is like the canopy of the Kedleston state bed, where the leaves in the fabric are cut in four ways for the bed of the ceiling of the canopy, and the cove is lined with the pomegranite section of the fabric. What is not clear is whether the curtains covered the posts or whether they were drawn back to show the carving and gilding of the posts.

From the 1760s the Polonaise was a fashionable form for beds and enough survive to show the development of the style. The earliest is that at Nostell Priory, but unfortunately the lightness of the original drapery was not re-captured when the bed was redressed 80–100 years ago. At Drumlanrig there is one made for the visit of the Prince Regent to Dalkeith in 1790 (Fig. 73). Round the dome are festooned valances caught up alternately by *choux* and trimmed with a typical ornamented bullion fringe. The state bed at Windsor Castle made by Jacob shows the form at its most elaborate about 1790, and at

Wimpole there is another related to a design by George Smith. A slightly later
one exists at Chatsworth, but it is not clear whether this is of English or
French origin. Acquired by the Bachelor Duke probably in the 1820s, it shows
how effectively a bordered chintz could be used and how two types of ornamented fringe could be combined together (Fig. 74).

Among a number of early 19th century beds four are particularly good. At
Castlecoole the original drapery in cherry taffeta shown in the photograph has
been carefully copied and the ornamented bullion fringe re-used so that one
still gets the kind of effect that was intended when the Prince Regent was
expected in 1821 (Fig. 75). The whole concept is rather heavy despite the
lightness of the material, and it is interesting to see how the upholsterer tried
to lighten it by revealing the gilded parts of the cornice. This was also done
quite frequently with the draperies for windows.

Some of the best examples of good upholsterer's work of the late Regency
period used to exist at Ashburnham Place, and two of the bedrooms are
illustrated here. Both are 18th century rooms, and indeed, in the first of them,
the Crimson State Bed Chamber, the original alcove for the bed can be seen
(Fig. 76). In this room, the bed, curtains and chairs were all done in the same
material. The main valance of the bed is stiff and heavily fringed and it is
ornamented with swags and bells that end in heavy tassels. The same pattern
is used for the deep curtain valances that hang from pelmet cornices placed
immediately below the cornice of the room covering the dead light, and the
curtains are held back by cords hanging from bold cloak pins (Fig. 77).

The second bedroom (Fig. 78) is even more evocative of the years about
1830 for as well as the upholstery, the original Brussels carpet with its bed
and hearth mats in a matching pile carpet and bed steps survived. The use of
tails, swags and bells both for the bed and curtain valances is clearly apparent,

95

74. A POLONAISE BED AT
DRUMLANRIG CASTLE, DUMFRIES-
SHIRE. Made for the visit of
George IV to Dalkeith Palace
in 1822.

XV. *SIR LAWRENCE DUNDAS AND*
HIS GRANDSON IN THE LIBRARY
AT 19 ARLINGTON STREET, LONDON,
BY ZOFFANY, 1769.
One of the most accurate mid 18th-
century renderings of a room in
a portrait: not only do some of the
pictures, bronzes and furniture
survive in the possession of the
Marquess of Zetland, but the artist
gives a good idea of contemporary
picture hanging, the use of fillets
with a plain wallpaper and of
reefed curtains.

XVI. *THE SITWELL CHILDREN*
BY COPLEY, 1787. French draw
curtains are shown.

and the upholsterer was allowed great freedom when redoing the earlier settee
at the foot of the bed: its draped valance matches the inner valance of the
tester of the bed, which is also an excellent illustration both of buttoning
and box pleating.

Compared with these the third Ashburnham bed (Fig. 79) shown here as
it was when in the Tobacco Bedroom at Haseley is a fairly simple design, but
the outline of the box pleated cotton valances trimmed with a linen and cotton
galloon is a particularly pleasing one and shows how successful the more
restrained work of that date could be.

Intentionally we have concentrated on the period before 1750 not only
because of the intrinsic interest of the beds themselves, but also because after
that date it is possible to find a greater range of upholsterer's work in more or
less original condition. After all even the state beds were not intended to be
seen in isolation but as part of an ensemble that included seat furniture and
curtains as well. Unfortunately very few pelmet cornices and valances survive,
although it is known they matched the beds, and it is rare to find any armchairs and side chairs en suite with the bed as they are at Clandon.

96

XVII. A VALANCE OF SPITALFIELDS
SILK IN THE WHITE DRAWING ROOM
AT HOUGHTON, ABOUT 1797. The
room is illustrated in Plate XXIV,
the style of the drapery is
comparable with that shown in
Figure 121.

XVIII. THE DRAWING ROOM AT
EATON HALL, CHESHIRE, IN 1826.
Buckler's watercolour shows one of
the elaborate interiors designed by
Porden and decorated by Gillows.
By then it was fashionable to
draw some of the seat furniture
out from the walls. Extra light at
night was provided in the urns set
in the niches flanking the end
window.

75. THE STATE BED AT CASTLECOOLE,
CO. FERMANAGH, ABOUT 1820.
Since this photograph was taken,
the original cherry coloured taffeta
hangings have been replaced, but
the trimmings have been re-used.
The flock wallpaper with its thick
gilt fillet is contemporary.

76. THE BED FORMERLY IN THE
CRIMSON STATE BEDROOM AT
ASHBURNHAM PLACE, SUSSEX, ABOUT
1825. Its predecessor would have
been set in the alcove.

77. THE CURTAINS AND VALANCES
FROM THE CRIMSON STATE BEDROOM
AT ASHBURNHAM PLACE. The
tie-backs for the curtains are hung
from cloak pins placed high up
the wall.

78. A BEDROOM AT ASHBURNHAM
PLACE AS IT WAS IN 1956. All the
upholstery dates from about 1825.
as does the Brussels carpet and
the pile hearth rug used under the
dressing table stool.

79. EARLY 19TH CENTURY HANGINGS
ON A BED FROM ASHBURNHAM
PLACE AS IT APPEARED IN THE
TOBACCO BEDROOM AT HASELEY
COURT, OXFORDSHIRE. The Brussels
carpet with its border, also from
Ashburnham, is contemporary.

Curtains

Marot's designs for interiors, beds and upholstery are so extravagant that it is hard to believe that they were ever executed in England, but it is clear from inventories of the most elaborately decorated houses and from upholsterers' bills that an attention comparable to that paid to state beds was lavished on all forms of upholstery including curtains, particularly· in bedrooms and dressing rooms. Inevitably window curtains have survived less well than the hangings of state beds, and complete contemporary pelmet cornices and valances are of the greatest rarity. How quickly the fashion for them caught on is not at present known, for even curtains in pairs were a novelty in France in the 1670s and 80s, the earliest reference to them so far recorded being in 1673.[18]

By 1700 at least three types of curtain were known in England. The simplest was the draw curtain, sometimes existing as a single curtain and sometimes in pairs. According to mid 17th century pictures they were sometimes hung by tape loops from a metal rod as can be seen in *The Blue Curtain* by Adriaen Van der Spelt (Fig. 80) and Pieter Janssen's *La Balayeuse*, or from crossed loops as in Honthorst's *Le Concert*. If rings were used, a curtain might be drawn on a cord running down the side of the window not covered by the material.[19]

Evidently on occasion the system of rod and rings was regarded as a decorative as well as a purely utilitarian feature. For instance, on December 11, 1705, Lapierre charged the Duke of Montagu for making two sets of window curtains of blue camlet "to draw upon pulley Rodds . . ." and in 1706 he supplied 76 yards of green silk cord together with five green tassels to draw curtains, suggesting that the cord was decorative as well as functional. A much fuller account exists in the Temple Newsam papers where all the fittings needed for the new dining room curtains in 1735 are specified. There were two large gilded brass pulley rods and the hooks to hold up the rods were also gilt. The curtains themselves were drawn on "$9\frac{1}{2}$ onsis of crimson In Grain Silk Rainwork Line" and there were 2 large brass pulleys. The curtains were hung on "36 large polished brass Rings Gilt," and there were also "4 small Brass hooks & 12 small brass Rings putt to the bottom of the Curtains to hang up when the Roome is cleaned."[20]

Lapierre's account with the Duke of Montagu also lists curtains "to draw in drapery" and for curtains "to draw up in festoons." At first one might take these to be the same thing, but as both terms continued to be used during the 18th century, it seems more likely that Lapierre meant two different forms of curtain, the former being what is now often called a reefed curtain and the second being a festoon curtain. Here, unfortunately, Marot is no help: in one of his plates he shows windows fitted with festoon curtains (Fig. 81), and in another (Fig. 82) he shows a variety of festoon curtains and valances, but he gives no explanation that throws light on the problem.

We cannot be dogmatic about this, and as Mrs Montgomery in *Printed Textiles*[21] uses different terms, her definitions as well as ours should be given. Drapery or reefed curtains, according to our interpretation, are made with draw strings set obliquely, so that when the cord is pulled, the pair of curtains is drawn up and part; whereas, a festoon curtain is one that is drawn up perpendicularly on a series of cords to leave the greater part if not all the window architrave visible (Fig. 83). Mrs Montgomery, on the other hand, uses the terms festoon curtain to describe our reefed curtain and the term Venetian curtain for our festoon curtain.

As terms in decoration are notoriously liable to change in meaning, this double definition is needed, because the evidence from documents is not entirely clear. However it is perhaps worthy of comment that while we have come across the term Venetian blind and Venetian shades (at Osterley in 1782),

80. *THE BLUE CURTAIN* BY ADRIAEN VAN DER SPELT. The artist shows his flower painting protected by a single curtain hung on loops from rings and a metal rod.

81. AN INTERIOR BY MAROT. This plate shows festoon curtains inset in the window embrasures and fitted behind a shallow pelmet cornice.

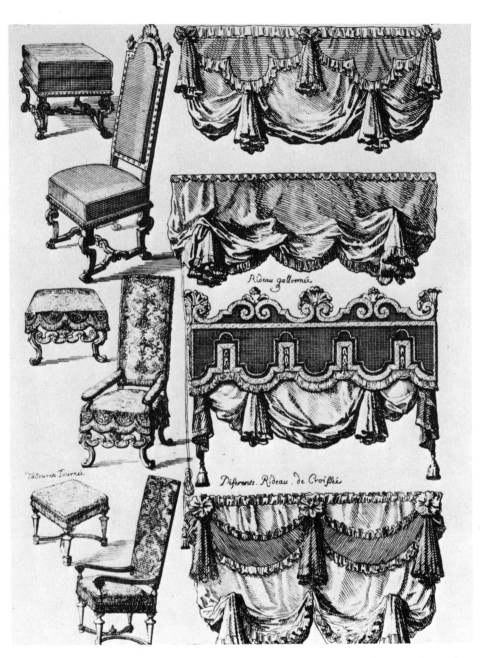

Rideau gallonnée

Tabouret Tournee

Diferents. Rideau. de Croiffée

82. DESIGN FOR UPHOLSTERY BY MAROT. He shows alternative treatments for festoon curtains and pelmet cornices.

which are true slatted blinds, we have only once come across the term Venetian curtain in accounts and inventories, and that is in the catalogue of Sir William Chambers's sale in 1796. There, most confusingly, in the dining room are listed curtains of striped cotton, "lined and fringed in the Venetian drapery taste" and in Lady Chambers's Dressing Room festoon curtains. And it is equally confusing that whereas the Osterley inventory lists three festoon curtains in the drawing room that are still *in situ* (and correspond to our definition), Vile and Cobb charged Sir Charles Hanbury Williams for making his damask into "festoone curtains made to open in the middle," thus corresponding to Mrs Montgomery's definition.[22]

In addition other variant terms are recorded. For instance, in 1767 Chippendale made two drapery window curtains of blue damask for Mersham, and the term "draw up" occurs in the Chandos inventory of 1725, at Blenheim in 1770 and at Hatfield in 1782. The former we take to be reefed and the latter to be festoon. The earliest reference of all, to a pull of crimson silk window curtains at Hampton Court Palace in 1699, could be either, although it might be presumed to be a festoon but for the fact that Lapierre was apparently making both kinds for Montagu a few years later.[23]

This reference and Lapierre's account suggests that there may have been no theory or custom about their use at that date, or at least no problem of

83. A MODERN FESTOON CURTAIN IN THE GREEN DRAWING ROOM AT CLANDON. It is shown partly drawn up.

height in the rooms for which they were intended. They were probably only used in the more important and so loftier rooms with very tall windows like those on the garden front at Hampton Court Palace or the north front at Boughton, and so they were probably sometimes fitted into the window architrave as they appear in Marot's engravings. However in Palladian houses, where the windows tend to be less tall in relation to the inner walls, festoon curtains appear at their most effective when there is plenty of "dead light" between the top of the architrave and the entablature and where they can be so fixed that when they are fully drawn up they almost clear the architrave, as can be seen in the Saloon at Uppark and the Gallery at Corsham Court (Figs. 201, 202). In the Corsham illustration the curtains are not fully drawn up so they break the lines of the architraves, but it can be seen that the fixings are placed just below the entablature. In a lower room there is usually insufficient dead light, and as George Lucy recognised when he was making changes at Charlecote in the early 1760s, "the hangings in Festoons they say will certainly darken the rooms."[24] Not everyone shared Mr Lucy's view, for it is clear both from William Verelst's portrait of the *Gough Family* in 1741 (Fig. 84) and Reinagle's picture of *Mrs Congreve and her daughters in their London drawing room* (Fig. 85) that they were used in rooms much more modest than the Saloon at Uppark, and then it was quite permissible for the festoons not to draw up clear of the windows.

103

84. THE GOUGH FAMILY BY
VERELST, 1741. The festoon curtains
are shown drawn up so that they
almost clear the window architraves.

85. MRS CONGREVE AND HER
DAUGHTERS IN THEIR LONDON
DRAWING ROOM BY PHILIP REINAGLE,
ABOUT 1780. This shows festoon
curtains used in a room where they
could not be drawn up clear of
the top of the window architraves.
The carpet stands clear of the
furniture ranged round the walls.
The fender is placed across the
fireplace and not framing the
hearth stone; and the fire irons
stand upright.

Quite apart from such practical considerations, the Uppark kind of arrangement appealed to patrons and architects dedicated to a theoretical approach to architecture. They did not want upholstery to break up the architectural design of a room, for the carved architraves to the windows were intended to complement those round the doors and the chimneypiece and overmantel. Also they wanted the detail of the carving, particularly if gilded, to be seen and admired. At Clandon in the Library even the shutter cases are decorated, and this would have been hidden by draw curtains (Fig. 86).

At Uppark, Clandon and Osterley the original mechanism for the festoon curtains still exists in several of the principal rooms. This consists of a board projecting for about six inches from the wall pierced with seven holes. Four of these are spaced out along the length of the board, and these correspond with four more at one end. Each hole contains a boxwood (later, metal) wheel, and over each wheel runs a draw string that runs down one side of the window. When the separate draw strings, which are knotted together at the end, are pulled down, they pull on the pear-shaped lead weights that are sewn into bags attached to the curtain lining at the bottom of the curtain, and the whole curtain starts to rise. When the curtain is pulled up into the desired position, the draw strings are secured by being wound round a pair of cloak pins placed a few inches apart in a figure of eight, as can be seen in Frances Cotes's portrait

86. A DETAIL OF A SHUTTER CASE IN THE LIBRARY AT CLANDON. This decoration would have been largely hidden by drawn curtains.

of *Paul Sandby* painted about 1760 (Fig. 87). Even cloak pins were the subject of careful attention, and decorative Rococo and Neo-classical examples can be seen in a bedroom at Blickling in Norfolk and in the State Bedroom at Osterley; and the Victoria and Albert Museum has some charming ones in cast brass decorated with enamel.

A reefed curtain does not have to clear the architrave and indeed is sometimes fixed inside it, so giving a softer effect as can be seen in Zoffany's picture of Sir Lawrence Dundas in his Arlington Street house (Plate XV, Fig. 88). However, as far as we know, no 18th century reefed curtains still survive in use, but Chippendale illustrates several beds with curtains that are "drawn up in drapery," as he described it (Fig. 89).[25]

With a festoon curtain the head and the board was usually hidden by a pelmet cornice and a valance, but, as has been said, very few early ones of any elaboration survive intact. Probably the earliest are those from Holme Lacy and now at Beningbrough: they match the valances on the state bed, but as the latter have been recovered in this century, they give a sense of the fineness of detail of the original finish and particularly of the working of the galloon.[26] At the Victoria and Albert Museum there is a valance from Dyrham that

87. PAUL SANDBY BY FRANCIS COTES, ABOUT 1760. An incidental detail in this portrait is the depiction on the right of the draw strings for festoon curtains wound round a pair of cloak pins.

88. AN 18TH CENTURY REEFED
CURTAIN. A detail from the painting
of Plate XV.

matched the state bed, but it may have been for the portières rather than the
curtains. At Clandon, a set of pelmet cornices still exists in the state bedroom
and they match the bed, but they have lost their valances. At Erthig interesting
valances apparently of caffoy and listed in the 1726 inventory survive in the
Gallery (Fig. 90). Another survivor, and possibly the earliest, is one in fretwork
upholstered in brown velvet and trimmed with green tassel fringe that is now
in the Victoria and Albert Museum.

Among the pelmet valances that Lapierre describes are some for blue camlet
curtains that were laced with broad and narrow gold colour lace; another set
in green taffeta were embroidered with three coloured gold galloon and furbe-
lows (flounces); a set of white damask curtains had the valances embroidered
with gold coloured orrice.

Probably the earliest surviving festoon curtains are those now in the State
Bedroom at Dyrham (Figs. 91, 92). They are not listed in the 1716 inventory,
but as their colouring and the working of the fabric in panels of yellow bordered
by red seems to relate to the state bed, they may date from soon after that.
They are thought to be made of moreen.

In view of Lapierre's account, it is surprising that we have not come across
more references to festoon curtains in the 1720s and 30s, and it is not clear
what allowance architects made for them in their designs. However they must
have been quite widely used, because they were sufficiently familiar for Hogarth
to include them in *Marriage à la Mode*, in the *Marriage Contract* scene
painted about 1743 (Fig. 93). At Marble Hill, the proportions of the window

107

89. A CANOPY BED DESIGNED BY CHIPPENDALE. Plate XLII from the Director shows curtains that are "drawn up in display".

wall of the Saloon and the arrangement of mouldings are such that they seem to call out for festoon curtains to pull the design together.

By the late 1740s festoon curtains were the most fashionable type to have, and most houses with any pretension had them somewhere. They occur in the inventory of Lord Townshend's house in Berkeley Square in 1755, and in Chippendale's bill for Dumfries House in 1759, to cite two examples.[27] By then it was usual to have the pelmet cornices carved and gilded, like those in the Drawing Room at Longford Castle, or covered in silk or painted with valances of the same fabric as the curtains, but few of those that survive are as splendid as those in the state bedroom at Holkham that match the state bed. The most famous are those in the Gallery at Harewood House supplied by Chippendale in the early 1770s (Fig. 94): there the carved and gilt cornices have carved and painted wooden valances imitating drawn-up festoons, a considerable *tour de force*, but their effect is partly spoilt because the original curtains have gone and been replaced by draw curtains that hide the architraves.

It might be supposed that festoon curtains would usually have been made of a fairly light material such as tammy, taffeta, lutestring, or cotton chintz. However, heavier materials were also used, as can be seen in the state bedroom at Osterley where they are of green velvet.

108

90. AN EARLY 18TH CENTURY
CURTAIN VALANCE AT EARTHIG,
DENBIGHSHIRE. Apparently part of
the caffoy furniture supplied for
the saloon and listed there in 1726.

They remained fashionable until the late 1770s or early 1780s. Adam used them in the Tapestry Room at Croome Court in 1769, then at Harewood in 1775 and at Osterley, as we have seen. The mechanism for them still exists in the library at Heveningham fitted up by James Wyatt in the early 1780s. However they were soon to be thought of as old fashioned, and when one learns of them being supplied to Bridewell House, Devon, by Seddon in 1792, it seems that either Seddon or the clients were not in touch with the latest fashions.[28]

Of course draw curtains had never completely dropped out of use, but they were not always supplied with valances. In Hogarth's *The Wanstead Assembly* (Fig. 95), which is supposed to show one of the richest rooms in the house and is presumably a fairly faithful impression of it, there are simple pairs of draw curtains. As an alternative to hanging these curtains from rings on rods, they were sometimes finished with what are now incorrectly called French headings or pinch pleats. A better name is *tête de Versailles*, but confusingly in France this kind of broad box pleating is called *tête Hollandaise*.

Writing about curtains in 1803, Sheraton said: "Festoon curtains, amongst upholsterers, are those which draw up by pullies, and hang down in a swag. These curtains are still in use in bedrooms, not withstanding the general introduction of the French rod curtains in most genteel houses. A festoon window curtain, consists generally of three pulls, but when a window is extensive they have four or five."[29]

The difference between the French draw curtains and the earlier type of draw curtains was that they overlapped at the top instead of merely meeting. Writing of drapery Sheraton said "These curtains are drawn on French rods. When the cords are drawn the curtains meet in the centre at the same time, but are no way raised from the floor. When the same cord is drawn the reverse way, each curtain flies open, and comes to their place on each side . . . "To effect this, the rod is made in a particular manner, having two pulleys at one end, and a single one at the other, which cannot well be described in words without a drawing of it."[30]

One of the earliest pictorial representations of them in England is in Copley's

109

91, 92. EARLY FESTOON CURTAINS
NOW IN THE STATE BEDROOM AT
DYRHAM. Although not listed in the
1716 inventory, the working of
the yellow and red materials seems
to link them to the state bed.
The fringes are 19th century.

93. *MARRIAGE A LA MODE* BY
WILLIAM HOGARTH. This shows that
festoon curtains were sufficiently
familiar to be included as a detail
in a satirical picture of fashionable
life by about 1743.

III

picture of the Sitwells painted in 1787 (Plate XVI) and they appear six years later in Sheraton's plate of the Carlton House drawing room (Fig. 96). And even as late as the early 19th century when Lord Palmerston had new curtains for the drawing room at Broadlands, he described them as "hanging down by the side of the windows in the modern style."[31]

By the next generation the draw curtain was so usual that the origin of the festoon curtain was forgotten and it became a symbol of the past. Thus a form of them appears in the view of the Cartoon Gallery at Knole in Nash's *Mansions in Olden Times* where all the figures are shown in 17th century costume, and they are also included in R. B. Martineau's painting *The Last Day in the Old Home* (Fig. 97), which is based on the Priests Room at Godinton in Kent, to suggest a survival from the past. To Lady Morgan, writing in 1862 of a house in Dublin, the survival of festoon curtains there was part of the old fashioned character of the house.[32]

One possible reason why they dropped out of fashion may have been that they were so bulky that unless a room was very large like the Gallery at Harewood, there was not enough room for elaborately draped valances as well as

97. *THE LAST DAY IN THE OLD HOME*, BY R. B. MARTINEAU. Here festoon curtains are intended to suggest an old-fashioned room.

the curtains. Sometimes in English houses one finds compromise attempts to modernise the curtains about this time. In the Palladio Room at Clandon, for instance, the mid 18th century pelmet cornices are still there, but the curtains are of lampas in a neoclassical design, as are the draped valances, and so probably date from the early 1780s when the Reveillon wall paper was put up.

Inevitably few elaborate late 18th century examples of drapery survive in more or less original condition, and when they are ordered today, it is seldom understood that the whole success of a well-made drapery depends on the skill of the cutter, and that considerable art and ingenuity is needed to make them hang naturally and with ease. Frequently modern ones have a sleek and over-symmetrical look that does not suggest the *drapery* of fabric at all: this should be avoided and particularly in a large room the freedom that Chippendale managed to express in wood should be aimed at. The only qualification to this is that in the more austere kind of Regency interior that approaches the French Empire style in feeling, a harder and more linear look is in character.

A simple drapery usually consists of one or more swags with tails to go at each end, and each part is made separately. Sometimes the join of the swags is ornamented with a "bell", that is a box pleat hanging down between them. There are two ways of handling this, one being to attach it invisibly, and let the points hang below the swag; and the second, which is more difficult to do, is to design the bell as a double box pleat and to make its outer edge join up with the bottom of the swag. The swags and tails are often lined with a contrasting material and colour, so that when the tail is correctly seamed and put up, it folds to reveal the two materials rising alternately towards the swag.

For early draperies we have to rely on engravings and the surviving evidence in the valances and heads of state beds. Several of them exploit contrasts of fabric and colour, crimson velvet and oyster silk in the Melville bed (Fig. 65), crimson velvet and embroidered silk in the Glemham bed and so on. The

114

Melville bed and the bed formerly at Hampton Court, Herefordshire, provide evidence of drapery in the Marot period. It seems that at that time the art of cutting was not particularly well understood (as we know from contemporary clothes), and in the Hampton Court bed the valance is just gathered at the top so that it does not hang very fully. The Melville bed is more sophisticated and more skill is shown in the arrangement of the swags: here they are combined with early forms of bells that hang from above the puckered "frieze". Sometimes flounces were used as a substitute for fringes, and this has been done on the new festoon curtains in the Green Drawing Room and Hunting Room at Clandon (Fig. 83).

The art of drapery was revived in France in the 1770s after an interval of nearly 50 years, but it may have taken some time to become established in England. There are even apparently a few designs surviving from the 1770s and 80s, but among the more interesting is one of 1786 showing alternative treatments for the windows at Grimston Garth, a house by Carr on the Yorkshire coast (Fig. 98).

The finest examples of drapery dating from the end of the 18th century are in the State Bedroom at Burghley (Fig. 99) and in the White Drawing Room at Houghton (Plate XVII). The Burghley bed room was fitted out for the Prince Regent's visit in 1790, and for the occasion a new state bed together with new window curtains were supplied by Fell and Newton. Although the bed was altered for Queen Victoria's visit, the carved and gilt pelmet cornice and the draped valance appear to be original; or if the material was renewed for the next Royal visit, it repeated the old design and the original trimmings were re-used. The Houghton room was decorated about 1797.

By the first decade of the 19th century even more elaborate effects were attempted, and, when Porden was at work in Gloucester House in 1807, he wrote to Lord Grosvenor: "I shall put the draperies under the active direction of Mr. Kay who will attend to everything your Lordship has said and who understands them both as a Painter and an Upholsterer." But evidently Mr. Kay was exceptional for the following year George Smith wrote: "In no part of his profession is the English upholsterer more deficient than in the arrangement and in the forms of his Draperies." He gave advice as to

98. ALTERNATIVE TREATMENTS FOR THE WINDOWS AT GRIMSTON GARTH, YORKSHIRE. A reconstruction by Francis Johnson of a drawing possibly by Carr of York, 1786.

99. A DRAPED VALANCE IN THE
STATE BEDROOM AT BURGHLEY HOUSE,
NORTHAMPTONSHIRE. Apparently
part of the decorations carried out
by Fell and Newton in preparation
for a visit from the Prince Regent
in 1790.

suitable materials and provided designs both for curtains and bed hangings
(Fig. 100).[33]

At Southill and Sezincote, both dating from about this time, there are
elaborate curtains and draperies that are faithful copies of the original design.
At Southill the curtains and valances in the Drawing Room (Fig. 101) are
combined in a single display of great imagination: originally of red sarsnet
lined with green manchester velvet to echo the wall panels of crimson bordered
with green, the curtains are made to look like reefed curtains (with cords
pulling them up at an angle of 45 degrees, but they are cut more fully so that
the material can be drawn up to the top of the pelmet cornice and be secured
by the eagle's claws.

At Sezincote the same idea is developed to form what was called a continued
drapery (Fig. 102), but here the curtains are of the French draw type and can
be pulled. To early 19th century French eyes a pelmet cornice seemed heavy,
and so there was a fashion for breaking it up with swags of drapery leaving
only sections of the cornice or pole exposed as was done here. At Sezincote

116

100. A CONTINUED DRAPERY AND
WINDOW CURTAINS. An illustration
from George Smith's *Collection of
Designs for Household Furniture*
(1805).

101. THE CURTAINS IN THE
DRAWING ROOM AT SOUTHILL PARK,
BEDFORDSHIRE. Replacements of
the original design of about 1800.

102. A CONTINUED DRAPERY IN THE DRAWING ROOM AT SEZINCOTE, GLOUCESTERSHIRE. A Victorian replacement of the original design and now replaced again.

there are three separate cornices, one for each window, and although the drapery that runs across the bow appears to be continuous, it is in fact achieved with no less than 13 pieces of material.

Of course this kind of display could easily degenerate into sheer vulgarity and costly extravagance as can be seen in some of the Gillow designs (Figs. 103, 104), and this is in fact what happened, particularly under the influence of books like those of George Smith (1826 edition). The market he was aiming at was certainly expanding, and, thanks to such publications, we know much more about changes in fashion, but the changes were on the whole regrettable, and usually the grander the work the more vulgar it became. Not only did carving become heavier and harder looking, but the result was often over-dressed, like the King's bed at Castlecoole (Fig. 75). Closely related to the designs and spirit of George Smith, this admirably illustrates the decline that had taken place since Holland first started work at Carlton House.

The room and the adjoining dressing room were both furnished and decorated for a prospective visit from the Prince Regent. A new flock wall paper in tone with the bed was hung and bordered with a heavy water gilt fillet. And in the dressing room there was a draped curtain at the window (Fig. 105). The

118

103. THREE ALTERNATIVE
TREATMENTS OF CURTAINS PROPOSED
BY GILLOWS, ABOUT 1825. (A detail
of a drawing in the Victoria and
Albert Museum.)

104. A CONTINUED DRAPERY
DESIGNED BY GILLOWS.

105. A DRAPED CURTAIN FORMERLY
IN THE STATE DRESSING ROOM AT
CASTLECOOLE.

XIX. THE REYNOLDS ROOM AT KNOLE. Mid 18th-century hangings and upholstery of stamped wool velvet.

XX. THE BLUE DRAWING ROOM AT HAM HOUSE, ABOUT 1675. The original effect of the hangings was of blue damask bordered with a darker blue embroidered velvet.

latter is of interest because it shows the breaking up of the cornice noted at Sezincote taken a stage further, for the drapery is merely hung from gilt ornaments and gathered up lightly in the centre, an arrangement that parallels a design in Ackerman's *Repository* for 1809 that shows draperies suspended from two gilt rosettes "doing away with the heavy effects of a cornice."

During the next twenty years draperies became even more elaborate and complicated. Among the good surviving examples are the valances in the Speakers' Parlour at Clandon (Fig. 106), apparently put up about 1820 when the room was refurnished as a formal dining room. A number of designs for curtains and draperies are included in the Wyatville designs for Windsor Castle: many have deep valances, very evenly draped with appliqué embroidery and heavy fringes. But even these must have been exceeded in elaboration by some of the curtains at Fonthill. In the Oak Parlour, for instance, Rutter describes outer curtains of purple silk damask, bordered with the royal tressure of Scotland, as indicative of royal descent; with inner curtains of scarlet moreen.[34]

In rooms such as these the upholsterer had won over the architect, but the 18th century architect had produced one insuperable problem, the Venetian window, and Adam's drawings always seem to skirt round it. So does the one plate given by Chippendale (No. 36) (Fig. 107): he proposed an elaborately carved cornice arched in the centre with a drapery of tails, swags and bells, but the drapery must have been fixed because there was not sufficient room to take the bunches of material. If the shape of the central window is not to be lost, it has to be fitted with reefed curtains or dress curtains that look like reefed curtains and the shutters have to be used. The side windows are usually

106. A DRAPED VALANCE IN THE SPEAKERS' PARLOUR AT CLANDON. A replacement of an original design of about 1820.

120

XXI. CRIMSON FLOCK PAPER IN
THE PRINCE REGENT'S BEDROOM AT
CLANDON PARK, SURREY, ABOUT 1735.
The colour has largely "flown"
from the stained ground so
creating a two-colour effect. The
pattern was a favourite one
throughout the 18th century and
exists in different colours in
damask and wallpaper.

XXII. A SECTION OF THE FLOCK
PAPER DESIGNED BY REVEILLON IN
THE PALLADIO ROOM AT CLANDON,
DATING FROM THE 1780S. The
room is illustrated in Figure 232.

A Design for a Cornice, for a Venetian Window

too narrow for a drapery of a swag and tail to be fitted inside the architrave, and a single curtain drawn to one side may have been used. Festoon curtains are never satisfactory in this position because of the difference in proportion between the dead light over the central and side windows.

There are various references to this kind of problem in contemporary letters, among them one from Elizabeth Anson to Lady de Grey sent from Shugborough in 1750. "The Window-Curtain in the Bow Window, I promised an account of" she wrote, "is divided as I thought, into two parts, & drawn up by three lines of a side—comme ca and these points hang down as low as the surface in the space between the two cornishes as ornaments & festoons of stucco." Evidently this was a reefed curtain, but at Blenheim, Duchess Caroline, when faced by round-headed as opposed to full Venetian windows, ordered "draw up Curtains lined & fringed, with arch'd heads." At Woburn in 1760 Samuel Norman made "a gaug'd damask head to the Venetian window curtain" in the State Bedroom.[35]

In American houses dating from the 18th century fixed draperies without curtains are quite frequently encountered, but we have not found references to their use in England in the 18th century perhaps because we have concentrated on customs in the larger houses. In the early 19th century there was a fashion for dress curtains, but in combination with inner curtains of a light fabric. Smith illustrates draperies suitable for the drawing room, which he says "should be of satin or lutestring, with undercurtains of muslin, or superfine cassimere; the fringe in contrast with the drapery."[36] They provided plenty of scope for display as can be seen in Buckler's watercolour of the drawing room at Eaton (Plate XVIII). A variant of this was to balance an outer curtain of satin or damask with an undercurtain of muslin or silk gauze. As far as we know no original examples of this kind of arrangement exist, but at Winterthur curtains of spangled muslin are to be seen.

Today little attention is paid to blinds, but in fact their history is as old as that of curtains and of fine upholstery, for the destructive quality of light was quickly realised. Lapierre's bill at Boughton includes "umbrellos," which were an early form of blind.[37] By the third quarter of the 18th century Venetian window blinds or Venetian shades, as they were also called, were frequently supplied, but whether they were made of wooden slats like the modern ones or were versions of festoon curtains is not always clear. Festoon blinds were also used and appear in Edwardian photographs of English houses, but few survive now.

However there are good examples in the corridors at Lyme Park. At Knole the blinds work on the same principle as festoon curtains, but instead of hanging in festoons they unfold like a concertina with fairly definite creases. The present ones are modern replacements, but they are of a type that appear to have been used in the house for many years, and elsewhere are now generally called Roman shades.

Spring blinds evidently came into use in the mid 18th century, for they are described as a new invention in the *London Tradesman* of 1747, and one is mentioned in the Felbrigg correspondence in 1752.[38]

One type that has virtually disappeared from England is the decorated blind. In recent years a few have been made, but apart from one in the Essex Institute, Salem, Mass, we do not know the whereabouts of any old ones. However they must have been usual as we have come across references to them on Trade Cards. John Brown, for instance, advertised "Blinds for Windows made & curiously Painted on Canvas, Silk or Wire: where is a good choice, & best painted of any in London, none excepted." And Bridport, a decorative painter and paper hanger at 18 Old Cavendish Street, Cavendish Square, advertised "Drawing Rooms decorated in the French, Egyptian, Turkish, Indian, Chinese & Gothic styles" and "Transparent Window Blinds in the above ways Ensuit with the Rooms."[39]

In French houses and Italian palaces one still comes on portières in use, but they are never seen in England, and apart from a brief revival in the second quarter of the 19th century, were apparently only used in the last quarter of the 17th and the first quarter of the 18th centuries. The earliest reference that we know to them is in 1691–92 when Thomas Roberts charged for making curtain rods for portières at Kensington. The portières themselves are listed in the State Bedroom in the 1697 inventory. Celia Fiennes mentions them in a house at Newmarket, and they are listed in the Dyrham inventory of 1717, in the Tapestry Room and State Bedroom. There they had valances, but at Cannons in 1725 they are stated to be "without vallance or cornice." Marot shows them in his engravings as matching the wall hangings and completely hiding doors (Fig. 20), and they also appear in the background of Marcellus Laroon's drawings. They are also recorded in the Gallery at Erthig in the 1726 inventory. When the Duchess of Norfolk was planning the decoration of Worksop in 1766, portières are mentioned in two rooms: in the notes about the Duke's room occurs "A Door of the same (blue indian silk damask) to slide on a rod is fixed to the Door going into the Dressing room & fastend to the Architrave on the side next the Bed to keep out the wind on that side." The other was in the South East Gallery.[40]

One of the very few references to their later use is in the 1845 description of Stowe in the Saloon; there were "long trailing curtains to each of the 4 doors (although they are of richest crimson silk velvet) formerly there were only crimson festoons with rich fringe over the doorways."[41] Not only is the reference to the curtains interesting, but the reference to the festoons is most surprising. Again the idea is familiar from Italian palaces, but is otherwise unrecorded in England in a neo-classical room.

Hangings

The use of hangings as a form of decoration as well as insulation dates back to medieval times, but fixed hangings only seem to have been introduced after the Restoration. In brick and stone houses the structure of the internal walls as well as the external was often left rough, and a wooden framework was constructed inside it, to form grounds for nailing, or sometimes it was plastered level with the face of the grounds. Sometimes a room to be hung with stretched material or tapestry, or later wallpaper, might be left with just the wooden

108. THE STATE BEDROOM AT
CLANDON STRIPPED DOWN. All the
main rooms in the house are
lined with wood hidden by the
hangings.

framework, or sometimes, as was discovered at Clandon (Fig. 108), all the main rooms were lined with wood, doubtless for warmth.

The method of fixing these hangings, whatever the fabric, was usually the same. First a scrim or canvas was stretched over each flank of wall and was cut out and tacked to the grounds of the framework round all openings such as doorcases, windows and chimneypieces. Having lined the room in this way, the scrim was often covered with a lining paper, and then the final covering of silk, wool or cotton was put on. When Vile and Cobb, for instance, were working at Buckingham House early in George III's reign they charged for hanging various rooms "with strong cloth and cartridge paper pasted thereon to keep the dust from the damask hangings."[42]

The traditional methods for hanging fabrics are still used today, but with the advent of modern central heating and the taste for hotter rooms, extra precautions usually need to be taken to see that the dust and dirt that is invariably present in old houses is not sucked through the fabric by the difference in temperature between the two sides of the hanging. If the sunk grounds are plaster, the wall should be lined with linen-backed paper over the battens, and it is important to tape the joints between the wood and the plaster before putting up the bump or domette lining; and only after this should the fabric be put up. This practice has been developed after disastrous use of the traditional method in a house with efficient central heating, but naturally it makes a form of decoration that was always expensive proportionately more now than it was in the 18th or 19th centuries.

Early wallpapers, which were after all called paper hangings, were treated in a similar way to fabric. However there were snags in using battens as Mrs Delany pointed out: "Whenever you put up paper, the best way is to have it pasted on the bare wall; when lined with canvas it always shrinks from the edges."[43]

Sometimes early papers were tacked, again a hangover from methods of working fabric. On the handbill for the Blew Paper Warehouse, issued about 1700, there are instructions how to put up panels of paper with and without borders: "First cutt your breadths to your intended heights then tack them at the top and bottom with small tacks . . ."; "But if you will putt up the same without borders, then cutt one of the Edges of each piece or breadth smooth and even, then tack it about an inch over the next breadth and so from one to another." (Butt joining was not then in use). "Gently wett them on the back

123

side with a moist sponge or cloth which will make them hang the smoother."[44] A fragment of an early paper found at Ramsbury beneath the Chinese paper was tacked like this and so was a flock paper at Clandon, which was not mounted on the grounds but tacked and pasted to the re-used dado panels that line the walls.

A rather later set of instructions for hanging Chinese paper were sent to the Earl of Hopetoun by James Cullen in the 1750s or 60s: "If the Indian paper is to be put up in a Room that is wainscoted it must have a linnen and the linnen must be covered with a smooth whited brown paper to prevent its cracking and then put on the Indian paper.

If it is to go on a Plastered wall the wall must be well siz'd and then covered with white brown paper.

To make the paste take fine flour and water and a little of allum, mix it exactly as for hasty pudding and when it boils it is fit for use.

If you can get no size its made thus: one pound of glue to about two quarts of water let it stand till soft then melt it over the fire."[45]

Not all papers were lined. In 1738 Sarah Byng Osborn wrote: "I am told if your walls are not thorough dry paper will be quite spoiled, and if they are dry the best way is to put the paper to the walls without any lining, if the walls are only a rough coat and not whited, but if they are whited, it will not do so . . ."[46]

On the whole lined papers have lasted better and also it is easier to restore them, because they can be taken down, relined like pictures, carefully cleaned and put up again. However after 1770 the old method was gradually abandoned, and paper was frequently stuck straight on the plastered wall, a process mentioned in contemporary bills, among them Robson Hale's for Althorp and Elliott's for Langleys. At Langleys Elliotts charged for "Pumice-stoning and sizeing the walls of the Drawing Room" before putting up the paper.[47]

Where it was the intention to upholster the walls with fabric or hang them with paper mounted on linen or scrim, the wooden grounds holding the scrim and tacks for the final covering needed to be covered, and this gave rise in the 1730s to the use of fillets or braids. The finest of these were carved wood, often water gilt and burnished, but as they were expensive, papier maché, cast lead, and, later, composition were also used. An added touch of sophistication was to pick out the gilding with a colour matching one of the principal colours used in the decoration of the room. This occurs both in the state bedroom at Nostell and in the Chinese Room at Ramsbury, where alternate gadroons are gilded and painted green. It was usual to place them above the dado rail and below the architrave moulding of the entablature, with often a double line in the vertical angles of the room; however they were seldom used on the external angle of a chimney breast as the material did not require tacking there. Where the fillets had to meet moulded doorcases or chimneypieces or other features with complicated outlines, they had to be specially carved, to follow the outline of the mouldings.

Having said this, it should be emphasised that exceptions can always be found. In the Gallery at Longford Castle (Fig. 109), for instance, where there is a fine Greek key fillet in carved and gilt wood, it is found double on the angles of the chimney breast, and it frames the doorcases in a clumsy way. The total effect is of too much fillet, and it seems more than likely that when Salvin altered the room in 1870 and the walls were rehung, the original fillet was copied to provide a much richer appearance, but one that strikes us as Victorian rather than Georgian. When a rich fillet was chosen, as in the Saloon at Woburn, it was only used for the horizontals, and for the verticals a simpler pattern was put up, a variant doubtless adapted from the use of fringes and braids, it being usual to have a narrower one for trimming vertical edges. In the Crimson Drawing Room at Hopetoun (Fig. 110), there is a particularly elaborate fillet of cast lead gilt that is used vertically, but not horizontally except round the doors, it being possible to bend the lead to follow the mould-

109. THE GALLERY AT LONGFORD CASTLE, WILTSHIRE. The original carved Greek key fillet made about 1740 was copied when more was required about 1870.

110. THE CRIMSON DRAWING ROOM AT HOPETOUN. The elaborate fillet of cast and gilt lead is used only horizontally.

ings of the architraves; it is also unusual because the design survives. In the Red Velvet Room at Saltram the complicated pierced design is used not only horizontally and vertically, but also round the doors, a generosity justified by the plain material but one that would probably be over-powering with a cut velvet or a two colour damask (Figs. 111, 112). It is interesting to compare the working of the fillet at Saltram with that shown in Zoffany's picture of Sir Laurence Dundas (Fig. 113). At Corsham in the Gallery the papier maché fillet is applied so as to simulate a double row of gilt nail heads and it repeats the pattern of the nailing on the seat furniture (Fig. 49); in the Cabinet there is only a single row.[48]

Fillets were always expensive. At Harewood, where Chippendale provided carved and gilt fillets, the bill for one room was £110-5-0 and for another £84-15-9, the first one working out at over 5/- a yard. The bill for 310 feet of "Rich raffle and honeysuckle composition border laid in wood and gilt in burnish Gold" provided for the drawing room at Hatfield in 1781 came to £50-7-6. Even the coarse moulded water gilt fillet used for the drawing room at Attingham in 1806 cost 2/6 a foot.[49]

However it was the kind of extravagance that 18th century patrons appreciated. In 1775, when Lady Sarah Bunbury was doing a room for her sister, the Duchess of Leinster, she suggested damask hangings that would cost £70, and then thought that a cheaper fabric with a carved gilt fillet might be more effective. Even so the fillet alone would have come to £40 at 2/- a foot. "The oak leaf border," she wrote, "is intended to make the most showy part of the room in case of a grey, green or white hanging."[50]

Papier maché was much cheaper and could be moulded into very effective patterns, as Chippendale shows in his plates CXCIV and CXCV. He charged 6d a yard for a fillet painted blue and white supplied to Mersham in 1767, and so presumably a gilt one would have worked out at 9d or 1/-. All the leading paper stainers supplied them—Crompton and Spinnage, for instance, used them in the Gallery at Woburn—and elegant designs still exist at Osterley, Kedleston and numerous other houses.[51]

By comparison the later composition mouldings used in great quantities at Chatsworth and Stafford House are somewhat coarse, but magnificent.

As an alternative to a carved or cast fillet, a plain or ornamented braid can be used. This was certainly done in the 18th century, for "8 dozen of narrow silk lace to go round the hangings at 3/-" was provided for the Duchess of Bedford's bedroom at Woburn in 1752. The lace was dyed to match the hangings.[52] At Chatsworth according to the 1764 inventory the green velvet hangings in the dressing room were bordered with gold lace and so were the hangings in an apartment at Wanstead decorated in the early 1740s. In a letter dated October 13, 1743, Charlotte Fermor wrote to her mother, Lady Pomfret: ". . . the new apartment is now furnishing with crimson velvet doubly bordered with a broad gold lace, and set in carved and gilt frames . . ."[53] In the Cabinet at Felbrigg, decorated in 1751, the fillet is of gilded cord.

Fillets and braids were frequently used with flock papers for decorative effect, even when they were not necessary, but there were also many paper borders printed, and they were thought appropriate for even the handsomest flock papers, as can be seen on fragments of paper from Clandon. There in a bedroom on the top floor a bold design was used, and as there was no chair rail, it seems one was implied with a strip of border. A more architectural printed border is used to separate the dado from the main area of the wall in the Print Dressing Room at Uppark.

We regard hangings and tapestry as among the most permanent forms of decoration, but something of the old portable tradition survived into the 18th century. In a very large house the Wardrobe might not yet have been reduced either to a cupboard or a junk room, but remained a place where valuable furniture was carefully put away. Particularly at the beginning of the century

III, 112. THE RED VELVET DRAWING
ROOM AT SALTRAM, DEVON. A gilt
fillet standing out against a plain
velvet, it follows the line of the
doorcase and of the chimneypiece.

there are references to beds and hangings not being up in houses when they were visited, equally some inventories list spectacular objects stored away in Wardrobes. This was evidently in James Cullen's mind as late as 1767 when he wrote to the Hon James Hope: "Herewith I shall enclose a sketch of a handsome bold papier maché border which in burnished gold will be 3s a foot—which may be fastened on the hangings by small screws & easily taken off & layed by in papers—this is only necessary where the hangings are taken off to lay by occasionally which I believe will not be attempted at Hopetoun, as My Lord is mostly at Home & besides the many large pictures hanging on it would make it difficult—the winter damps in large rooms sometimes will milldew the hangings."[54]

Where it is planned to have heavy pictures in a room that is hung with fabric or paper it is important to provide suitably strong grounds into which to screw the brackets for the rods below the architrave moulding of the entablature. It is the need for this preparation as well as the desire not to waste money on material that will never be seen that is one of the reasons why the hanging of pictures in a room was so carefully planned.

This kind of economy was usual in country houses and not just an expedient of later generations. At Hopetoun, for instance, in 1766 one of the entries on a *Memorandum of work Yet To Be Done* was "The whole room is to be hung except under the pictures & glass frames." It was even thought worth planning a room to be hung with flock paper in a similar way as could be seen in the mid 18th century saloon at Lydiard Tregoz in Wiltshire. When Porden was altering old Gloucester House for Lord Grosvenor in 1806, he wrote to his

113. A DETAIL FROM THE PICTURE OF SIR LAWRENCE DUNDAS. (Plate XV.) Zoffany shows the gilt fillet used both horizontally and vertically; it follows the outline of the chimneypiece as in the Red Drawing Room at Saltram.

patron on September 3 that year suggesting that the walls at Gloucester House should be lined with rough framing over which the canvas for the hangings could be stretched; "This will be more expensive than plaster," he continued, "But it will be ready for use immediately, and will afford proper means for fixing the pictures, and for changing their situations, as often as your Lordship thinks is proper. On plaister walls that is not quite so easy," and in another letter he mentions not putting material where there would be large pictures.[55]

It was typical of 18th century attention to detail and care for expensive objects that when Chippendale was working for Sir Lawrence Dundas in Arlington Street he supplied not only tassels to make a decorative feature of the hangings but also put "Canvas & Carteridge paper behind your 8 large Picture Frames, to prevent the frames and Nails scratching the Damask, when they shall be hung on it."[56]

At the time when stretched hangings were introduced, even the grandest houses had few pictures other than family portraits, and consequently the hangings had to make a much more positive contribution to a room than they were to do later. So from the beginning upholsterers began to devise ways of creating rich effects based either on painted or printed decoration or early forms of hangings. The most usual of these was to alternate widths of fabric contrasting in texture and design. It was a form popular in Renaissance Italy and France and was probably introduced into England in the second half of the 16th century. Probably the earliest surviving example is not in upholstery but in wallpainting, at Clifton Tower, Kings Lynn. Only fragments of this late 16th or early 17th century scheme exist, and it is now easier to judge the

128

effect in the hall of Treasurer's House, York, which was copied from it. The inventory of Charles I's possessions prepared before the sale lists numerous examples in upholstery, but none now exist.

Paning and panelling of fabrics continued to be fashionable after the Restoration and various examples can be seen on state beds and chairs made between 1680 and 1715, but wall hangings are much rarer. At Ham in the Blue Drawing Room (Plate XX) the hangings listed in the inventory now appear as cream coloured damask bordered with embroidered velvet, but in fact the original intention was blue framed by darker blue. Even finer are the hangings at Penshurst (Fig. 114) presumably made about 1695 and done as part of the decoration of a state bedroom. They consist of panels of rose damask with an appliqué design in velvet and coloured silks. When seen beside the day bed and the chairs that are upholstered en suite, they bring to life the incredibly elaborate rooms illustrated by Marot and the kind of interior seen by Celia Fiennes at Chippenham Park. She described the best drawing room there as having "a very rich hanging gold and silver and a little scarlet, mostly tissue and brocade of gold and silver and border of green damask round it," with curtains and portières of green damask. A more modest example is the fragment from Ivy House, Worcester, in the Victoria and Albert Museum, that consists of widths of flock paper and leather.[57]

As an alternative hangings were sometimes panelled and edged with orrice or gold lace. There are various descriptions of this kind of decoration in the

114. HANGINGS AT PENSHURST PLACE, KENT, ABOUT 1695. Rose damask with an applique design in velvet and coloured silks.

late 17th century: the Grand Duke Cosimo noticed hangings of sky blue damask with divisions of gold lace in the Queen's Closet at Whitehall, and at Windsor in the Chamber of State Celia Fiennes described the green velvet bed "strip'd down with very thick gold orrice lace of many hands breadth." As late as 1764 the Chatsworth inventory lists hangings in the ante-room and state dressing room as being of velvet bound with gold lace.[58]

The rich taste of the time is particularly apparent in the few surviving examples of leather hangings *in situ*, for they combine a feeling for pattern and contrasts of texture with a shine not unlike that of contemporary graining. Accounts and inventories show that they were widely used in the second half of the 17th century, but they were seldom as elaborate as the set of pictorial hangings at Dunster Castle.[59] The geometric pattern in the Marble Dining Room at Ham put up about 1675 and the rather later hangings in the Entrance Hall at Dyrham are both more typical. One of the most interesting examples is in the closet at Honington in Warwickshire (Fig. 115), where the panels are filled with panels of chinoiserie leather, an idea derived from contemporary lacquer rooms, like the closet at Drayton and the rather later room at Burton Agnes, where the panelling incorporates a lacquer screen. Beneath the over-painted panelling are traces of alternate grained and gilded decoration.

To admirers of Palladian architecture such elaborate effects must have seemed baroque and barbarous as well as unnecessarily extravagant, for they competed with and distracted attention from the architectural design of a room. However they admired rich bold patterns that must often have been over-

115. LEATHER PANELS INSET IN THE WAINSCOT OF A CLOSET AT HONINGTON HALL, WARWICKSHIRE, ABOUT 1670.

130

powering when put up in the 1720s and '30s. Dust and light have softened those that survive intact, and when one encounters them now, the tendency is to be overwhelmed by them and not to notice how coarse and repetitive are many of the designs. Early Palladian taste was more concerned with proportion than pattern.

In trying to establish what fabrics were used on what occasions, there are many difficulties, for while damasks and velvets, for instance, have changed their character comparatively little in the course of the last 200 years, many silks like lutestring, and woollen materials like caffoy, moreen and harateen, have dropped out of use, and only a few experts are fairly clear what they were like and would recognise them immediately. This means that we have a one sided view of 18th century interiors and consequently an unbalanced one. At Houghton, for instance, there are the cut and plain velvets that go with the state room furniture, but we have only the haziest idea of what went with the admirable simpler walnut and japanned furniture that fills the other rooms.

To add to our difficulties the 19th century habit of gilding painted furniture continues, and almost all 18th century seat furniture is upgraded when it comes on to the market by being upholstered in a more expensive material than would have been used originally. Consequently we are no longer used to seeing good quality woollen materials on good furniture, and so when it comes to serious restoration, a great deal of research needs to be done not only on the nature of the materials mentioned in bills and inventories but also on what fabrics were thought appropriate in what rooms.

Here as in so many places we can only scratch at the surface of the problem and pose a question rather than provide an answer, but by compiling a hierarchy of materials by weave, price and use, we hope it will be possible to have a clearer impression of the great range of materials and particularly woollens used in the 18th century.

Of the silk weaves used in furnishing the principal ones were velvet, damask, brocade, satin, taffetas, lutestring, tabby and sarsnet. Among the main woollen materials were moreen, camlet, harateen, tammy and caffoy. But this is not as straightforward as it might appear for many of the silks and the woollens were mixed materials, and in any short account there is bound to be some over-lapping. Also there is watering to be considered as a finish.

Of the silk velvets Genoa cut velvets were the most sought after, for they came in up to three or four colours on a satin or ribbed silk ground. However they were not all made in Genoa but in Lyons and Spitalfields too. Naturally the more colours used the more expensive the material became, and probably the most costly recorded in England was the seven colour velvet used in the Queen's Bedroom at Kensington Palace in 1688–89: the velvet alone cost £619. However one is more certain with the velvet used on Queen Anne's bed made for Windsor in 1714 and now at Hampton Court: thought to be Spitalfields, it has a cut and uncut silk pile in crimson and gold on a voided satin ground and cost 42/– a yard (Plate XI). The condition of the bed is a pale reflection of the original, but a piece of unused material on view at the Victoria and Albert Museum gives an idea of the brilliance of its colouring. [60] The green cut velvet in the drawing room at Longford Castle cost 25/– a yard in 1741.

In the first quarter of the century a plain Genoa silk velvet cost about 32/– a yard, but crimson tended to be about 4/– more. The price did not rise much in the next quarter of the century, for when the Duke of Bedford bought "the richest crimson velvet" for clothes in 1752 he paid 27/–. [61]

Not all velvets were silk, for considerable use was made of woollen velvets. Often called Utrecht velvets, but erroneously because they were never made there—the term is really *velours de trecht*—some came from Haarlem but more from Rouen and Tournai. They are still occasionally encountered in houses decorated in the second or third quarter of the 18th century. Much the finest examples are the cut wool velvets in the saloons at Houghton and Holkham.

131

Sometimes the wool was mixed with linen as occurs in the sample at the Victoria and Albert Museum. Few old cotton velvets have been recognised, but at Buckingham House in 1799 the covers of the sofas and cushions in the saloon were of "white cotton velvet painted with flowers" by Princess Elizabeth.

Related to woollen velvets were a number of other materials with a pile, but they present considerable problems of identification. Quite often in inventories there are references to caffoy and also to camlet. Apparently the only documented example of caffoy to survive is on a set of chairs now in the Gallery at Erthig and originally in the Saloon that is so described in the 1726 inventory (Fig. 90). However there are a number of references to its use including the family drawing room to the south of the Saloon at Houghton, which was hung with yellow caffoy. Mrs Delany mentions having crimson caffoy in her drawing room in 1744. And in 1765 the saloon furniture at Stowe was upholstered in crimson caffoy and also one of the bedrooms was done in it.[62]

There were also caffoy wallpapers. Early in the 18th century Abraham Price advertised "a Curious Sort of Imposed Work Resembling Cassaws;" in 1755 Mrs Delany mentions "mohair cafoy" paper; and in a letter to Walpole in 1761 Gray refers to mohair flock paper at 1/- a yard, adding "the pattern is small & will look like velvet."[63]

The combination of mohair and caffoy together raises the problem of mohair. In medieval times it was evidently a material made of goat's hair, and the material that is sold as mohair today is one with a pile and is made of goat's hair, which gives it a harder wearing texture than pure silk velvet and a more glossy appearance than woollen velvet. The pile can be plain or have a cut pattern or be stamped, which the French call gauffrage, like wool velvets. However recently Mr Peter Thornton has suggested that modern mohair and the material described as mohair in the 17th and 18th centuries are quite different, for he interprets mohair as being the same as *moiré*, i.e. watered, and he regards it as a watered silk material.

Certainly it seems that not all old mohairs had a pile, for Abraham Rees, for instance, in *The Cyclopedaedia or Universal Dictionary of Arts, Sciences and Literature* (1819) says mohair is the hair of a kind of goat and continues: "some give the name to the camblets or stuffs made of this hair: of these there are two kinds: the one smooth and plain; the other watered like tabbies; the difference between the two only consists in this, that the latter is calendered, the other not. There are also mohairs both plain and watered . . ."

Of camlets he says some are of wool, silk or hair, but no European ones are pure hair and they come as figured, waved (i.e. moiré) or water, which confusingly is not moiré but a smooth lustrous finish. Mr Thornton has disagreed with us about the contribution of the goat, but most encyclopedists mention the goat in connection with mohair and mohair in connection with the goat, and also a room occupied by the wife of the 3rd Earl of Manchester in 1675 is described as "hung with six pieces of haire, called silk watered moehaire . . ." The tradition of doing rooms and beds with mohair continued, for as late as 1762 Lady Kildare mentions using it in her new dressing room at Carton.[64]

The pile material we call mohair, Mr Thornton suggests is plush, but again plush may have changed its commonest meaning, for it is now generally used to describe a material with a longer pile than velvet and a more silky appearance. Rees describes plush as a sort of velvet made of wool, wool and camel's hair, wool and goat's hair, all silk, or all goat's hair. Some of the silk plushes he says "have a pretty long knap on one side, and some on both."

Moquette might come to mind in this context as well, but it seems that in the 18th century it was generally used in connection with carpets of the Wilton type (i.e. with a pile) rather than to describe upholstery material.

Unfortunately no documented examples of 18th century mohair exist, and one of the few rooms done with a material with a pile is the Reynolds Room

132

at Knole (Plate XIX). And it is not certain whether it should be described as stamped mohair, stamped woollen velvet or caffoy. And just to complicate matters there is at the Victoria and Albert Museum a piece of similar fabric described as "stamped woollen plush" (T. 169–1969).

Good silk damask was considerably cheaper than silk velvet and was usually about 15/– to 21/– in the middle of the 18th century. For instance, the original green damask in the Gallery at Longford Castle cost 12/– in 1740, the crimson damask at Hopetoun cost 13/6 in 1766 but was "a quantity much below the markett price;" and in 1775 Lady Sarah Bunbury quoted damask as costing 14/– a yard. The crimson genoa damask used at Buckingham House cost between 17/– and 18/– in 1763—246 yards came to £219-15-11; another order of 540 yards of crimson genoa damask cost £481 10s 1d and 319 yards of green genoa damask cost £231 5s 6d.[65]

In addition there are a number of references to three and four coloured damasks, which suggests a material of damask weave that is brocaded. Indeed in 1764 Lady Holland wrote to Lady Kildare: "I propose hanging (my drawing room) with a damask or brocatelle of two or three colours." Other references to it are in the journal of the Duchess of Northumberland, who saw one in the Drawing Room at Audley End, and in the journal of Lady Shelburne who saw a four colour damask in the drawing room at Castletown; Lady Holdernesse had one of "quattre couleurs."[66]

What was even more extravagant was to use a brocaded silk like the one that still survives in the Red Drawing Room at Syon and recorded in old photographs of the Great Room at Brocket.[67] Of earlier brocaded hangings little has survived in England, but they must have existed in the richest houses. At the Victoria and Albert Museum there is a piece of brocade of bizarre type dated about 1700–1710 that was once a portière; at Knole there is a contemporary settee upholstered in a bizarre silk (Fig. 116). Some of the richest brocades used at that time were immensely expensive: the "rich blue and gold brocade" used on Queen Anne's coronation chair cost £9 a yard in 1702.[68]

But not all damasks were silk; often they were a mixture of silk and wool or silk and linen even in the finest houses, and they were about half the price. At Dumfries House in 1759 the superfine Genoa damask cost 13/6, and the silk and worsted damask for a bed 6/6. At Mersham in 1767 Chippendale charged 7/– for a blue 'mix'd damask' and he also supplied 'mix'd damask' for curtains at Nostell. According to Celia Fiennes a bed at Ashtead Park done in worsted damask looked "pretty and with a gloss like camlett of a light ash coullour." At Bedford House in 1771 the Red Drawing Room is described as being hung with flock paper and having curtains and upholstery of crimson mixed damask.[69]

The term Nassau damask and Norwich damask also occur. The former was a material evidently much disliked by Lady Kildare, who records it cost 9/– a yard and it is recorded as an alternative to silk for covering chairs on a design by James Wyatt. Horace Walpole records that Norwich damask was used in the Picture Gallery at Houghton and his own Gallery at Strawberry Hill. This was almost certainly a wool or worsted damask, and probably very like the well-preserved red material still hanging in the Cabinet at Felbrigg (Fig. 208).[70]

Again as with the woollen velvets and caffoys, old woollen damasks have tended to disappear from houses, partly because they were used more and partly because they attracted moth. However at the Victoria and Albert Museum there are a number of examples of materials variously described as brocaded worsted damasks, glazed worsted damasks, or calimancos, and wool damasks. T. 410–1966 is a plain red wool damask chair seat; T. 363–1966 is a striped worsted damask panel or glazed calimanco thought to be Norwich; T. 288–1962 is somewhat similar but glazed, whereas T. 352A–1960 is a brocaded and glazed worsted damask; in addition there are examples of watered worsted damasks to which reference will be made later. Although none of these

116. BIZARRE SILK USED FOR THE
UPHOLSTERY OF A SETTEE AT KNOLE,
ABOUT 1700-1710.

samples can be related directly to what is described in the past, at least they give an idea of what they were probably like. On the whole the brocaded worsted damasks have a certain sheen about them and it is difficult to see why Lady Kildare had such a dislike of the still unidentified but no doubt similar Nassau damask. The plain wool damask on the other hand is a much more acceptable material and would have gone well with flock paper.

Taffeta was widely used for hangings and curtains, but evidently regarded as a second class silk and suitable for rooms with a feminine cast. It seems to have cost about 8/6 to 11/– a yard. At Houghton, for instance, the bed in Lord Cholmondeley's dressing room was of painted taffeta, and at Osterley there is a bed done with painted Chinese taffeta. Contemporary attitudes to it are admirably illustrated by a letter from Lady Kildare to her husband in 1759. Writing about the lasting qualities of India taffeta, she said "If anybody says it [does not last], send them to look at that at Goodwood, which has been up forty year. In short, it is as cheap *silk* furniture as one can have. I know you will smile at this, but 'tis really true."[71]

Apart from the Osterley bed with its window curtains and cushions, probably the best example is a bedroom at Houghton where the walls are en suite with the bed (the curtains are a modern replacement *c.* 1938) (Fig. 117). Mrs Powys

134

117. THE TAFFETA BEDROOM AT HOUGHTON. The bed curtains are modern, but otherwise the painted taffeta appears to be mid 18th century and is a very rare survivor of a once fashionable material.

describes a room in the Duke of Cumberland's Chinese House in 1762 as hung with painted satin, and the Duchess of Northumberland describes Lady Strafford's closet at Wentworth as having hangings of straw coloured satin painted with sprigs of natural flowers.[72]

A form of taffeta that was widely used in fashionable houses was lutestring or lustring, which was a taffeta *lustré*. A plain ribbed silk heavier than modern taffeta *faille*, it was given a glittering finish by being smeared with beer over a brazier. Chippendale charged 6/6 a yard for it in 1768 when he supplied curtains at Nostell. It was also imitated in wallpaper, for Lady Holdernesse's ante-chamber was done with red and white lutestring paper. Lutestring or lustring first became popular in the late 17th century and indeed a Royal Lustring Company was established in William III's reign. However it enjoyed a second period of popularity in the 1760s and 70s: in 1775 Lady Sarah Bunbury wrote "It is the fashion to have lutestring curtains."[73]

At that time there are also a number of references to the use of satin for furnishing. Both Mrs Delany and Lady Mary Coke comment on it at Luton Hoo in the 1770s. Later, round about 1800, plain satin with a small repeat design was fashionable. Mrs Powys records a visit to the house of a Miss Heathcote in Bath in 1803: "She has an elegant house in the Crescent, and he (Mr Wheley) has one in St James's Square in Bath, which tho' most elegantly furnished, after he returned from Paris, finding paper hangings were there called vulgar, immediately took all down and hung with satins." The previous year the younger Chippendale supplied a yellow and black satin for the curtains of the Picture Room at Stourhead at a cost of 13/6, blue satin with black spots for the Cabinet and yellow satin for the ante-room (whereas the blue silk damask for the saloon cost 23/–).[74]

Apart from calico and chintz one of the materials most frequently mentioned was moreen, which was a woollen material. Chippendale charged between 2/4 and 2/8 a yard for it in the 1760s. It was evidently a favourite material of the time for Lady Holland, or Lady Caroline Fox as she then was, described it in 1759 as "Very pretty furniture" and it was thought suitable by Chippendale to be used in Lady Wynn's Ante-Room at Nostell in 1767 and on a set of mahogany French armchairs. It is seldom seen today, but at Erthig and Scotney Castle there are moreen curtains; and at the Essex Institute, Salem, Mass, there is a crimson moreen bed hanging of about 1770.[75]

Harateen and serge cost about 1/9 and were used for simpler jobs. At Nostell for instance the housekeeper's bed was done in harateen and the case covers were made of serge, and at Holkham serge was used to line tammy curtains.[76]

The use of watering has already been mentioned in connection with the vexed question of mohair. Indeed the French word *moiré* was originally used to describe a kind of watered mohair, but, as in so many aspects of decoration, the word has changed its meaning over the years. In England it is usual to describe a watered silk as *moiré*, but in the past tabbying was also used; this was derived from tabby, a thick silk that was usually watered. Today watering is only done on silks or on materials of silky appearance, but from the late 17th century it was used on a much greater range of silks and woollen materials, including many wool damasks and moreens. The effect was achieved by passing the material through a pair of heated rollers cast and engraved to match so that the ribs of the material are crushed to form the *moiré* or watering. The same method was used to create a vermiculated effect similar to that more familiar in rusticated stonework, but it could be equally well adapted for other impressed patterns, as is still done today. Indeed this is the basis of stamped woollen velvets, the pattern of which is made by the interaction of two rollers.

A hierarchy of materials based on prices gives some idea of how they were used, but inventories, particularly those with valuations, give a fuller idea of their disposition through a house. That for Sheffield Park, Sussex, in 1766 is particularly interesting. There were two drawing rooms, the first with tapestry hangings and damask curtains and upholstery, and the second with damask hangings, curtains and upholstery, and their contents were put down at £30 and £42. In the Breakfast Room, Shooting Room and Dining Room the curtains were serge. The contents of the Red Damask Bedroom, which had paper hangings, were put at £65–10–0; the Blue Damask Room, which had tapestry hangings, was valued at £36–14–0. After that came Lord De La Warr's room done with crimson moreen at £35, the Crimson Morine Chamber at £29, the Green Mohair Room at £25–13–0, and the Blue Camlet Room at £22–3–0. The two daughters' room had silk beds and crimson serge curtains; the housekeeper's bed was chintz and the cook's green linsey, and they were put down at £15–0–6 and £7–16–0 respectively.[77]

From about 1730 wallpaper began to compete with material as an acceptable form of decoration in a room in an up to date house, and designs were sufficiently imposing to attract patrons of Leoni and Kent. However it was not a new invention, for the earliest fragments of wallpaper to be found in England date from the early 16th century. But it is only from the late 17th century that it is possible to compile a fairly comprehensive history based on fragments, trade cards like that of the Blew Paper Warehouse in Aldermanbury and other records. Even so, despite the extensive researches of Mr Eric Entwisle, large areas of pre-1730 papers are so rare that their evidence is still of historical and archaeological rather than practical value, for few have been reproduced.[78]

Apart from imported chinese and chinoiserie papers, the earliest type to be used in important rooms was flock paper, which was a rather different material from the flock paper sold today. At the present time virtually all flock paper is made with nylon or a mixture of nylon and wool, and it has a distempered ground that is usually solid in tone. Eighteenth century flock on the other hand was usually of wool, although it was also sometimes of mohair and, by the third quarter of the century, occasionally of silk, as can be seen in the French paper in the Palladio Room at Clandon; its ground was generally painted in distemper so that it had a matt ground, but it was sometimes painted and then varnished or sized. The sheets used were generally small, elephant being 20 in. x 27 in. and double demy being 22½ in. x 35 in., and although these were usually mounted up into strips 12 ft. long, the effect was much livelier and less uniform than modern paper. Paper of unlimited length was only introduced in 1797.

Good flock paper was not cheap, although prices varied according to the complexity of the patterns, the number of colours used and whether it was single or double flock. The Duke of Bedford, for instance, paid 4/– a yard for flock paper in 1754; Gray told Walpole in 1763 that blue mohair flock cost 1/– a yard; Chippendale charged 9/– a piece for Norwich crimson damask flock when supplying Nostell Priory in 1768; and in 1770 Chambers reckoned flock paper cost 8/– a yard.[79]

The technique of flocking is supposed to have been invented in France in the 1620s and introduced into England in the following decade. The early examples are all rather crude in execution as well as design, and in fact some of them are not on paper but on linen or canvas. At the Victoria and Albert Museum there are three late 17th century examples of flocking on linen including one of a hunting design in red, a crude ancestor of a pictorial cotton print, and an ornamental design in red, blue and gold.[80] At Winterthur there are two rooms done with flocked canvas and several examples exist in Holland, notably at the Rijks Museum and the Lakenhall Museum at Leyden.

Most of the flock patterns dating from the 1730s are derived from velvet, and indeed they were made to match fabrics. This was a staple part of the paper seller's trade: Thomas Bromwich, for instance, put on his trade card: "Makes and Sells all manner of Screens, Window Blinds and Covers for Tables,/ Rooms, Cabinets, Stair-cases, Hung/ with Gilt-leather, or India Pictures,/ Chintz's, Callicoes, Cottons, Needlework, & Damasks Matched in Paper, to the /utmost exactness at Reasonable Rates."[81]

At first there seem to have been comparatively few patterns, and one still produced by Warners in silk as "Campagna" and by Coles as "Amberley" exists in various colours.[82] In damask it survives on the bed from Belhus, Essex, now at Christchurch Mansion, Ipswich, and in flocked paper in George II's Breakfast Room at Hampton Court Palace, in fragments from the Privy Council Room and in several versions at Clandon. There are minor variations in detail between the different examples, presumably due to differences in the carving of the blocks, but the general pattern continued to be fashionable until the late 1760s, damasks being chosen for the State Bedroom at Hopetoun and the Gallery at Corsham. It was revived again in the 19th century and this century.

The paper in the Prince Regent's room at Clandon admirably illustrates the stained character of the paper (Plate XXI). The actual design is in crimson wool flock and the ground was stained to match it, but over the years the colour has "flown" from the ground, so that the effect now is like a cut velvet on a contrasting ground rather than a ton-sur-ton effect as was originally intended.

No guidance can be given as to when it was considered suitable to use a ton-sur-ton fabric or paper and one with a contrast between the pattern and the ground, like the damask in the Drawing Rooms at The Vyne, where the design is crimson on ivory; no doubt it depended on the pictures available and whether it was for a room of parade or a drawing room.

However there is one detail connected with these bold patterns that is worthy of comment, the habit of dropping the pattern or staggering the design. It is not known when this was first done in England, and although it might be presumed that it was in the 1740s when asymmetrical patterns started to become fashionable, one example is recorded in the *Tea Party at Lord Harrington's House* painted by Charles Philips in 1739 (Fig. 118). The picture has a naive quality that suggests an attempt at truth, and it is interesting to see how the "Amberley" type hangings are carefully depicted with the pattern dropped. Two sophisticated examples are the brocaded silk in the Red Drawing Room at Syon put up in the 1760s and the one formerly in the Saloon at Brocket. At Syon alternate widths of the running design are dropped so that each pair joins up to form a complete, symmetrical design. At Brocket the dropping of the pattern gave sufficient variety without breaking the continuity of the small garlands that support the larger sprays. The Reveillon paper in the Palladio Room at Clandon (Plate XXII) was obviously designed to be hung so that the subsidiary garlands join up. The subtlety of effect is one that most people would take for granted, but the point is neatly made by comparing these three with the arrangement of the panels in the White Drawing Room at Houghton (Plate XXIV), where the design is not staggered.

During the 1740s designs were adapted from lighter printed cottons, and there were not only various interesting technical experiments like those carried out by John Baptist Jackson, but a much greater variety of papers were produced. They were admirably suited to rising rococo taste and probably had a

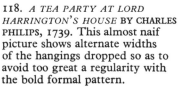

118. *A TEA PARTY AT LORD HARRINGTON'S HOUSE* BY CHARLES PHILIPS, 1739. This almost naif picture shows alternate widths of the hangings dropped so as to avoid too great a regularity with the bold formal pattern.

138

particular appeal to women, like the Duchess of Manchester, who as early as 1741 had a house at Englefield Green "no bigger than a nutshell" with all the rooms done in paper.[83]

Indeed English papers were so successful that they were exported not only to America but to France as well. In 1753 Aubert "graveur en bois à Paris" advertised "papiers veloutés aussi beaux et aussi parfaits que ceux d'Angleterre;" and in 1754 Madame de Pompadour chose English flock paper for her wardrobe and for the corridor that led from her apartment to the chapel at Versailles and in 1758 put up similar paper in her bedroom at Champs. English blue paper was thought particularly chic about 1760, for Madame de Genlis remarked that ladies "even relegate to storage their magnificent Gobelin tapestries to put English blue paper in their place."[84]

The craze for paper killed the taste for some older forms of wall treatment particularly leather and tapestry. Thus in 1754 Lady de Grey took down leather from a pavilion in the park at Wrest and put up paper in its place. And a few years later Horace Walpole thought there would be a chance of getting tapestry "in the country where People all disdain tapestry, because they hear, that Paper is all the fashion."

However it is difficult to get a feeling as to when different types of material and paper would have been used in a house. Obviously it depended very largely on cost whether silk or mixed damask was chosen or flock paper, but it is very hard to appreciate the 18th century distinction between uniformity and monotony, and how uniformity in a room or in an apartment was related to the house as a whole. At Houghton, for instance, one must have been strongly aware of the transition from cut velvet in the Saloon to green velvet in the State Apartment, and from cut velvet to more modest caffoy in the family drawing room; but then this has to be balanced with other ideas and traditions, among them that green was thought to be the most restful of colours and the tapestry was considered warm and so traditional in a state bedroom, which itself was the most important of the state rooms. At Holkham the impression is much the same: the Saloon is hung with cut wool velvet; the original Great Drawing Room to the east is hung with cut silk velvet, and the Cabinet beyond with damask; the balancing Drawing Room, now hung with Edwardian cut velvet, was originally hung with crimson damask, the bedroom is hung with tapestry and the upholstery is cut velvet. At Woburn, on the other hand, the principal apartment was all done in blue damask.[85]

In a less formal house there might be more variety, and certainly one gets a sense of this in Mrs Powys's description of Fawley Court in 1771 which was quoted on page 26.[86]

Among the more successful innovations of the last quarter of the 18th century was the increasing use of borders both in paper and fabric and the false panelling of rooms. Originally inspired by the pilaster strip used in France in the late 1750s and first employed by Chambers in the Saloon at Buckingham House in 1761, this way of treating a wall became increasingly widespread. Painted borders occur on furniture about 1770 and on painted papers and chintzes about the same time: the fashion for them probably ante-dates the arrival of the French decorators in the mid 1780s, for Sophie Von La Roche describes a bedroom at St Leonards Hill in 1786: "It is hung with a delicate monotone pale-blue-chintz, with a border of the sweetest flower-garlands embroidered in blue of the same shade on a white ground, similarly the curtains, quilts on both the beds, and chair-covers."[87] A similar idea but in a different vein was carried out by Holland in the Chinese Drawing Room at Carlton House, a room engraved in 1793 but not illustrated by Sheraton until 1803 (Fig. 96).

Much of the most elaborate example of this kind of decoration is not in England, but in a room from W. P. Kops's House in Haarlem now in the Rijks Museum, Amsterdam (Figs. 119, 120, 121). Not only the hangings, but

121. THE CURTAINS AND VALLANCES. The borders used for the curtains and valances are woven in different widths and in two designs so that they could be used horizontally and vertically. The curtains come to the top of the skirting.

the curtains and the seat furniture survive in their original condition and together with the carpet and the boiserie give an admirable idea of the effect Holland set out to achieve. The furniture and the materials were imported from France about 1790, and the whole scheme is one of surprising complexity. The plain pale blue silk wall panels are bordered with a broad band so designed that it has to be woven in a vertical and a horizontal version. The curtains are made up in the same way, the plain fabric being bordered with two weavings. The valances, however, have a narrower border and are of a broad weaving of the tissue used for covering the chair seats and backs, which consist of an enlargement of the main motif used in the vertical border. The chairs themselves are edged with a narrower border. It is unlikely that such an elaborate conception would have been often attempted, but at least this room provides the ideal. By chance another panel of the fabric can be seen at the Victoria and Albert Museum (Plate XXIII).[88]

Possibly the earliest surviving scheme of this kind in England is the Chinese Room (Fig. 122) at Ombersley in Worcestershire, which, it has been suggested, may have been fitted up by Marsh and Tatham, a firm who had experience of working with Holland. The proportions of the room are quite English, but

119. A ROOM FROM W. P. KOPS' HOUSE IN HAARLEM, ABOUT 1797. The furniture and materials were imported from France.

120. THE WALL PANELS AND CURTAINS IN THE HAARLEM ROOM.

141

122. THE CHINESE ROOM AT
OMBERSLEY COURT, WORCESTERSHIRE.
An English version of a Louis XVI
effect, possibly fitted up by Marsh
and Tatham, about 1812.

the design of the pier glasses, the super-portes and the placing of the panels
of Chinese embroidery suggests that the decorators were striving after a Louis
Seize effect.[89]

It is interesting to compare this room with the drawing room at Moccas
Court, Herefordshire, a room originally designed by Anthony Keck and redecorated about 1793 possibly by Eckhardt (Fig. 123). A somewhat similar
arrangement used to exist in the drawing room at Longford Hall, Shropshire,
but of the wall paper designed by J. B. Fay, printed by Reveillon, and supplied
by Elliots there are now only some fragments in the Victoria and Albert
Museum.[90]

These English versions of Louis Seize interiors were no doubt strongly
influenced by Holland's own work of the late 1780s. However virtually all that
we have to go on now are what exists at Southill supplemented by descriptions
of its original treatment. In the Boudoir there are still the "5 carved and Gilt
Moulding Pannels with rich carved angle ornaments," but of the original green
and white damask only one panel survives in another part of the house and
that has faded to cream. In Mrs Whitbread's Room (Fig. 124), which adjoins
it, the original black and gold frames still exist, but the "rich chintz calico,
bordered with calico border" and the matching curtains have gone. Gone too
are the original hangings for the drawing room, which were of red sarsnet
bordered with green velvet, a heavier combination than is perhaps normally
associated with the 1790s and one that looks forward to Walsh Porter's re-
vamping of Carlton House and Porden's work at Grosvenor House. The
Canaletto Room at Woburn was another essay in this kind of taste, for it was
originally decorated with gilt panels framing green satin.[91]

The grandest surviving example is undoubtedly the White Drawing Room

142

123. THE DRAWING ROOM AT
MOCCAS COURT, HEREFORDSHIRE.
Panels of arabesque wallpaper
possibly by Eckhardt, about 1793.

124. MRS WHITBREAD'S ROOM AT
SOUTHILL. The black and gold
frames were originally filled with
chintz.

143

at Houghton, which was redecorated to take panels of superb Spitalfields silk given by the Prince of Wales to Lord Cholmondeley (Plate XXIV). Originally hung with green velvet to match the state bed, in the late 1790s the walls were fitted with gilt mouldings to frame the silk, single widths being used for the narrow panels flanking the chimney-piece and several widths for the wider panels on the end walls. Each panel is elaborately bordered in silk, and the same border is used for the draped curtains.[92]

There must have been a great many variations on this kind of scheme, and many of the simpler ones must have had great charm. At Shugborough in Staffordshire there is a very pretty example, possibly done by the Eckhardts: the main paper is a moiré pattern, the border is plain, and inset from the edge of the paper is a cut-out border of flowers (Fig. 125). At Townley Hall, Co. Louth, one bedroom has a moiré paper bordered dark green, the join being covered with a border of flowers (Fig. 126).[93] One of the bedrooms at Broadlands, in Hampshire, which is also done with a moiré paper, has the walls divided into panels with two borders, an outer one of a ribbon design and an inner one of flowers. Probably all these rooms originally had curtains to match, and no doubt considerable imagination was displayed in their design: at Daylesford, for instance, in 1799, the curtains in Mr Hastings's study were of yellow and white cotton "with a rich flower'd bordering and Medallions of Flowers in the corners of the curtains."[94]

There are two other forms of hangings that should be mentioned, albeit briefly, those forming tent rooms and those done with pleated or puckered hangings. Of the former type only two early 19th century examples survive in England, but it seems that the idea started in France and was always more fashionable on the continent than here. The earliest was probably the tent bedroom at Bagatelle decorated for the Comte d'Artois by Bélanger in 1786,

125. THE BOUDOIR AT SHUGBOROUGH, STAFFORDSHIRE. A moiré paper with an inset cut-out border of flowers, about 1790.

126. A CORNER OF A BEDROOM AT TOWNLEY HALL, CO. LOUTH. An early 19th century moiré paper with a coloured border, the join being masked out by a cut-out border of flowers.

and it seems that Percier and Fontaine took up the idea, illustrated it and used it in the Council Room at Malmaison. It then became part of the vocabulary of decoration. Probably the earliest English design is one of about 1800 among the Crace drawings in the Cooper Hewitt Museum Collection in New York (Fig. 127), which shows a tented alcove, but Gillow's designs (Fig. 128) and the two survivors are later. At Shrublands in Suffolk there is a bedroom decorated as a striped tent about 1833 (Fig. 129), and, as there is a *bateau* bed with a canopy, it seems more likely that the whole room was inspired by a French design. The other room (Fig. 130), at Cranbury in Hampshire, is dated about 1835–45 and is less martial in feeling. Done in cotton and lavishly trimmed with tassel fringe and tassels, the whole room is a remarkable example of late Regency upholstery and close in feeling to the bedrooms formerly at Ashburnham Place.[95]

Such rooms were obviously exceptional extravagances, but it is likely that quite a number were done with pleated or puckered hangings at the end of the 18th and beginning of the 19th centuries. Again the idea is probably French in origin and introduced to England by the French decorators working under Henry Holland. Significantly the earliest recorded reference to a room done in this way is in a description of Mrs Fitzherbert's house in Pall Mall by Mary Frampton in 1785: she commented on the puckered blue silk hangings from which "the now common imitations on paper were taken." Three years later Sheraton describes fluting on a sofa bed: "It must also be observed that the best kinds of these beds have behind what the upholsterers call a fluting which is done with a slight frame of wood fastened to the wall, on which is strained, in straight puckers, some of the same stuff of which the curtains are made."[96]

145

127. A TENTED ALCOVE, ABOUT 1800.
A design by Crace & Co.

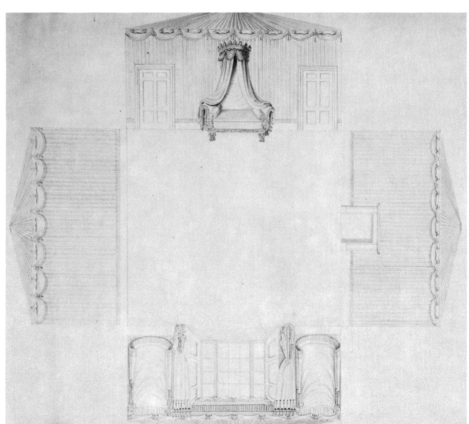

128. A DESIGN FOR A ROOM WITH
RUCHED HANGINGS AND A TENTED
CEILING, ABOUT 1820. From the
collection of Gillow drawings.

146

No old examples of this kind of decoration are known, and probably the
best known is that in the State Bedroom at Osterley (Fig. 71), which is now
thought to have been first done about 1863. The hangings in the Boudoir at
Belton decorated by Wyatt are a replacement of what was there before, and
it is not known when the originals were put up. In recent years a variant of the
idea has been revived in rooms at Houghton and Chatsworth, and in both cases
the fabric is hung in loose pleats.

Another idea that was apparently used in the late 18th century was to have
loose hangings, but again they are only known from drawings. Two examples
are for libraries, one in Steuart's proposals for Attingham and a second in
Playfair's 1793 designs for Cairness in Aberdeenshire. George Smith shows
designs for hanging fabric in loose "mantles" after the antique and also
draperies that hark back to the tent; and among the Crace drawings there is
a design for a boudoir with an apse where the walls are shown draped in pale
pink and green.[97]

147

130. THE TENT ROOM AT CRANBURY
PARK, HAMPSHIRE, ABOUT 1835-45.

Chairs, Covers and Cushions

It is perhaps inevitable that the framework of a chair should be studied
before its upholstery, and during the past 50 years a great deal has been discovered about the development of design and the identity of makers, but little
attention has been paid to upholstery. Now, however, this is a much more
difficult subject to pursue because the contents of so many old-established
houses have been scattered, and examples of original upholstery illustrated in
earlier books on furniture have been restuffed and recovered. There are signs
that a shift in interest is starting, but, as virtually nothing has been written on
the topics described here, our account is bound to be somewhat tentative in
character. The topics consist of the line of upholstery, buttoning, nailing,
cushions, case and loose-covers.

However, the 18th century approach to chairs in general is best conveyed
not through these details but through the complicated trade with France.
During the first quarter of the century the French chair-makers developed a
bewildering variety of forms of chair, but importing into England was an
expensive and tiresome business. There are quite a number of references to
this in contemporary correspondence, and they reveal what pains people took
to get what they wanted. For instance, when Lord Fitzwilliam wanted seat

148

furniture in 1771, he asked the advice of Lord Grantham, who was then in Paris, and the latter replied: "Everybody I have consulted is clearly of opinion that any furniture that is not gilt is not worth the carriage, risk and trouble." But having given the details of two sets, he went on: "The painting and varnishing of either set will come to £1 for chairs and so on; the stuffing will be done better in Paris but will increase the cost of carriage . . . I am of opinion it is not worthwhile to send for them but rather to get the shapes and carving of some already in England imitated. I would recommend Mello's house in S. Audley Street as the best I have seen and equal to any here." Yet a few years later, in 1775, Lady Sarah Bunbury wrote to her sister in France: "If you have not got a set of proper chairs already, you may get for half the price as pretty a chair, couch etc."[98]

Sometimes the frames alone were sent over and finished off in this country. At Heythrop Mrs. Powys saw French sofas in the drawing room that had been gilded in England. Similarly Lady Mary Coke wrote in 1769: "I've got my chairs from Paris without being beholden to anybody, they have paid the duty, but I don't intend to have them covered with the damask, or have the frames gilt, till after I return from abroad."[99]

The Line of Upholstery

"The stuffing and covering on Chair or Settee-Bed is indeed the nicest Part of this Branch; but it may be acquired without any remarkable Genius."

The London Tradesman, 1747

With the decline in attention paid to upholstery, one of the things that has been lost is a developed sense of line. Consequently one of the risks that has to be taken with a piece of furniture retaining its original upholstery but is in need of restoration is that it is quite likely to lose its original quality of line when restored. Again, as in so many aspects of decoration, it is virtually impossible to describe what is meant with any degree of accuracy, and all one usefully can do is to comment on a series of photographs mainly drawn from

131. A MAHOGANY CHAIR FROM THE TREASURY, ABOUT 1730. The line of the seat is well defined by the nailing and the piping. This cleanness contrasts with the effect of the tufting, but the actual tufts have been replaced by buttons.

132. A CHAIR FROM THE STATE BEDROOM AT HOLKHAM. The precision of the upholstery and the flatness of the seat is emphasised by the vertical and horizontal nailing.

such a fundamental source as the *Dictionary of Furniture*. This is splendid as far as the development of the design of the frames of chairs is concerned, but few are upholstered correctly as far as line is concerned.

For the early Georgian period, the mahogany chair from the Treasury is a good example of a good line in the seat (Fig. 131). It is well defined by the nailing and piping, and there is a firm vertical edge at the corner; and this cleanness contrasts 'with the tufting of the seat and the back (although in this case the floss silk tufts have been replaced by buttons). The same precision is to be seen in the chair from the State bedroom at Holkham (Fig. 132) where the nailing continues up the outer edges of the front and the seat is virtually flat. In Fig. 134, a slightly later example from Southill, the same kind of seat is found on the curve, the double line of the nailing, the line of the piping and the curve of the top of the seat all being in harmony. In a chair at Nostell (Fig. 135), the horizontal line of the seat rail is carefully emphasised by the two rows of nailing and the precise edge is marked in by rows of nails at the angles that continue slightly above the upper horizontal row. In a chair formerly at Brocket Hall, Hertfordshire (Fig. 136), the good line of the seat (again with tufts replaced by buttons) is kept but the original nailing has been replaced by a gimp that distracts the eye and does not create a precise enough line.

With a neo-classical chair in the French taste the edge of the seat was also often piped, but if a softer look was desired, the swell of the seat would carefully follow the horizontal line of the chair both at the front and the side, rising straight and then curving back on the flat of the seat, as in the chair formerly at Langley Hall, Norfolk (Fig. 137), but not curving outwards and then going flat as in the old photograph of a chair at the Victoria and Albert Museum (Fig. 138) where the line of the seat does nothing to complement the line of the frame.

Obviously line in upholstery changed with fashion in the design of chairs, but it would be harder to find a better example of line in a mid 18th century chair than the one shown in Figs. 139–141. A chair of middling quality without any carving or moulding on its legs, it is covered in wool damask.

133. A MID 18TH CENTURY ARMCHAIR FROM HAM HOUSE. A comparable chair of middle quality upholstered in original cut wool velvet.

134. AN ARMCHAIR FROM SOUTHILL. The curve of the seat, the lines of the nailing and of the piping are in harmony. The original tufts have been replaced by buttons.

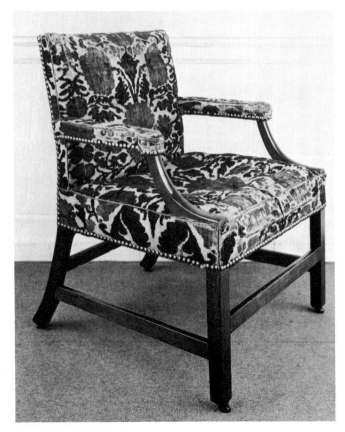

150

If it is examined in silhouette, it will be seen how the line curves out quite boldly at the top of the back and reaches its greatest fullness about a third of the way down; and from there tends to taper away to the seat rail, and the swell of the lower part tends to be less than the swell at the top of the back. The effect is of the chair having a full busted look about it. And the curve from the top to the greatest fullness is about equal to the curves from the centre to the sides of the chair.

The line of the nailing down the side of the back does not follow the rake of the back, because it is somewhat exaggerated in this example, but follows the front line of the frame; and it is also nailed on the front of the chair as well, the nails alternating to avoid a conflict between their shanks.

The seat, unlike the back, is not tufted, because there is no strain on a flat surface as there would be on a perpendicular one. If the seat rails were wide enough, it was often the practice on a more elaborate chair to put in a double row of nails, one at the top and one at the bottom of the seat rail, but in this case they go round the corners and do not repeat themselves vertically at the two front corners, which was also frequently done.

Where the material masking the seat rails joins the platform of the seat it was usual to use a piping of the same material, as is seen here.

Looking at the back it will be noticed that this chair has a recessed panelled back, and the whole of the framework of the chair is separately upholstered. This is unusual for most chairs, particularly when re-upholstered, have their backs covered with material from one side to the other hiding the panel.

With a chair with padded arms it is important not to get the arms looking mean and scrawny, but to swell out so that they do not meet the back apologetically but balance the generous look of the back of the chair.

In a short space it is impossible to describe the methods of achieving a good line, but it is instructive to look not only at earlier examples like the chairs

135. A CHAIR FROM NOSTELL PRIORY, YORKSHIRE. The smooth horizontal line of the seat and the seat rail is emphasised by the two rows of close nailing, and the vertical nailing emphasises the precise edges of the chair.

136. A CHAIR FORMERLY AT BROCKET HALL, HERTFORSHIRE. The original nailing has been replaced by a gimp that disturbs the eye and does not create a precise enough line.

151

137. A CHAIR FORMERLY AT LANGLEY PARK, NORFOLK. Here the swell of the seat rises more or less straight from the edge of the chair and then curves back almost flat.

138. A MID 18TH CENTURY CHAIR UPHOLSTERED IN ORIGINAL WOOL DAMASK. Although the original tufts are lost, it can be seen how their placing complemented the line of the chair.

139. THE SILHOUETTE OF THE CHAIR. The curve of the padded back is particularly good.

140. THE BACK OF THE CHAIR. It is now rare to find the framework of the chair upholstered separately from the recessed panelled back.

141. A CHIPPENDALE CHAIR, ABOUT 1765. Based on Plate XXII in *The Director* (3rd Edition). The thin flat seat shown here in an old photograph does not complement the lines of the chair. Now re-upholstered.

142. THE ARMCHAIR FROM THE CLANDON SET.

143. A CHAIR EN SUITE WITH THE STATE BED AT CLANDON.

144. A CHAIR AT LYME PARK. A good example of late 17th century line in upholstery and use of trimmings.

XXIII. A section of a panel of Lyons silk, about 1785.

XXIV. The White Drawing Room at Houghton.

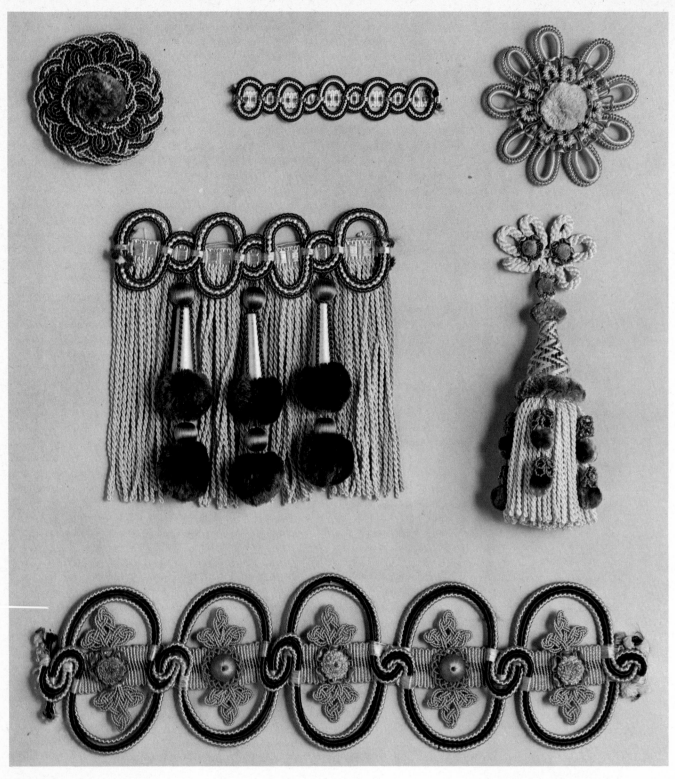

XXV. SAMPLES OF TRADITIONAL TRIMMINGS MADE IN LONDON IN THE 1960S BY B. A. CLARKE LTD.
Top left: an ornament to trim curtains. *Top middle*: "embassy" gimp, copied from a guilloche pattern which was used at the Dutch embassy. *Top right*: an ornament to embellish the choux on draperies at Daylesford, Gloucestershire. *Middle left*: a fringe and gimp made for Sezincote, Gloucestershire. *Middle right*: a tassel to trim the corner of a hand-painted cushion in the Queen's Private Audience Chamber at Buckingham Palace.

Below: a reweaving of an early 19th century gimp used at Haseley Court, Oxfordshire.

141. THE BACK OF THE CHAIR. It is now rare to find the framework of the chair upholstered separately from the recessed panelled back.

142. A CHAIR EN SUITE WITH THE STATE BED AT CLANDON.

143. THE ARMCHAIR FROM THE CLANDON SET.

144. A CHAIR AT LYME PARK. A good example of late 17th century line in upholstery and use of trimmings.

associated with the state bed at Clandon (Figs. 142, 143), a chair at Lyme (Fig. 144) and others at Hampton Court Palace, but at an English carved gilt rococo chair that has been acquired quite recently by the Victoria and Albert Museum (Figs. 145, 146, 147). It is one of the few chairs that can be identified in contemporary pictures, for it was Cosway's sitters' chair, and so it is possible to learn certain lessons about upholstery from its history. When acquired by the Museum it had been recovered in a modern copy of a late 18th century French silk, and the seat, back and arms were more or less flat; but it is quite clear from the portrait of Mrs Draper that it looked quite different in the 18th century. It was then upholstered in a red damask and instead of being finished with a gimp was boldly nailed. Also the back and arms had a swell to them that complemented the scrolling design of the chair; and the back was tufted, for one of the tufts appears above Mrs Draper's shoulder. Some of the spirit of the chair in the picture has been recaptured by the Museum in the re-upholstering, but there is still not enough swell to the back, and the tufts instead of following the line of the back form too rigid a pattern of their own.

By carefully studying pictures and the best surviving examples it is not too difficult to develop an eye for what is good in upholstery and what is not, and then, when faced with the problems of repair, it will be possible to explain the kind of result that is desired.

146. THE CHAIR AS IT WAS WHEN ACQUIRED BY THE VICTORIA AND ALBERT MUSEUM. A copy of a late 18th century French silk has been used.

147. *A PORTRAIT OF MRS DRAPER BY RICHARD COSWAY, ABOUT 1777.* The discovery of the painting suggested that the chair had been Cosway's sitter's chair. The colour of the upholstery suggested the use of the crimson damask and the use of nails instead of gimp. But the fullness of the base and of the arms has not been completely recaptured.

145. AN ENGLISH CARVED AND GILT CHAIR AS RECENTLY RE-UPHOLSTERED IN CRIMSON DAMASK.

Buttoning

Today buttoning usually means the deep-buttoning found on Victorian upholstery, but in fact the idea dates back to the second half of the 17th century and appears to have been familiar to upholsterers working for Louis XIV. However the buttoning that they did was float-tufting.

The easiest way to see the difference is to compare the leather squabs on the library chairs at Osterley (Fig. 148) with the interior of the Ashburnham bed (Fig. 76). The tufting on the squabs is so lightly done that there is only sufficient pull on the leather to hold the stuffing in place and keep the squab in shape. Invariably the upholsterer took care to place his tufts in relation to the line of the chair, as can be seen in the chairs and sofas from the Gallery at Corsham (Fig. 149). The number of tufts is dictated by the width of the chair, so that if, as here, there are three in the top row, it is usual to find two in the second and three in the third; and it should be noted how the top three are not in a row but equally spaced below the top of the chair.

All that is missing from the Corsham chairs are the original tufts, but they can be seen on the Osterley squabs. Made of a small hank of spun, looped, and crimped silk approximately an inch long, they are bound in the centre with more silk, to which are attached one or two linen threads or strings. When the latter are drawn through the upholstery and knotted at the back, the hank tends to open like a flower and becomes almost circular.

It is not often easy to tell how pronounced an effect of buttoning 18th-century upholsterers wanted, particularly on sofas, but judging by the design for one at the Gallery at Osterley, the tufting was intended to be a positive part of the design.

Inevitably the tufts tended to break off their strings so few examples are now as complete as the Osterley squabs. Sometimes they have been replaced

148. A CHAIR FROM THE LIBRARY AT OSTERLEY. The leather squab is original and retains its original tufts.

149. A CHAIR IN THE GALLERY AT CORSHAM. The number and placing of the tufts on the back of the chair is dictated by its width and on the settee (Figure 49) it can be seen how the placing of the tufts complements the line of the back.

156

by self-covered buttons, but it is not certain that they were ever used in the 18th century.

True deep-buttoning appears as part of the Rococo revival of the 2nd quarter of the 19th century. Known in France as *capitonné*, it was frequently used to give a sumptuous and voluptuous effect. Compared with float tufting it is much more regular, more stuffing and more material are used, and the silk tufts are replaced by covered buttons. When their threads are pulled tight, much tighter than in 18th century work, a definite trellis pattern of deep pleats forms between the buttons.

Nailing

Today the gilt or lacquered brass nails used for good upholstery are frequently imported from the continent and are machine made. In the 18th century they would have been hand made and show the usual evidence of such work, being not absolutely even; and they had forged iron shanks, which are square and not round in section.

They can be put on in two ways. The more usual form is what is called close nailing: that is to say one nail is placed next to another. But in good 18th century examples it will be noticed that any impression of overlapping is avoided, and there is a very slight breathing space between nails.

Vardy in his *Designs of William Kent* illustrates typical examples for the second quarter of the century (Fig. 150), and at Kedleston the chairs in the State Bedroom show this kind of effect in practice. The nailing on a gilt gesso chair made about 1720 (Fig. 151) is exceptional both from the point of view of the size of the nails used and the width of the spacing. At Hopetoun in the Red Drawing Room the covering of the chairs is close nailed over a fringe no doubt repeating the original treatment, and the same kind of finish can be seen on a suite of needlework chairs formerly at Cusworth Hall, Yorkshire (Fig. 152). Later 18th century nailing tends to be much smoother and more even, as can be seen from Hepplewhite's plates, but his fancy designs seem to have been more popular in America than England.

150. A DESIGN FOR A CHAIR BY KENT. Vardy in his engraving underlines the importance of the space nailing in the design.

151. A GILT GESSO CHAIR, ABOUT 1720. The nails are of exceptional size and wide spacing.

152. A CHAIR FORMERLY AT CUSWORTH HALL, YORKSHIRE. The needlework is original and the nailing was backed with a short fringe of which traces remain.

Cushions

Just as the line of the upholstery of a chair should complement the line of its frame, it is important that the cushion or cushions should be in keeping. They vary considerably in thickness not only according to the date of a chair but according to its type. The thinnest form of seat cushion is a pancake squab, which is really a pad little thicker than the cord or piping used to edge it, and it is often float tufted. This is the usual form of squab for a chair with a rush seat.

For a chair with a cane seat made in the second half of the 18th century or first half of the 19th century a bordered squab is usual. This should be made of horsehair with a layer of wadding on top and is usually between one and two inches thick depending on the delicacy or solidity of the chair. The edge of a bordered squab is made firm by the cutting and sewing of the material and is piped or corded on both edges. It was customary for the cover to be of the same fabric as the curtains, except, of course, if they were on library chairs as at Osterley. Also at Osterley there is a set of painted satinwood chairs with cane seats that retain their original squabs covered either in Chinese painted or embroidered silk (Fig. 153).

The cushion for a late 17th or early 18th century chair with a cane seat is made on the same principles, but should be a little thicker than a pancake squab, flat on the underside and slightly curved on top. It is usually attached to the chair by knotted tassels at the back and front, or tapes through the canework.

158

Evidently some late 17th century cushions had valances, but as far as we know none survive in England. They are implied in Marot's designs for stools and a set of Dutch-style chairs at Clandon have valanced upholstered seats that copy the form of their upholstery shown here in a 1927 photograph (Fig. 154). However again Lapierre's account to the Duke of Montagu provides confirmation for this idea, for he charged for six cushions to six cane chairs with valances all round and laced with broad and narrow silk lace. Apparently the fashion for valances continued, for the Chandos inventory taken in 1725 mentions window seats as "Squabs with falls to the windows."[100]

An English bergère or hunting chair may have side squabs as well as seat and back squabs depending on its size. The seat squab is two or three inches deep. However mid-18th century French chairs, like those in the Drawing room at Goodwood which are upholstered in their original cut velvet (Fig. 155), require a cushion rather than a squab: this is often as deep as five or six inches and, unlike the squab, should be soft and springy. The best ones are filled with down and lambs wool or white horse hair and wool covered with soft leather before being covered with silk. The practice of leather lining dates back earlier than the late 17th century when it was followed by Lapierre. When he upholstered an easy chair for the Duke of Montagu, the account specifies filling a sheepskin cushion with down and then covering it with damask. Later cushions of this type were usually trimmed with a barrel gimp, that is to say two rows of a narrow gimp one each side of the cord or piping.

Inspired by French examples, certain mid 18th century arm chairs with upholstered arms and seats had bolsters, but apart from the engraving in Ince and Mayhew (Plate LX) and a chair at Ham they are rarely seen (Fig. 156).

There are no general rules about cushions for sofas and settees, but it is remarkable how many of those illustrated in books on furniture appear to have lost all or part of their original complement. Chippendale in his note on the

153. A SATINWOOD ARMCHAIR AT OSTERLEY. The squab is covered in its original painted Chinese silk.

154. A CONTINENTAL CHAIR AT CLANDON. Upholstered seats with valances of this type are recorded in early 18th century prints.

sofas he illustrated in Plate XXIX wrote "Four designs of Sofas. When made large, they have a Bolster and Pillow at each end, and Cushions at the Back." Possibly some sofas primarily intended as part of the architectural design of a room, like those in the drawing room at Kedleston, never have had back cushions; but in other cases a grand settee might have three back cushions, the central one being slightly larger than the other two and following the line of the back. Few have kept both their original bolsters and pillows, but examples do survive, and a number of pillows retain their original tassels at the corners.

Frequently bolsters on 18th century sofas have been remade, and most of those seen today are of Regency type and very tailored in appearance: the ends of the roll are finished with a piping, and on the end face the material is carefully pleated to lie flat and usually secured in the centre with a broad flat button, sometimes with a tassel attached. Earlier bolsters tend to be looser in appearance. On the cut velvet sofas at Holkham, for instance, the bolsters are not piped at the end of the roll, and there is no break between the roll and the slightly rounded and less precisely pleated end (Fig. 157).

Couches and day-beds may have a bolster and a pillow, but an alternative shown by Ince and Mayhew in Plate LXIV was to have three graduated cushions (Fig. 158). The day-beds in the Gallery at Longford, which have a thick squab, have three cushions at each end. Similar sets of cushions were often made to show on state beds: richly embroidered and en suite with the counterpane, they were much too fine for use and may have been shown at the foot of the bed. Three sets are on view at the Victoria and Albert Museum.[101]

Case Covers and Loose Covers

The modern loose cover on a chair has a more complicated history than most people realise, for as a case cover it came into use in the 17th century. Not only were fine fabrics costly and the total length needed for the hangings and upholstery of a room considerable, but with an insistence on uniformity it was important to keep the wear even and exclude as much light and dust as

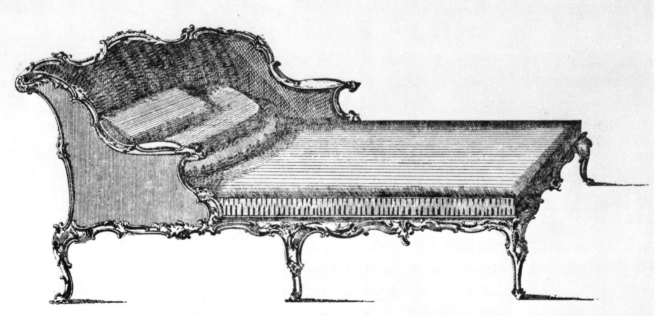

possible. Consequently from the 17th century onwards fine seat furniture was invariably supplied with one or two sets of covers. For instance at Lyme Park, the inventory of 1687–8 lists cloth cases on the chairs. In the early 18th century it was usual for the case covers to be of the same colour as the show fabric. At Cannons crimson damask chairs had case covers of crimson shalloon. Later big checks became fashionable. For the chairs in the Tapestry Room at Croome Court, Chippendale supplied calico dust covers and covers of fine crimson half inch check, together with chamois stockings to protect the gilt legs. His chairs in the Great Room at 19 Arlington Street had leather cases that cost 1 gn. each and crimson check covers that cost £6 for eight.[102]

Very few old case covers still exist, or, if they do, have not been identified, but there is one at Winterthur illustrated by Mrs Montgomery in her *Printed Textiles*. This is made of a linen or cotton print produced by Robert Jones of

157. THE SOFA BED FROM THE STATE BEDROOM AT HOLKHAM. The original bolsters have softly gathered ends rather than more regular piped ends as is usual with Regency bolsters.

158. A COUCH FROM INCE AND MAYHEW'S *UNIVERSAL SYSTEM* Three graduated cushions are shown.

160. THE GREAT PARLOUR AT STRAWBERRY HILL. The watercolour shows red or pink and white check case covers on the settees.

161. THE YOUNG PRINCES AT BUCKINGHAM HOUSE BY ZOFFANY. It is interesting to find that some of the case covers were still left on for a royal portrait; albeit an informal one.

Old Ford in England in 1761. And at Attingham Park there are attractive striped ones possibly dating from the second quarter of the 19th century still in use. However there are many to be seen in 18th century conversation pieces and portraits, among them J. H. Mortimer's Group of *Sergeant-at-Arms Bonfoy, his Son, and John Clementson* (Fig. 159) in the Mellon Collection, where the covers are of a typical blue and white check. They are also to be seen in the drawing of the Great Parlour at Strawberry Hill (Fig. 160). And when Zoffany painted the young Prince of Wales and his brother Prince Frederick at Buckingham Palace, some of the case covers were left on (Fig. 161).

It is particularly interesting to see them in the Zoffany, for it shows that in the largest houses they were in use almost all the time and only removed for special occasions. And naturally Mrs Delany, proud housekeeper that she was, would have followed the convention. However it did mean that if she had a sudden unexpected visit from someone like the Lord Lieutenant of Ireland as happened in 1745, there was a great deal to do: "To work went all my maids, stripping covers off the chairs, sweeping, dusting etc."[103]

Sometimes the practice was reversed, and it was the loose covers that were for show and put on for special occasions. At Boughton the 1697 inventory lists in the Drawing Room in the Great Apartment eight walnut chairs with blue damask cases and gold fringe; the 1707 inventory lists cases of crimson damask trimmed with gold and silver fringe in one room and "false cases of needlework" in Lady Anne Popham's room. Contemporary examples survived at Kimbolton Castle until recently: in the Small Drawing Room there was a set of chairs with detachable covers of crimson cut velvet that matched the wall hangings (Fig. 162).[104] And at Erthig there is a set of chairs with loose covers of caffoy and even the headless nails in the frame on to which the covers were hitched survive.

The modern chintz cover is a descendant of the mid 18th century linen check cover and probably came into use in the late 18th or early 19th century. A good description of their use in 1842 is given by Augustus Hare who was writing of Curraghmore in Co. Cork: there Lady Waterford "has made the drawing-rooms very pretty & comfortable, with chintz covers on all the chairs and sofas, and all sorts of china and ornaments scattered about." Evidently the chintz was never intended to be removed, even on formal occasions, for Lady Waterford's idea was to make the room cosy as the early Victorians understood the term, an idea far removed from James Wyatt's intention when he designed the room 70 years before.[105]

159. *SERGEANT-AT-ARMS BONFOY, HIS SON, AND JOHN CLEMENTSON BY J. H. MORTIMER.* The chairs have typical loosely fitting case covers in blue and white check.

162. THE SMALL DRAWING ROOM AT KIMBOLTON CASTLE, HUNTINGDON. A copy of an old photograph showing early 18th century loose covers of crimson cut velvet on chairs formerly at Kimbolton. The velvet is supposed to have been part of that acquired by Lord Manchester on his embassy to Venice in 1707.

Braids and Trimmings

In most aspects of decoration there have been fundamental changes of emphasis over the last 250 years, but perhaps the one where the change is most noticeable is in the use of trimmings, that is to say braid, lace, orrice, gimp, fringe and tassels. Today their cost is so high that they tend to be used sparingly and usually with at least a degree of reluctance, certainly seldom with the generosity and freedom that is characteristic of work at the beginning and end of the 18th century. However good trimmings were always an expensive part of any job. The Duke of Bedford, for instance, spent over £470 on trimming for one bed in 1702. And when new curtains were ordered for the drawing room at Hawarden Castle, Flintshire in 1812, the bill came to over £300 for the curtains and the drapery: the 60 yards of crimson cloth for three pairs of curtains cost £72. 9s. 0d. while 117 yards of gold coloured silk lace £35. 2s. 9d. and 35 yards of fringe £36. 15s. 0d.; making only cost £4. 10s. 6d.[106]

However since then two things have changed; first, the emphasis laid on upholstery in all forms and, second, the ending of the tradition of making fine trimmings. The finest trimmings used at the end of the 17th century and beginning of the 18th century must have been made by professionals, but evidently a great quantity were made by ladies. At Badminton, for instance, the first Duchess of Beaufort had "divers gentlewomen commonly at work

164

upon embroidery and fringe making, for all the beds of state were made and finished in the house." And in the early 1680s Lady Carr had her new bed trimmed "with white thrid (thread = linen) fringe of her own making." And this custom lasted right through the 18th century. When Mrs Delany could not get a set of white tassels under eight or nine shillings, she wrote: "you may get the nobs turned in wood, of what shape you like, and cover them with some of your own tufted knotting, which will be prettier than anything you can buy; and if you cover them with a case of cloth, it may be slipped off when dirty to wash." Her friend, Miss Hamilton, did "a very pretty fringe" for her chintz covers, which she "made up with two knotting needles." Even Queen Charlotte had a frame for making fringe that she showed to the Duchess of Portland.[107]

It is this tradition that helps to explain Sarah, Duchess of Marlborough's very detailed instructions about the use of trimmings. When she ordered a piece of furniture, it was not left to the upholsterer to finish it off as he pleased: the Duchess gave precise orders about lengths, quality, price and use of the trimmings. The scale of Blenheim soon brought home to her the vast amount of money involved in such work.

The run-down of the craft in this century makes restoration increasingly difficult, particularly if, let us say, new curtains have to be matched up with old hangings. Some historic examples, like the tassel fringes on the King's Bed at Knole or the State Bed at Clandon, could not be made in England now, and most of the trimmings available on the retail market have a mechanical and lifeless look that makes them a disappointing finish for fine 17th and 18th century furniture. This may sound depressing, but as with gilding, there is no cheap and easy way to get the right effect.

The illustrations in Plates XXV, XXVI give a good idea of the best quality of work that was done in London until the end of 1970 and they also give an idea of the general characteristics of trimmings. A, B, D, H, and L are all gimps, which are made by spinning and over-spinning so that the cord produced is so hard that the pattern can be pinched with pliers as in the gothick gimp (A).[108]

C, E, F, and J are different types of fringe. C is a wool bullion fringe that is first double spun to make a cord on the same principle as a gimp and then it is woven into a fringe. Attached to it is an ornament, which consists of alternating bundles and bows, each one made by hand and sewn together. The bows are strips of copper covered with spun silk and then worked into shape. Leaving aside the time needed to produce a single complete ornament, it would take about an hour to make enough bullion for a yard of fringe 9 inches deep and another hour to weave the bullion into the fringe.

In E the weaver has used a mixture of coloured silks to make a fringe with a fan heading and the trellis is all tied by hand. F is a block (i.e. different blocks of colour) fringe with a gimp heading and is ornamented with hangers of floss silk.

J is a copy of an early 19th century fringe from Attingham and was made for the curtains replacing those shown in the drawing room at Sezincote, (Fig. 102). Two kinds of bullion are used, and the heading is a guilloche gimp that is woven in with it. The ornaments are made like tassels.

The tassel is much the most complicated element. Starting with a turned mould that may consist of as many as six pieces of wood, the tassel maker has first to cover it with silk and tie it, possibly even snailing it, that is weaving a pattern on it as in K. Occasionally the snailing is done with a basket pattern of silk-covered metal strips that match the ground colour. Then the skirt has to be made out of the specially woven bullion fringe and sewn on; after that the cut ruff is made and wired on. The tassel in K is a small one, four inches from top to bottom, but it is easy to see why it might be a complete day's work by a highly-skilled craftsman. And when a bed like that from Ashburnham

Place needs 18 small tassels and six large ones, it is easy to see why the author of the *London Tradesman* of 1747 wrote that women trimmings makers "make a very handsome livelihood of it, if they are not initiated into the Mystery of Gin-drinking."[109]

Over the years the basic patterns and techniques have not altered very greatly, and with a little experience it is not difficult to distinguish trimmings made about 1700 from those made about 1750, 1800, 1850 and 1900. Undoubtedly the most interesting were those made at the end of the 17th and beginning of the 18th centuries when not only silk but a great deal of silver and gold was used in the finest work, not only in fringes but in orrice, galloon and lace. Orrice is a gold and silver lace woven on a loom and sometimes finished off on a pillow like thread lace. Galloon and lace are both braids also woven on a loom. The extravagance of this kind of work on the King's Bed at Knole is overwhelming, but as it has darkened so much, the fineness of contemporary gold and silver work is best illustrated in a contemporary length of orrice put away at Boughton, presumably a relic of one of the Duke of Montagu's beds.

The surviving state bed from Boughton at the Victoria and Albert Museum is hung with red silk brocaded with gold, and it is trimmed with gold fringe in two widths, the narrower one being used for vertical edges as was invariably the practice. The silhouette of the bed is fairly severe, and no elaborate effects are sought by the upholsterer in his working of the trimmings.

However with the Melville bed the trimmings are used to play up the elaborate silhouette, and just as there is a striving after three dimensional effects in the design, the braids and tassel fringes are used to emphasise this (Figs. 66, 67). It is interesting that the flat strapwork patterns, which could have been done in galloon, are done with double lines of orrice which is less solid and allows the white ground to show through and make a contrast in colour and depth with the tufts that form part of the braid. The fringe is tasseled, which also allows the ground to show through, and, to give extra emphasis, it is lined with a single line of braid. The fringe on the valance is double to give a greater sense of weight.

There is a splendid freedom about fringes at this date and they exist in such variety that it is impossible to give a comprehensive account of them. On the Hornby Castle suite, for instance, the fringe (Fig. 163) is multicoloured and the hangers holding the little tassels are of different lengths. Some fringes were woven to be serpentine and others sought variety in texture. For instance one fringe has tassels of two types, one being floss silk and the other crimped silk, that are arranged in a pattern 2 floss—1 crimped—3 floss—1 crimped—2 floss and so on. The sense of vitality and variety that this gives is comparable with the contemporary carved mouldings that catch and break the light.

Not only were fringes shaped, but they were used to form patterns on upholstery. There are particularly fine examples of this kind of effect on a chair from Lyme, and on another in Col. Colville's collection (Fig. 164). Another favourite device was to trim the edges of a back of a chair and to apply it in a scallop pattern at the base of the back as can be seen on chairs formerly at Rushbrooke Hall and in the Ambassador's Bedroom at Knole (Figs. 165, 166).

Round about 1710 there was a reaction against such Baroque exuberance and costly extravagance, and Queen Anne's bed at Hampton Court Palace appears almost austere when compared with the Melville or Dyrham beds. The strongly architectural design of the cut velvet is all important, and the trimmings are subservient to this: braid is only used to outline the cornice and border the curtains and is not intended to be eye-catching.

The reaction also affected the use of orrice, galloon and lace, but to a lesser extent, for they continued to be used on state beds as can be seen at Houghton and at Kedleston. The trimmings for the Houghton bed and curtains cost over

166

163. A detail of a settee from the Hornby Castle suite. It shows the use of a multi-coloured fringe with tassels of different length.

164. A CARVED AND GILT CHAIR UPHOLSTERED IN ORIGINAL CRIMSON VELVET, ABOUT 1695. Its impact is largely made by the rich trimming of the back and seat with an ornamented fringe.

165. A SWAGGED FRINGE ON A CHAIR FORMERLY AT RUSHBROOKE HALL, SUFFOLK.

166. A CHAIR FROM THE VENETIAN AMBASSADOR'S BEDROOM AT KNOLE, ABOUT 1686. The cut velvet upholstery is trimmed with tassel fringe doubled and swagged at the base of the back and round the seat.

£1200 in 1732, the pattern of the lace being worked over vellum. At Kedleston the curtains and the counterpane are decorated with orrice. And lace continued to be used for edging wall hangings; a use recorded in accounts and in contemporary pictures but not known to survive *in situ* in a country house.

Most of the trimmings made between 1720 and 1790 are intended to underplay rather than overplay a design and they tend to be more evenly made and smoother. For instance, on the Erthig bed the fringe to the valance is quite deep, but it is smooth and not tasselled, slight variety being given by the occasional knotted strand.

This is not a true knotted fringe, which was a favourite form throughout most of the 18th century, and yet so understated that if one was not told of its details one would never suspect the extravagance of labour involved in making it, an extravagance so great that it has probably not been made in living memory in England. It is woven like a normal fringe except that the bullion loops are not twisted, and when they are cut, the bullion is knotted by hand so that only the ends unravel and hang free. As can be seen on the Uppark bed such a fringe gives a scarcely visible layered effect, the ends being softer than the head of the fringe (Fig. 167). The Uppark example is decorated with fly ornaments, as was usual, and these consist of hangers with a series of ties of floss (that is unspun) silk. On a bolder bed, or one with a richer patterned fabric, a heavier fringe would be usual. On the Cut Velvet Bed at Hardwick, which was designed by Vardy about 1745, there is a particularly fine knotted fringe with a gimp heading and it is decorated with hangers and bows, flys and ties of balls. It is not known what this cost, but the two kinds of fringe used on the state bed at Woburn in 1760 cost 27/- and 30/- a yard. The cheaper is described as the "best blue Belladine Silk Crape Fring, with a large double gymp head, buttons, and hangers enriched with diamond head."[110]

Naturally Adam would not have wanted upholsterers' trimmings to dominate his designs, but at Osterley excellent examples are to be seen of how he used them to underline his ideas and how he carried through his designs down to the small detail. In the Etruscan Room, for instance, the festoon curtains (which may or may not be original) are trimmed with a block fringe in black

168

167. AN ORNAMENTED KNOTTED
FRINGE ON A CRIMSON DAMASK BED
AT UPPARK, 1754.

and white to suit the colouring of the room, and the same mixture of black and white is repeated on the tassels that finish off the curtain cords.

With the return to fashion of elaborate drapery in the last 10 or 15 years of the 18th century, there was a revival of interest in trimmings and they began to play a more dominant role in the upholstery designs. Fringes became deeper and heavier with the ornaments making stronger contrasts; tassels became larger and more elaborate. Frequently the trimmings were chosen to make direct contrasts with the fabrics used, whereas in the middle of the century they had either matched or been fairly close in tone. As there was a fashion for smooth fabrics, including satins with small regular motifs, the trimmings often held the attention, particularly if the fabric was draped. This is well illustrated on the Castlecoole bed, where the hangings are a copy of the original cherry taffetas and the fringe is original. The latter has a bold gimp heading and the ornaments are set so close together that they set the rhythm and the bullion becomes of secondary importance.

More sensitive examples of high class upholstery of the 1790s are to be seen at Powderham Castle. A pair of day beds are covered in embroidered silk and the mattress is outlined with a deep gimp somewhat similar to the one shown in Plate XXV.

169

Mourning Decorations

The most familiar relics of 18th and early 19th century funeral decorations are the hatchments that still hang in many churches displaying the arms of the local family painted on a square of board or canvas set in a black wooden frame often originally covered with puckered black crape; but they were by no means the only or the most elaborate part of the equipment needed for the funeral of a person of consequence 200 or 300 years ago. Here we are not concerned with the details of the procession or the arrangements in church, but must concentrate on the rather fragmentary details of what was done in a house. Much the fullest account of a grand funeral is that published by Francis Sandford in the *Funeral of the Great Duke of Albemarle* in 1670, a funeral ordered by the King and, as far as the lying in state at Somerset House was concerned, organised by the Royal Wardrobe. The illustrations[111] (Fig. 168) and description throw considerable light on the scattered references found in family papers.

"The Three Rooms at Somerset House were furnished in manner following: The First Room was hung with Bays from top to bottom, adorned with Escucheons, and furnished with Sconces, and Wax-Candles unlighted; and Formes placed about it, covered with Bays.

"The Second was hung with Cloath, adorned with Escucheons, and furnished with Scones and Candles, unlighted, the Forms about it covered with Cloath; at the upper end, a Haute-pass floored with Bays, a Canopy of Black Velvet, the vallance Fringed, the Pendant within half a yard of the Ground; a Majesty-Escucheon of Taffata, a Black Velvet Chair with Arms, and a Footstool.

"The Third Room was hung with Velvet, floored with Bays, adorned with Escucheons, and Black Sconces, with White Wax Tapers, and at the upper

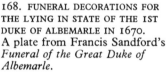

168. FUNERAL DECORATIONS FOR THE LYING IN STATE OF THE 1ST DUKE OF ALBEMARLE IN 1670. A plate from Francis Sandford's *Funeral of the Great Duke of Albemarle.*

end upon a Haute-pass, a Bed of State of Black Velvet was placed with Black Plumes at the Four corners of the Tester; at the Head a Majesty-Escucheon, and another in the midst of the Tester. Upon the Bed was placed a Coffin covered with a fine Holland-Sheet of Eight bredths, and Eight ells long, and over that, a Pall of Black Velvet of Eight breadths, and Eight yards long, and thereupon the Effigies of the Duke" . . . in armour, wearing his coronet and robes, and the Garter.

"About Five foot distant from the Bed, was a Rail covered with Black velvet and close to the inside of the Rail, were placed on both sides, the Bannerols, three Banners, and a Guydon, and at the Foot, the Standard, and Great Banner; between these on the Sides, were also placed Twelve Black Stands, with as many Silver Candlesticks, with large White Wax Tapers in them.

"At the Bed's Feet, was a little Table covered with a Carpet of Black Velvet, and thereupon were placed the Coat of Arms, Sword, Target, Helm, and Crest, Gauntlets, and Spurs. Between the Standard and the great Banner, hung a Crystal Branch with Twelve Sockets, and therein as many Tapers of Wax.

"In this Room . . . the Tapers were continually burning when it was exposed to sight, which was every day (except Sunday) during the space of about three weeks." 40 Gentlemen, 20 a day were on duty, 4 in the 1st Room, 6 in the 2nd, 10 in the 3rd, 5 on each side of the rail of the Bed of State with their backs to the wall.

Another very elaborate funeral for which there is plenty of detail is that of the 1st Duke of Marlborough in 1722. Five rooms at Marlborough House were prepared for the ceremonies: the Great Hall, where distinguished mourners were received, was hung "from the Painting downwards to the floor with Black Bays adorned with Escutcheons Crest and Badges of the Order of the Garter, furnished with black Sconces and Wax candles." The second room, which was hung in a similar fashion but ornamented with different heraldic devices and lit with silver sconces, contained "a Canopy of Black Velvet laced round the vallance with gold, adorned with Black plumes of feathers on the top, and under the Canopy on an assent of three degrees a Chair of State covered with black velvet . . ." The Duke's body lay in the third room on a bed in a crimson velvet coffin; over the coffin was a black velvet pall and on the pall was set a complete suit of gilt armour. Over the body was a canopy trimmed with plumes of black velvet. The fourth and fifth rooms were reserved for the nobility and others invited to the funeral.[112]

There is much about these ceremonies that strikes us as macabre, but the clue to them is provided by Misson writing in the late 17th century for he says "Upon this occasion, the rich Equipage of the Dead does honour to the Living."[113]

He also describes a lying-in-State, "Among Persons of Quality 'tis customary to embalm the Body, and to expose if for a Fortnight or more in a Bed of State." Celia Fiennes gives an account of the lying in state of Queen Mary in 1695, which took place at Whitehall nearly two months after her death. The bed itself was of purple velvet and so were the hangings of the room; the ante-chamber was hung with purple cloth, and elsewhere the hangings were black.[114]

The preparations in a country house were obviously not as elaborate as those made by the Wardrobe, but usually the house was hung with black baize. On the death of Sir Ralph Verney in 1696 for instance, it was ordered that the Hall at Claydon should be hung with black baize, "the entry from the Hall door to the Spicery door, and the best Court porch, likewise the Brick Parlour top to bottom," where a dozen chairs and three great tables to be covered with black. And in April 1697, Sir John Verney wrote to William Coleman "Pray let all the Black Bayes that's around the Hall, the Entry and the Summer Parlour be taken down, and off the Chaires, and Stooles, Tables and Standes (if you can measure it, do) and make it up in a bundle and sent it up to me by the

Carrier . . . for the Escochens About the Hall lay 'em up untill I come down, & then we'll distribute 'em among the Tenants. Doe not meddle with the Hatchment over the Doore in the best Court . . ."[115]

As in the Duke of Albemarle's funeral, the heraldic element was obviously very important, and this emerges in the account of a Sheldon family funeral in 1684, for the "Scocherer" were put up at Weston in the Hall, Staircase, Dining roome and roome of State."[116]

Most of the references are to black hangings, but there were evidently half mourning decorations as well. When Saint-Simon married in 1695, the company was not received in his mother's house because she was in half-mourning and the house was hung with black and grey. It is this that probably explains the references to grey hangings in the King's Apartment at Kensington Palace in 1697. There is a similar mixture of black and grey in the accounts relating to Harcourt House, London, after Lord Harcourt's death in 1727. There hangings were put up for 12 months in the Hall and Staircase, in the Great Dining Room and Eating Parlour, the Dessing Room and Her Ladyship's Dressing Chamber, but they were not all black. Black baize was used for the Hall and Staircase, a fine cloth with a blue ground in the Eating Parlour, light grey cloth in the Great Dining Room, dark grey cloth in the Dressing Chamber and fine whitish grey cloth in the Dressing Room. In these two rooms the hangings went from the ceiling to the ground, and the curtains, valances, portières and chairs all matched and in one room the floor was covered over too.[117]

There is no mention of a mourning bed, but one might have been expected. It is not known when they were first introduced, but one is recorded in 1624 as "A bedstead of black velvet with taffeta." On this the widow received the condolences of her family and friends, a most macabre event to judge from the descriptions of Evelyn and Liselotte. Evelyn's is of Queen Catherine's mourning bed used on Charles II's death: "There came over divers envoys and great persons to condole the death of the late King, who were received by the Queen-Dowager on a bed of mourning, the whole chamber, ceiling to floor, hung with black, and tapers were lighted, so as nothing could be more lugubrious and solemn. The Queen-Consort sate under a state on a black foot cloth, to entertain the Circle (as the Queen used to do), and that very decently."[118]

Liselotte's description dates from 1701 and is particularly interesting because she describes her clothes. "I had to receive the ceremonial visit of the King and Queen of England wearing the strangest apparel: a white linen band across my forehead, about it a cap which tied under my chin like a veil, over the cap *les cornettes*, and over them a piece of linen that was fastened to the shoulders like a mourning-coat, with a train sevel ells long. I was dressed in a coat of black cloth with very long sleeves; ermine, two hands wide, bordered the cuffs. There was more ermine of the same width down the front of the coat from throat to floor, and a girdle of black crepe reaching to the ground in front and a train of ermine, seven ells long.

In this get-up, with the train arranged to show the ermine, I was placed on a black bed in an entirely blackened room. Even the parquet was covered and the windows hung with crepe. A great candelabra of twelve candles was lit, and there were ten or twelve candles burning on the chimneypiece . . ."[119]

That this was not just royal etiquette is born out by Lady Bute's description of what happened after her grandfather's death in 1726. "The apartments, the staircase, and all that could be seen of the house, were hung with black cloth; the Duchess, closely veiled with crepe, sat upright in her State-bed under a high black canopy, and at the foot stood, ranged like a row of servants at morning prayers, the grandchildren of the deceased Duke—Profound Silence reigned, the room had no light but for the single wax taper, and the condoling female visitors, who curtseyed in and out of it, and whose duty it was to tender in person their sympathy, approached the bed on tiptoe, and were clothed, if relations down to the hundredth cousin, in black glove morning for the occasion."[120]

If a family did not own the mourning hangings or bed, and could not borrow them from a friend, they could be hired, and this was done when the 2nd Duke of Bedford died in 1711. Baize for two staircases and the hall and black sconces for Southampton House were hired for £15, and another £20 was spent on "black cloth hangings, curtains, chairs, stool, shovel, tongues etc" for the Great Parlour. These evidently remained up for 12 months, the length of the hire. The bedroom furniture on the other hand cost £30 for two years. Many of the things used in the decoration of Marlborough House in 1722 were also hired. The "48 black Japanned sconces & scroles round the Hall," and the "black velvet canopy over the chair of state," the "69 large plate sconces & double scrouls" for the State Room, together with the 380 yards of new black velvet, the velvet Bed of State and even "A Dukell Crownett Guilded & a crimson velvett cap with a large Gold Tassell" were all hired for 25 days, the two lots of sconces costing £5 and £21, the canopy £5, the velvet hangings £142–10–0 and the bed £10. It was quite usual to hire, for on the trade card of Robert Green of St Margaret's Hill, Southwark, issued in 1752, it announces that he "Sells & lets all Manner of Furniture for Funerals . . ." including velvet palls, hangings for rooms, large silvered candlesticks and sconces, tapers and wax lights.[121]

On reading this account many might think these references have no bearing on decoration or on the interpretation of interiors today, but they are important for two reasons. Firstly they underline once again the symbolic aspects of decoration and the emphasis on a hierarchy in all aspects of life in the 17th century and for much of the 18th century as well. But secondly they may provide an explanation of why certain pieces of furniture are found to have been painted black at some point in their history. At Knole for instance the feet of the King's Bed are painted black; at Firle the frame of a portrait is decorated with black chevrons; at Clandon there is a George I table that should be gilded but is black. However no beds have survived and of the hangings all that is known are fragments of black velvet found on the wall of the State bedroom at Lyme.[122] We cannot prove it, but it is at least worth bearing in mind that all four may have been so treated to fit in with mourning decorations 200 years ago.

Chapter 5
Colour and the painter's craft

Introduction and Books

Colour is the most difficult aspect of decoration to write about because there are no absolutes. For three hundred years people have been trying to codify colour by producing increasingly complex charts and tables, but helpful as these can be in planning series of colours, they cannot provide the full answer when it comes to decoration, for colour is as much to do with light as pigments and is never constant. Taking, let us say, white, there is not one recognisable tone but an infinite number of shades that vary according to the surface on which they are laid, the way they are put on, the light in which they are seen, and with time. With colour, familiar labels like Wedgwood Blue and Adam Green may seem to help, but in fact no two people would agree precisely what they mean, and most of the time neither Wedgwood nor Adam would approve of the dreary results produced in their name. Thus, much of this chapter must be written in a tentative way, and the comments on how effects were achieved in the past and the suggestions that may help people now should be treated with the same understanding as an advanced cookery recipe. Memorable cookery is based on flair and freedom of interpretation, and so is the best decoration: slavish adherence to the pattern books seldom produced the most successful results.

However it is important to attempt to order the information that is available, and this is a task that English writers have been attempting to do since the 1670s. The earliest author, and apparently the most successful, was John Smith, whose book *The Art of Painting in Oyl* first appeared in 1676. Subsequent editions of this book were published in 1687, 1705, 1723, 1753, and the last, revised by Butcher, came out in 1821. In 1685 appeared *A Short Introduction to the Art of Painting and Varnishing* by an anonymous author and only identified by the name of the publisher, George Dawes, and this was followed in 1688 by Stalker and Parker's *Treatise of Japanning and Varnishing*.

Two 18th century books with practical information are the *Laboratory of the Arts*, by Godfrey Smith, which was published in 1735 and 1755, and Robert Dossie's *The Handmaid of the Arts*, which came out in 1758 for the first time and in new editions in 1764 and 1796. Both books are fairly clearly indebted to John Smith's *Art of Painting in Oyl*, and of the two Dossie provides rather more information about colours. Not only does he list the main ones and their subdivisions, including, for instance, in the yellow section English and Dutch pink, gamboge, masticot, orpiment and gall stone, but he gives a great deal of detail on how the colours were made and how they reacted to different vehicles and dryers. House decoration was not in the forefront of

174

either writer's mind, for there was at that time widespread interest in theories of colours and the relationship of one colour to another in the spectrum. This is also seen in the way artists laid out their colours on their palettes, a subject that was discussed by F. Schmid in the *Burlington Magazine* in 1966 where he said "Extensive preoccupation with systematic and standardised methods of painting in the 18th century may explain the enthusiastic outburst."[1]

The earliest English theory of colour was that introduced by Sir Isaac Newton to the Royal Society in 1675 and published in *Optics* in 1704; he was followed by, among others, J. C. le Blon, who was particularly interested in colour printing and published an account in English called *Coloritto, or the Harmony of Colouring in Painting, reduced to Mechanical Practice*, and Moses Harris, whose *Natural System of Colours* was first printed in 1766. Harris's book was dedicated to Reynolds, but in the reissue of 1811 this was altered to Benjamin West.[2] Almost certainly always a scarce book because of its hand-coloured plates and possibly even unknown to Adam, its publication in 1766 at a time when Adam's use of colour was becoming more adventurous may be coincidental; but it is conceivable that Adam referred to it or to some other colour theory. Harris arranged his colours in two circles, shaded in intensity outwards, first the three grand primitive colours as he called them, red, blue and yellow; and next the intermediate, orange, green and purple. The author refers to his system "opening a door whereby further information may be obtain'd respecting the mixing and blending of colours, and seems plainly to point out the reason why the science or systematic knowledge of colours in general hath been so dark and occult, as there has been no form, or mode, for mixing the various teints wanted in a vast variety of subjects painted. Many ways are commonly try'd by the young artist in mixing, or compounding teints, and nothing but experience in consequence of many attempts can set him right, and this is a difficulty with which he is always seazed, when his ideas are fixed and deeply bent on some other subject."

In the early 19th century a spate of books was produced, and although there appears to be no complete collection of them anywhere, a selection of titles that we have come across gives an indication of the interest in the subject at that time. The work of Professor Tingry of Geneva appeared as *The Painter's and Varnisher's Guide* by P. F. Tingry in 1804 and was reissued as *The Painter's and Colourman's Complete Guide* in 1830. M. Gartside produced *An Essay or a new theory of Colours* in 1808; G. Field's *Chromatics: or an essay on the analogy and harmony of colours* appeared in 1817; the *Painter's and Varnisher's Pocket Manual* was printed for Knight and Lacey in 1825; Reade's *Theory of Colours* in 1826; Nathaniel Whittock's *The Decorative Painters and Glaziers Guide* in 1827; D. R. Hay's *The Laws of Harmonious Colouring Adapted to House Painting and other Decorations* in 1828; Arrowsmith's *House Decoration and Painter's Guide* in 1840, and in 1841 W. M. Higgin's *The House Painter or Decorators Companion*. Robert Haldane's *Workshop Receipts* was published in 1883.

This sounds overwhelming, but it suggests that if these manuals were correlated, they would be of considerable assistance to those trying to identify colours from accounts and inventories and match them in restorations. For instance, it is interesting to find in Dossie's book that egg-shell paint was actually derived from egg shells: "Take egg shells and peel off the inner skins. Then levigate the shell to a proper fineness, and wash over the powder."

Patrick Syme's *Nomenclature of Colours* (2nd edition 1821) is particularly interesting, because he was trained as a flower painter and wanted his book to be useful to those concerned with the arts and sciences, particularly Zoology, Botany, Chemistry, Mineralogy, and what he called Morbid Anatomy. He listed 108 colours, providing samples of each and explaining how they are mixed and giving illustrations, one animal, one vegetable and one mineral. He identified 8 whites, 8 greys, 7 blacks, 10 blues, 11 purples, 16 greens, 15 yellows, 6 oranges, 18 reds, and 11 browns, each shade being illustrated. For instance the whites are described as, snow, reddish, purplish, yellowish, orange-coloured, greenish, skimmed mild and greyish: the greys are ash, smoke, French, pearl, yellowish, bluish, greenish, blackish, and so on.

In recent times systems even more complex than Harris's and Syme's have been produced, and, according to the authors of the *Methuen Handbook of Colour*, over 8,000 colour names are current in the British Isles. They give 1266 colour samples and list colour names which they relate both to the samples and to the Monsell system and to British Standard colours. This is helpful to anyone wanting to check on a colour, but inevitably as there are fashions in names, some of those found in old books are not given in the *Handbook*. For instance ceruse, flake white, and Bougival white given in the *Painter's Manual* do not appear. Nor do we know that the names absolutely correspond even if they are given.

The whole subject is one that has to be approached with caution, for it is not enough to know the range of colours: it is equally important to understand that they will look different in different situations and lights.

Mediums and Methods

To all intents and purposes only five mediums have to be considered today and they are oil, tempera, soft distemper, oil bound distemper and emulsion paint (which we have chosen not to discuss). However before the establishment of factory-mixed paints at the beginning of the century, the whole craft was organised on different lines. First there was the making of the pigment. Then there was the vehicle to consider, the vehicle being the medium that made the colour fluid. And there was the dryer as well, for the medium often needed an additive to make it dry. And that is why books like John Smith's and Robert Dossie's concentrate on the nature of colour, for as the *London Tradesman* says "Of the Herald, House and Coach-Painter;" ". . . The chief Secret lies in grinding, mixing and compounding the Colours; as to the laying them on, it requires no Art, but an even Hand to carry the Brush up and down according to the Grain of the Wood. This Branch is now at a very low Ebb, on accounts of the Methods practised by some Colour-Shops; who have set up Horse-Mills to grind the Colours, and sell them to Noblemen and Gentlemen ready mixed at a low Price, and by the Help of a few printed Directions, a House may be painted by any common Labourer at one Third of the Expense it would cost before the Mystery was made public . . ."[3] When he says mixed, he does not mean mixed with a vehicle and ready to apply, but concentrated like the stainers that some decorators use when mixing special colours today.

John Smith gives plenty of detail, because he envisaged his book being of assistance to gentry "that live far remote from great Cities where Painters usually reside, (who) may sometimes have occasion to play the good Husband in preserving such ornaments of their Habitations as are most exposed to the violence of Rain and Wet, . . ."[4] He describes the grindstone that was needed, the muller or grinder, the voider to clear the stone of ground colour, and the ox bladders for storing ground colour and so on. If this sounds elementary to us we must remember that a painter in a remote place would be expected to tackle an extraordinary range of work. For instance Thomas Collier who was a painter in Penrith in the early 1780s advertised himself as follows "who in particular takes likenesses; Paints Coaches, Chariots, Post Chaises, & either in common or High Varnish. . . . He also continues Pedigrees; Paints Arms, Ensigns, Moon, and Coffin-plates; Funeral Escutcheons, and Achievements; Japans; Gilds in Oil, Bronze, and Burnish Gold. . . . Exactly copies, carefully cleans, repairs, or varnishes Old Painting, Prints, or Japann'd Work, likewise, Colours in Distemper or Oil, all manner of Stucco, ornamented Rooms,

Ceilings, Halls, Temples, Staircases etc., in variety of Colours, properly adapted to suit the Furniture of the Apartment, and shew the Ornaments to best advantage . . .''

Recently the Society for the Preservation of New England Antiquities has been carrying out research into these old methods of making paints and suggested that they should be revived for restoration work, and perhaps in time they will be; but making the paint is only part of the problem and so it may be helpful to start by describing one method used for painting walls or woodwork today that is based on a combination of personal experience and historical precedent.[5]

Here the preparation of the surface is just as important as the final coat, and this can be divided into four stages. The first consists of putting on a white lead primer. After this all holes and cracks should be filled with Alabastine or some such filler, which then needs to be carefully rubbed down when dry so that a smooth surface is obtained. A coarse glass paper (No 1) should be used first and then a No 0 or "flour" if an extremely fine surface is required. Next the surface should be sealed with a coat of transparent shellac polish. At least a day should elapse between each process.

Only after that should two coats of undercoat be applied. As white eggshell paint tends to discolour and darken when used by itself, it is better to use a mixture of 50 per cent white eggshell and 50 per cent flat white undercoat as the last undercoat before the final colour is put on. If a coloured undercoat is used it should be a very much paler version of the final colour.

The final coat should have the stainers added and be given a flat finish. It can be thinned with pure turpentine, and sometimes a very small quantity of linseed oil can be added (say a teaspoon to half a gallon): this will allow the paint to "flow" more easily if it seems too "ropy" (i.e. thick and streaky). Oil will tend to give a gloss appearance, and so it should be used very sparingly, because the stainers used for tinting the white paint contain a certain amount of oil in any case.

This may sound a very long drawn out and so a costly process, and there is no denying that it is, but it is the only way to avoid a dead mechanical finish that is so unpleasing in a large room in an old house. The antipathy to a mechanical finish is not just a 20th century decorator's fad, but is a noticeable feature of rooms retaining old paintwork. This is commented on by Morgan Philips in his recent paper where he says "Most of us now understand that old paint has not only colour but a ropy textured appearance, usually showing pronounced brush marks." Loudon refers to the matter obliquely when writing of the graining of woodwork in 1833: all woodwork should if possible be "grained in imitation of some natural wood, not only with a view of having the imitation mistaken for the original, but rather to create an allusion to it and by a diversity of lines to produce a kind of variety and intricacy which affords more pleasure to the eye than a flat shade of colour."[6]

To give a greater sense of depth and texture to the colour, the final coat of paint may be applied in different ways, the most usual of which are brush graining, stippling, glaze painting and dragging. All these fashionable finishes, like the actual method of painting described above, are based on historical precedents. The object of brush graining is to create a soft effect and break up the colour and, although now frequently done in pale colours, whites and off-whites, it derives from the commoner kinds of graining done in the 18th and 19th centuries when wood in general was suggested rather than a specific type of wood being imitated. Although the brush strokes are now more pronounced than they would have been in the 18th century, they create an effect similar to that achieved with the 18th century paints in which the pigments were less finely ground and so the medium was not as smooth as it is today.

The object of stippling is much the same, but instead of the paint being applied in sweeps and strokes, the fresh paint is stamped on with a stippler, that is a brush with a rectangular head. It is not known when this technique was introduced into England, but it is probably Italian in origin, being a useful way of imitating effects of stone on plaster. It is a technique that requires at least two painters working in close collaboration for, as one applies the colour, the other has to stipple it while the edges are "alive"; once they start to dry they form hard edges that cannot be stippled out.

With glaze painting, one or more very thin coats of the final colour is laid on a white or pale coloured ground, so that the ground glows through the translucent top coat. The number of coats depends on the degree of translucency required. It is not known when the technique was introduced into English decoration, but it was certainly familiar by the middle of the 18th century, for Dossie in his *Handmaid to the Arts* gives a description of it: "The most considerable of the more general properties of colours after purity and durableness . . . are transparency and opacity: for according to their condition, with respect to these qualities, they are fitted to answer very different kinds of purposes. Colours which became transparent in oil, such as lake, Prussian blue, and brown pink are frequently used without the admixture of white, or any other opake pigment; by which means, the teint of the ground on which they are laid retains in some degree its force; and the real colour, produced in the painting, is the combined effect of both. This is called glazing, and the pigments indued with such property of becoming transparent in oil, are called *glazing colours* . . . The property of glazing . . . is of so much importance . . . that no other method can equally well produce the same effect in many cases, either with regard to the force, beauty, or softness of the colouring . . . Colours which have no transparency, such as vermillion, King's yellow, etc. are said to cover . . ."

It has never gone out of favour, but it is a method that is very difficult to analyse through scrapes, because the glazes are so thin that they hardly ever survive and also because they are effected by the action of the oils in the paint.

Nowadays it is fashionable to finish off a glazed effect by drawing the brush in vertical sweeps, a development that has come to be known as dragging. It is a form of brush graining, but it is carried out more boldly and can produce an effective result in a large room.

To anyone concerned with restoration who encounters these techniques used in historic interiors today, the questions that immediately spring to mind are firstly "are the results authentic" and "are the methods authentic". The answer to both cannot be an unequivocal "yes", for the mediums are not exactly the same as those used in the past, and consequently results have to be achieved in a different way. Nor indeed have the methods been conceived for restorations: they have been worked out for the decoration of private houses before there was a demand for the kind of "academic restorations" that is now developing in England. However they do correspond to the methods described in the books mentioned at the beginning of the chapter.

For instance, Butcher's description in 1821 of how to paint a room white "three times in oil" is a very similar process to that described here, for the alteration of the mixture of each coat gives a result similar to that of the two undercoats and top coat.[7]

In France in the mid 18th century it was the practice to use many more undercoats in an elaborately decorated room, particularly when water colour rather than oil paint was used, and it was undoubtedly this care for detail that produced the very subtle effects of light and colour on old boiserie. In Michel Gallet's description of the *cipolin* method, he lists five stages: the first was to treat the natural wood with a boiling mixture; then followed between 7 and 9 coats of Bougival white carefully polished with doeskin; next the undercoats were smoothed with pumice, and the carvings and mouldings were carved out again; and then the final colour was put on.[8]

We have not discovered any bill for English work listing so many coats, but David Adamson's bill for painting at Osterley, which can be taken as good evidence about high class work, lists as many as six coats on occasion. However what is particularly interesting about this account is that it suggests that more oil paint than we would expect was used and that there was a definite attempt to create contrasts between flat and shiny paint. Four coats were the usual number used, but on the dining room ceiling there were five coats of oil "finished Pink colour" and on the ceiling of the principal staircase, the ornaments were done in five coats of oil dead white and the grounds in six coats of oil picked out in green.

In 18th century letters there are no doubt many unpublished accounts of painting a room, but one given by Rowland Belasis in a letter dated April 10, 1767, to Lord Fauconberg who was then involved in remodelling Newburgh Priory in Yorkshire is of considerable interest. "While I was at Mr. Southcotes at Woburn Farm", he wrote, "I saw a Room painted Blue, as the man seem'd to understand his Business I took notice of his methods with a design to give you what information I could, the method is as follows he first put up Coarse lining & pasted upon it the common Light Brown paper, after that the same sort of paper that was put up in your Drawing Room, the room was painted three times over, & everytime as much paint was made as would paint the room once, & I was told that they put no more size into the paint than was necessary to fix the Blue & hinder it from rubbing off with the hand. This method succeeded so well that it is all one colour, & looks extremely well . . ."

One important difference between old and modern methods is in the nature of the top coat. Today commercial oil paints can be bought with a matt, an egg shell or a gloss finish, but that is a modern development. In Butcher's day the matt surface could only be achieved by adding an extra coat of "flatting, or dead white, which is to be laid on the above 3rd colour, or 2nd colour, as you think proper." For this "take Nottingham-white, and mix it with turpentine only," but a little nut-oil could be used because it was a quick drier. When mixed this had to be used straight away, because "if it stands to set, it will leave a mark."

This was confirmed by Wyatt Papworth in 1857 for in a lecture to the RIBA he described methods of painting and described the object of the flatting coat as "to prevent the gloss or glaze of the oil and to obtain a flat dead appearance . . . It must be understood that a flatting coat is not considered as a coat of paint; being wholly of turpentine, it is by exposure to the air evaporated, leaving a thin coat of pigment which is only required for effect, not for use."[9] And Haldane when giving his estimates quoted for 4 coats unflatted and 4 coats plus flatting.[10]

It is not absolutely clear when the fashion for a flat or matt finish came in, but it may have been in the 1720s or '30s as part of the Palladian innovations and was then generally called dead colour. The London Tradesman refers to "When it was the Taste to paint the House with Landskip Figures, and in Imitation of varigated Woods and Stone, then it was necessary to serve an Apprenticeship to the Business, and required no mean Genius in Painting to make a compleat Workman; but since the Mode has altered, and Houses are only daubed with dead Colours, every Labourer may execute it as well as the most eminent Painter."[11]

Not only did the taste for graining die, but also the fashion for lavish use of varnishes that complemented the taste for the high polish of walnut, and this explains why dead white is not given in lists of colours. Dossie, for instance, mentions white flake, white lead, pearl white, Troy white, egg-shell whites, calcined hartshorn and Flowers of bismatt, but not *dead white*.

However in the Osterley bill to which reference has already been made the terms "oil flat white" and "oil dead white" both occur. Presumably they are interchangeable.

Just as modern oil paint is a rather different material from that used in the 18th and 19th century and has to be handled differently, distemper and water paint referred to in old accounts is not the same as modern distemper, for the latter is oil bound. The older form is sometimes now called soft distemper and its basis is ball whiting broken down over heat with size and water. It gives a drier, fresco-like effect that appeals today but did not necessarily suit 18th century taste: for according to a mid 18th century dictionary in the Victoria and Albert Museum "The greatest disadvantage of distemper is, that it has no glittering, and all its colours look dead." But unlike true fresco as used in Italy, which is done in a water medium on damp plaster, so that the colour becomes part of the plaster, it is applied to dry plaster.

The effect of oil bound distemper is not unlike that of emulsion paint, which has generally superseded it in recent years. The range of colours available in emulsion is broad, but it seems impossible to achieve subtleties of texture with it, and it is for that reason that it is not recommended for the kind of work described in this chapter.

The Problems of Painting Architectural Decoration

The complexity of the mediums and methods of painting is matched by the need for careful planning when painting a room of architectural distinction. Just as completely solid colour is seldom effective in a large period room, a single tone from floor to ceiling seldom produces the best results for it does not seem to enhance the classical language of the mouldings. However as classical architecture is by its nature highly adaptable and infinitely varied in its details, there is not just one way of painting it, and it would be both wrong and dangerous to try to lay down a rule. And whereas it is not impossible to trace fashions in colours and patterns and relate them to accepted architectural styles, it would be rash to try to differentiate between, let us say, a Palladian and a neo-classical way of painting a room. Sometimes one suspects a room was painted at a certain date, but as our knowledge stands at present it is impossible to give precise guidelines.

As in all 18th century decoration, the main point is to create a satisfying balance between the different elements of a room, while allowing each architectual element to make its proper statement. This is a matter of being sufficiently familiar with the architectural language to know when to play up contrasts of light and shade, where to make definitions and where to create sufficient emphasis to catch the eye. Moreover it is vital that not only the director of the work, but the painter should understand the object: it is difficult to create the right balance of tones even when the painter is experienced and understands the idea; but if he is reluctant to see what is involved, it is better to abandon the attempt.

This is not just a modern problem. Now that few people are prepared to learn the Orders, it is not surprising that most painters should find this type of work fiddling and uneconomic, but the kind of detail we are about to describe was invariably done by well trained and experienced craftsmen. The painters, for instance, who executed Robert Adam's schemes, were highly skilled, and as we know from the Osterley bill, their work was expensive by the standards of the time. However, often when one sees an Adam house today, it is obvious that their work has been repainted or touched up in the remote or recent past by less skilled hands, possibly in the wrong medium, and in the process the original magic and balance has been upset, if not completely destroyed.

The basic principles of painting a room of classical design are best understood if a room of appropriate character with or without pilasters as in the drawing of Plate XXVIII is compared with, let us say, James Gibbs's Corinthian order as engraved in 1728, or at least a simplified version of the complete order.

The wall surface, whether it is wood panelled or plaster, corresponds to the base, shaft and capital of the column. The dado and skirting correspond to the pedestal, and the entablature corresponds to that of the full order.

When painting such a room, the flat of the skirting should be the darkest tone, and if not marbled, be painted a blue-berry black rather than a dead black. In a neo-classical room the skirting was sometimes painted in a darker shade of the colour used for the main walls. In one of Adam's designs for the Eating Parlour at Headfort, for instance, the skirting is dark green and the walls light green.

The skirting mouldings and the dado mouldings should correspond with the cornice and architrave of the entablature. If the entablature is enriched, the mouldings of the skirting and the dado are also usually enriched; and so if the former is picked out in gold or with colour, the latter should be too. The dado itself is usually white, but if it is painted a colour as in the Saloon at Clandon, a shade darker than that of the main fields of the walls is used instead. Provided that the colours used, or the tones of the same colour if there is only one, are properly balanced, the relationship of horizontals and verticals will be correct.

Frequently one sees a cornice in a Palladian room painted as if it was part of the ceiling instead of the wall, and if this is done it is quite impossible to create a right balance. However it is dangerous to be categorical about this in earlier rooms for there are possible precedents in the Commonwealth and Charles II periods for treating the entablature as part of the ceiling: at Forde Abbey the cornice and frieze are part of the ceiling in the Saloon but the architrave is part of the wall (Fig. 169): at Ham, in the Blue Drawing Room (Plate XX) the cornice and frieze are white plaster, like the ceiling, but the architrave is the top of the panelling and is grained and gilded; and the same happens in the Marble Parlour. Of course this may be the mistake of a later painter, for in the Queen's Room at Sudbury the whole of the alabaster

169. THE SALOON AT FORDE ABBEY, DORSET. A mid 17th century interior where the cornice and frieze are treated as part of the ceiling and the architrave as part of the wall.

entablature to the overmantel had been painted over to match the rest of the entablature (Figs. 170, 171). [12]

The most difficult part is the picking out of the entablature and here the cost of the work may be a limiting factor, for the time involved is even more considerable than the price of gold leaf. The example illustrated is marked for elaborate picking out, and this would only be carried out in a state room like the Green Drawing Room at Clandon (Plate XXIX). The entablature is divided into three sections, the cornice at the top, the frieze in the middle and the architrave at the bottom.

Taking the cornice first, it is suggested that the fillet at the top should be gilt in order to define the break with the bed of the ceiling. The next member to pick out is the cyma reversa, which should be gilt in part to show up its enrichment, as should the lower cyma reversa. If the modillions are carved, the only parts that need to be picked out are the scrolls at each side of the acanthus leaves, but the spine of each acanthus leaf and its tips can also be gilded: the bed, which the bracket supports, may also be gilt as may the complete patera. And if it is desired, the bed to which the patera is stuck, may be painted a colour: this is usually the same colour as used in the ground of the frieze. Part of the ovolo moulding may also be picked out, so that the eggs stand out from a gilt or coloured ground. The faces of the dentills and the

170, 171. THE CHIMNEYPIECE AND OVERMANTEL IN THE QUEEN'S ROOM AT SUDBURY HALL, DERBYSHIRE BEFORE AND AFTER RESTORATION. The alabaster cornice had been painted over, so that it matched the main frieze and so went in with the ceiling rather than with the wall treatment. The room is illustrated in Figure 233.

astragal may be gilt too, so that the latter emphasises the slight break between the cornice and the frieze.

The frieze, if it is ornamented, may be given a coloured ground or the ornament may be gilded. Innumerable variants occur, but among the unusual ones is the use of an olive green for the ornament in the frieze of the Drawing Room at Blair Castle. With a doric frieze, the ground of the metopes may be coloured to emphasise the two plane effect of the architecture.

The architrave requires less picking out than the cornice, but it is usual to gild the fillet that marks the break between the frieze and the architrave and to partly pick out the lower cyma reversa and also the bead of the bead and reel ornament if it exists.

A door and its architrave should be treated with similar care and its enrichment painted in the same way as the main entablature. One effective way is to paint the door itself in three tones of a colour: if this is done, the stiles and rails should be in the darkest tone and the panels in the middle tone; the mouldings should be in the lightest tone or picked out in gilt or in white or occasionally in a contrasting colour. These tones need very careful marking out, for if the relationship between the colours is not right, the whole door can look out of key and the panels appear to leap out in front of the stiles and rails.

The same method can be applied when painting a panelled room whether the walls are stuccoed or wainscotted. But, as can be seen in the Saloon at Clandon, the colour of the dado has to be taken into account (Plates XXVII, XXX). If two tones of colour are used for the stiles and the rails and for the fields of the panels, and a cane colour is used for picking out the mouldings, the dado looks more effective if painted a darker tone of the colour used for the stiles and rails.

The elaboration of window architraves and shutters depends not only on architectural style, but, as we have seen, on changes in curtain style as well. Generally the degree of enrichment is the same as on the doors and door architraves, and this should be reflected in the painting and any picking out that is done, but it should be remembered that the architrave will be largely hidden if draw curtains are used. One of the points of a festoon curtain was that it revealed the architrave, but when in the late 18th century the draw curtain became fashionable, it was no longer necessary to enrich the architrave.

As yet no 18th century instructions for painting a room in the way we have described have been discovered, and the only reference to the use of three tones of colour is among the Osterley papers. However there are many rooms still existing which provide all the visual evidence that is needed, and sometimes the evidence survives in a more durable form than paint. It is more than likely that Inigo Jones understood the principles, and that as a man of the theatre and as an admirer of mannerist architecture he would have exploited them. We cannot point to any interior by him that demonstrates this, because none survive in an untouched condition, but these qualities are fully apparent in the facades of the pavilions at Stoke Park, Northamptonshire, almost certainly designed by him for Sir Francis Crane, the manager of the Mortlake tapestry manufactory. There, ironstone is used for the podium, the giant pilasters, the columns, the window architraves and the cornice and architrave of the entablature; and a white Weldon stone is used for the main walls, the capitals and the frieze.

Georgian taste was more orthodox, but the appreciation of colour and texture was based on the foundations Jones laid. And some of the characteristic devices appear surprisingly early. The Balcony Room at Dyrham (Plate XXXVII), although now much darkened, appears to be in more or less original condition and so provides an excellent illustration of balance in colour and paint at the end of the 17th century. Perhaps the two best examples from the next generation are the Cupola Room at Kensington Palace (Fig. 172) and the Marble

XXVI. FRINGES AND GIMPS.
Top: gothic gimp, a reweaving of
an old gimp. *Middle left* and *right*:
"shell" gimp. *Middle centre*: ornamented bullion fringe made for
Nicholas Stone's Hall at Cornbury,
Oxfordshire. *Below left*: a silk
trellis fringe. *Below right*: a fringe
with black "flies" on the hangers.

XXVII. THE SALOON AT CLANDON.
Scrapes revealed the colouring of
the entablature and the lightest
and darkest blue used for the
walls. The colouring of the ceiling
is original as is that of the
entablature. The walls have been
repainted. The marbling of the
plaster overmantel was done to
match the marble chimneypiece.

Parlour at Houghton (Plates XXXI, XXXII). At Houghton the chimneypiece
and overmantel with its relief by Rysbrack are in white marble and they are
set against a ground of grey-white marble. Black and gold *porto venere* is used
for the blocking course to the columns and for their pedestals; the shafts of
the columns are *brèche violet*; the skirting mouldings, dado mouldings, base
of the columns and the capitals are white marble (and the architrave and cornice
of the frieze are also white). The rich carving and gilding of the frieze balances
the darker tone of the shaft of the column. Within the two arches that flank
the chimneypiece the marble facing is cut in two sections to imply a dado and
so a division in the main wall, the join lining up with the top of the cyma
reversa that heads the dado moulding on the column. A similar approach to
columns is apparent in the serving tables and the lining of the back wall. This
is a concept of the utmost sophistication, and, although unrivalled, could be
taken as an impeccable precedent.

At Kensington one finds the same principles worked out in paint. The
scheme is principally in an off white or stone colour heightened with bistre
and gold, and great play is made with tromp l'oeil. The fluting of the pilasters,
for instance, is all in tromp and so is the carving of the mouldings to the bases,
as is all the carving of the mouldings of the entablature. The top fillet is gilt,
so are the tromp masks on the cyma recta, the carved cyma reversa, the rosettes
on the corona, the ovolo, the dentils and cyma reversa. The frieze is picked
out in tromp; so is the fillet, the cyma reversa and the bead and reel of the
architrave. And to add to the subtlety and vitality of the whole scheme much

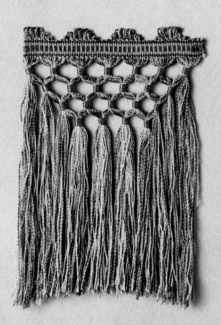

CYMA RECTA
CYMA REVERTA
CORONA

CYLLS
CAVETTO

FRIEZE

BROKEN WHITE

A ROOM OF THE FIRST HALF OF THE EIGHTEENTH CENTURY

D

L

BROKEN WHITE

L

BROKEN WHITE

D

L

BROKEN WHITE

D

BROKEN WHITE

L

L

BROKEN WHITE

BROKEN WHITE

D

L

D

D

BROKEN WHITE

of the gilding is not solid but hatched.

The use of colour as revealed at Clandon is also of the greatest interest (Plate XXVII). Areas of both the darkest and lightest blue were discovered, the former as one would expect on the dado, and the palest in the recessed panels; the middle blue used for the walls creates a balance between them. The skirting is blue black; the skirting mouldings and the dado mouldings are a cane colour, and this is also used for the mouldings to the recessed panels, on the door architraves and as the main tone in the entablature. However as there is no gilding in the room, a stone colour is used for the cyma reversa in the cornice, for the modillions, ovolo, dentils and lower cyma reversa and again in the architrave for its cyma reversa and its three astragals of bead and reel. The ground of the frieze relates to the tone of the dado. The use of Italian red for the grounds to the paterae in the cornice is an unusual detail.

The gilding of the entablature in the Green Drawing Room is also a good illustration. Here all is original except the top fillet to the cornice added in 1968 to increase the sense of definition between the wall and ceiling and the whitening of the ribbons of the pulvinated frieze.

The picking out of enriched door architraves was planned to create a similar kind of balance, and there could be no more splendid example of this than in the main door in the saloon at Houghton. How the tradition continued is well illustrated by the painting of the doorcases in the Tapestry Room at West Wycombe (Plate XXXIII). A slightly later example of great subtlety is to be seen in the state bedroom at Blickling in Norfolk, which was redecorated in 1779 (Plates XXXIV, XXXV, XXXVI). Here the alternate leaves in the dado rail and in the mouldings of the architraves of the doorcases are picked out, as are the leaves in the friezes of the doorcases, where they are of two patterns. It is seldom that such well planned and well preserved picking out survives, and the answer could be that it is double gilt.

It would be logical to presume that the coming of the neo-classical style revolutionised or at least modified ways of painting. However the basic principles of the kind we have been enumerating continued to be followed. The colours changed, of course, and, again in pursuit of harmony and balance, Adam used much more colour on his ceilings. His best painted work continued to have a painterly vitality as appears on the recently uncovered ceiling from the Adelphi at the Victoria and Albert Museum, but probably generally there was a tendency to a drier more precise finish than would have appealed to Kent's generation. Doubtless more will be discovered about this, but at this stage it would be dangerous to divide the 18th century into two distinct periods.

Gilding

Gilding is and always was a great extravagance, and anyone considering using it in architectural decoration should take warning from 18th century bills not only for the sums involved but from the proportional relationship of the gilding accounts to bills for other aspects of decoration. For instance the value placed on the stucco of the Saloon ceiling at Cannons in 1725 was £250 and on the gilding £155; Thornhill's painting that was incorporated was valued at £500.[13] When the drawing room at Osterley was painted in the early 1770s, the painting of the ceiling cost £66. 12s. 11¼d.; and the gilding was no less than £262. 3s. 3d. If the proper effect is to be achieved, there is no cheap way that can be recommended, and it cannot be too frequently stressed that gold paint should never be used for any object of even the most modest quality. Unfortunately this is not understood in England; indeed there are few craftsmen and few patrons who understand that art at all.

There are two kinds of gilding used on plaster and wood, water-gilding and oil gilding, and, just as their grounds are differently prepared, they are used

XXVIII. A SECTION OF A PANELLED ROOM. A drawing done by Peter Hood to show the use of different tones to bring out the architectural character of a room of Gibbsian type and to create a sense of balance.

to achieve slightly different effects. Broadly speaking in England oil gilding is used for architectural decoration and water gilding for furniture and picture frames.

In the case of water-gilding the carcase has to be built up with many coats of white gesso, and after each coat has been allowed to dry and harden, it is rubbed down to a satin-like smoothness. When a perfect surface has been achieved, it is finally given a coat of coloured bole and this influences the colour of the gilding as well as providing the gold leaf with a suitable base. When the bole has dried and hardened, it is merely wetted with weak sized water (hence water gilding) so that the gold leaf, which has been cut with a special knife to the appropriate size, can adhere. In John Smith's day a book, which consisted of 24 leaves 3 inches square, cost 2s. and he calculated this was enough to cover 216 inches of work. The books are still of the same dimension, but beaten thinner.

When the leaf is first laid, it gives a shaggy appearance for there are always particles of gold that have not stuck, and this has to be brushed off to leave a clean smooth surface that is ready for burnishing with agate. It is this ability to be burnished that is the great point of water-gilding: a skilled gilder can achieve a variety of effects in a small area by burnishing some mouldings to get the maximum play of light and leaving others matt, so creating a contrast of light and shade. In addition he can tool or cross hatch the ground or gild over sand to provide greater contrasts. Indeed from its very nature water-gilding is not suited to large flat areas and is best seen on a modelled surface.

Usually only one layer of gold is used, but from various 18th century accounts and books it seems that when a very rich effect was desired more than one might be applied. For instance, the mirror from the Tapestry Room at Croome Court is described in the accounts as "Gilt in the very best Double Burnish'd Gold", a process described by Sheraton as follows: After the burnishing of the first coat "proceed to a second lay or coat of gold as lay the first, which will cover all the defects of the first lay occasioned by burnishing, and having waited till this second coat be dry, burnish as before; and if there be any defects of gold, such places must be repaired. Some recommend to have the work done three times over, but twice will do as well, if carefully done."[14]

As in all things there are exceptions, and in two quite important categories of furniture water-gilding does not seem to have been used. Not all the gilding on early 18th century walnut and mahogany was water-gilt: generally speaking where the wood was veneered and very highly polished, the parcel gilding would be done in the way we have described, but on certain famous pieces like the chairs attributed to Giles Grendey at Longford Castle, which are heavily carved, the picking-out is done in oil-gilding. And the same is true of the architectural side tables of the Kent period. Rather surprisingly the very rich chairs (Fig. 173) that Chippendale made for Sir Lawrence Dundas's house in Arlington Street are described in the account "Gilt oil gold".[15]

In addition to furniture of this type, much 18th century furniture that we see today gilded was originally intended to be painted and picked out in contrasting colours. By the early 19th century this was not only no longer fashionable, but owing to the fragile nature of painted furniture had become shabby and was not considered opulent enough and so it was gilded. To quote only one documented example, the Chippendale furniture in the drawing room at Burton Constable, which was originally blue and white, was gilded by Thomas Ward in 1830.[16] Sometimes such furniture was merely oil gilt or, even worse, painted with gold paint by the house carpenter.

Oil gilding is a simpler process and therefore cheaper in time, but the amount of gold used is the same as in water-gilding. Again the ground needs to be smooth, but it does not have to be as fine, and instead of being prepared with layers of gesso, is merely painted. Over this size is laid on and it is usually tinted with a colour to influence gold. Some sizes can be ready for use in half

173. A CHAIR MADE BY CHIPPENDALE
FOR SIR LAWRENCE DUNDAS.
Surprisingly it was described in
the original accounts as "Gilt oil
gold". (One chair from the set is in
the Victoria and Albert Museum.)

an hour, but in others it may take as long as 72 hours to reach the tacky stage
that is right for the application of gold leaf. The basic principle here is the
slower the drying of the size the greater the brilliance of the gold, a 24 hour
size being acceptable for good quality work. Oil gilding can never be burnished
to achieve the flash seen in the best water gilding, but a 24 hour size produces
a sufficient brilliance, even if with time it gets imperceptibly darker, particularly
if a room is much used.

On the other hand it is a much less fragile finish than water gilding and if
care is taken can be revived by washing. Water gilding on the other hand can
never be dampened. The protection that can be used with both techniques is
to add a final thin coat of parchment size. This was often done in the past and
it is still done today. Among the documented examples are chairs supplied by
Samuel Norman for the Crimson Drawing Room at Moor Park and listed in
an inventory of 1766 as follows: "10 very rich Elbow Chairs Gilt complete
the best Burnish'd Gold and Varnish'd 5 times over . . ."[17]

Probably the most extensive example of the 18th century use of oil gilding
in architectural decoration is at Houghton, where throughout the state rooms
the carved mahogany ornament is parcel gilt. There the effect is now one of
sober richness for inevitably over the years some of the original brilliance has
faded and the gilding has toned down. A slightly later example of great interest
is the Norfolk House Music Room with its *soi-disant* French-style panelling:
even if its proportions do not proclaim its English execution, to an experienced

187

eye its gilding also gives it away for it has the dull uniformity of old oil gilding and none of the contrast and flash of even the shabbiest water gilding. Unfortunately the original bill does not mention the type of gilding.[18]

Today we are slowly recovering from a timorous attitude to gilding that developed in the first quarter of this century as a reaction against its over use and misuse from the 1820s onwards, but we still find it difficult to appreciate the Baroque use of different colour golds as in the Double Cube Room at Wilton. Occasionally references to colours of gilding occur in 18th century documents,[19] but few examples survive and today very few colours are made. Indeed because of the scarcity of English and French leaf, most of the best leaf used today is Italian, and when used by the furniture trade is usually rubbed down to let the bole influence the colour much more strongly than would have been the case in the 18th century in England.

Nor do we make much use of lacquered silver, a technique frequently used in the late 17th and early 18th century to simulate gold. This was done not only because it was a cheaper method, but it gave a translucency and depth that is attractive. In his *Art of Painting in Oyl* Smith says "the common Painters do now generally in gilding use more silver than gold, in most works that are not much exposed to the Air, to which they afterwards give the colour of Gold, by means of the lake varnish." Recently the technique was revived at Sudbury Hall where a very large picture frame on the staircase was in need of extensive restoration.

Untreated silver was almost never used for architectural decoration because of its tendency to tarnish, and we have come across few references to it. However, as always, there are exceptions, a notable one being the Yellow Damask Drawing Room at Harewood House, Yorkshire, which was fitted up by Chippendale in the early 1770s.[20] The chairs were yellow and white, the upholstery and hangings yellow damask; the fillet was "finished in Burnished Silver & varnished", the cornice was picked out in silver, the girandoles were silvered and so were the cloak-pins. When George Lucy was making improvements at Charlecote in the 1750s it was suggested that he should have doors and cornice picked out in silver; but he refused, because it would tarnish in a room where there was not a constant fire. Apart from the silvered stands occasionally found supporting late 17th century lacquer cabinets, silver is not often seen on furniture, but at Erthig there is an outstanding silver gesso table, and looking glass made about 1725.[21]

The reaction against gilding in this century is not the first there has been since 1660, but again, as with so many fashions, it is not easy to be precise about the cycles, because it is largely a matter of chance whether one finds illuminating comments. The *London Tradesman*, for instance, says: "as Gilding at present seems to be out of Fashion, there is Employment but for few Hands who do not understand carving . . .;"[22] but perhaps this was based on the lightening of architectural decoration in general as well as on the fashion for painted furniture. Adam too, except in some of his most opulent rooms in houses like Syon and Osterley, used less gilding than we presume today, and, although some of his ceilings are now picked out in gold, the more robust ones were probably originally painted white, or in tones of white or combinations of colours. This is borne out both by Lady Mary Coke, who felt it was worth pointing out that there was no gilding at Luton Hoo[23] and by Horace Walpole, who noted that "there was not a morsel of gilding at Portman House" in 1782. A surviving example of this taste is to be seen at Heveningham where there is no gilding in any of the original rooms.

The revival came with the French decorators working for Holland and the Prince of Wales's circle in the late 1780s and 90s, and thereafter there was an increasing use of gold, working up to a crescendo in the late 1820s, '30s, and '40s, in such schemes as the state rooms at Stafford House, the 6th Duke of Devonshire's new rooms at Chatsworth and so on. Not only were new rooms more highly gilded, but earlier rooms that appeared too sober were enriched. At Attingham, for instance, within 20 years of its completion, a new generation, finding Steuart's refined decoration too cool, added brilliant but coarse fillets to the walls, picked out the entablatures and added opulently gilded furniture.

For gilding metal an entirely different process was used; and "was" should be emphasised, because mercury gilding, or fire gilding as it is sometimes called, is forbidden as there is a danger to health from the fumes given off by mercury. When this was done, the intensely heated piece of unpainted metal was dipped in an amalgam of gilt and mercury. The heat made the pores of the metal open, and as the metal cooled down the pores closed up again gripping the gold, so that it was ready for burnishing when cool. This was a skill at which the French excelled and which, with the exception of Matthew Boulton and the French *fondeurs* working for Holland, was seldom equalled in England. Today when metal is gilded, it is usually done electrically.

Many aspects of the uses of gilding have already been discussed in the section on *Painting Architectural Decoration*, but there are several that deserve separate treatment, including the gilding of pulvinated friezes.

The frieze in the Green Drawing Room at Clandon has already been mentioned (Plate XXIX). Here both the bay leaves and the ribbons were gilded, but when the room was restored, it was decided to whiten the ribbons to create a contrast and to match much of the other detailing of the entablature. A slight contrast of this kind is effective, but there is a danger that the result will become spotty if more elaborate picking out is done. However, sometimes the central spine of each leaf and the acorns, if it is an oak leaf frieze, or the berries, if it is of bay, are gilded.

The gilding of a fluted column can be done in two ways: this is not a question of right or wrong but of the effect that is desired. If a very rich effect is desired, the flutes should be gilded as in the State Bedroom at Blickling (Plate XXXV): the gilding of a concave surface and the contrast of light and shade that exists in each flute both heighten its impact. However to achieve a more restrained result it is better to gild the surfaces between the flutes because not only are they much narrower, but they are convex and do not create such a brilliant effect as can be seen in the boudoir at Attingham (Plate III).

Graining and Marbling

The author of the *London Tradesman*'s lament about the decline in skill in house painting in the second quarter of the 18th century needs to be seen in relation to changes in fashion and the Palladian reaction against the kind of finishes given to wainscot and plaster throughout the second half of the 17th and first years of the 18th centuries. The tradition of such elaborate forms goes back to at least the latter part of the 16th century, but we have had to confine ourselves to fashions in graining and marbling about 1700 and about 1800.

There are modern accounts of methods available including John P. Parry's *Graining and Marbling* (1949), but anyone who specialises in graining and marbling develops his own ways and secrets, and it is difficult to generalise. The basis of marbling is for the painter to work up from a ground colour that relates to the predominant colour of the marble that is being imitated or suggested. Thus a dove-grey marble or *bordillo* would usually be grounded in pale grey, and the figuring and veining worked in paler and darker tones of grey, with extra touches of very dark grey and white. This can be done both in oil colour or water colour, and if in the latter beer is often used as a medium. To marble successfully in water colour, you have to work quite fast, because it has to be completed before the ground dries. The first task is to brush in the ground in broken tones, and stipple it with the end of the brush, so that one tone comes through another. At this stage it is possible to keep the ground damp by dabbing with a sponge.

Having got the ground in, a start is then made on the composition of the veining, which should not all run in the same direction. This is brushed in with a trembling hand to get a broken line. To get the colours to blend a badger-softener is used, and if the veins show signs of running, quick use of a sponge will repair the damage. The figuring is built up with a combination of brush work, softener and sponging.

The two main dangers with marbling are the tendency to carry on too long and over vein it. The other is not to have observed marble closely enough, and so not to know how the veining works through different planes. Veining in marbling should not continue in the same line through a moulding, but be broken as would a piece of real marble.

When dried, it can be protected with varnish or a thin coat of beeswax.

The basic methods of graining are identical to those of marbling, the craftsman using his skill to copy examples from nature. However one speciality that should be mentioned is over-graining. By this is meant over-graining a natural wood like oak to simulate a finer one like walnut, the oak grain being exploited and enriched and allowed to show through the painted glaze. An ambitious example that has been recently restored is the Galerie Henri II at Fontainebleau, where the old wainscot and seats below Rossi and Primaticcio's panels have been over-grained to simulate walnut.

Although many of the old methods are still in use, illustrations of the best historical examples have never been collected together, but many have appeared in *Country Life* and references to a great number are given in Edward Croft-Murray's *Decorative Painting in England*.

Some of the survivors from the 1660s and 1670s are surprisingly crude, which may be partly lack of skill, but also it is because not all painters were trying to create a naturalistic effect that would deceive the eye; some wanted to create an attractive texture and colour that would suggest rather than deceive. And to the Baroque mind there was the extra pleasure of having been taken in and then admiring the skill with which the deception was made.

The graining of the King's Dining Room at Drayton is a fairly straightforward attempt to play up the essential character of the early bolection panelling to emphasise the differences in the working of the grain in the fields, the stiles and rails. At Ham there is much greater variety of effects, but considering the emphasis on display in the furniture and the upholstery, the results are crude. Some rooms are brush grained with the mouldings gilded, others are marbled white, but the oddest effects are in the Duchesse's Private Closet and the Green Drawing Room. It is likely that the graining is intended to suggest olive wood for it has a large dark figure with splashes of gold-leaf underpainting that break through the top glaze.

Towards the end of the century not only did the painters become much more skilled, but they attempted much more complex schemes combining imitations of different woods and marbles. It might be thought that these were complete fancy on the painter's part, but Celia Fiennes described the hall at Chippenham Park as being "wainscotted with Walnut tree the pannells and rims round with mulberry tree that is lemon coullour and the mouldings beyond it round are of a swete outlandish wood not much differing from Cedar but of a finer graine."[24] At Hill Court, near Ross-on-Wye, not only is the Cedar Parlour done in this fashion, but there is a room painted in comparable style. In the Cedar Parlour, the fields of the panels are cedar, the mouldings oak, and the stiles and rails veneered in walnut. In the Painted Room (Figs. 174, 175) the fields of the panels are painted to simulate curiously figured marbles of the types occasionally seen incorporated in 17th century Florentine cabinets, the mouldings in which they are framed are painted to simulate white marble, and the stiles are painted in a chinoiserie style. The whole effect is now bright because the room was restored a few years ago and the discoloured varnish removed

174. THE PAINTED ROOM AT HILL COURT, HEREFORDSHIRE. Painted about 1700, the fields of the panels simulate figured marbles; the mouldings simulate white marble and the styles are painted in a chinoiserie manner.

175. A DETAIL OF A DOOR IN THE HILL COURT ROOM.

and redone. At first glance it may seem a little too polished, but this is probably very close to the effect intended, for Stalker and Parker say "What can be more surprizing, than to have our Chambers overlaid with Varnish more glossy and reflecting than polished Marble."[25]

The Hill Court room may have been painted by Isaac Bayley, who decorated the hall at Stoke Edith in 1705. There the fields of the panels below Thornhill's decorations were much larger, but they were also done in imitation of marble. He asked 1/- a yard for cedar colour and walnut tree neatly done, 1/6 for black marble and white in nut oil, 2/- for greenstone, 3/6 for rockstone, which must be the type seen at Hill Court, and 5/- for lapis lazuli. And by chance this can be compared with two other bills that are more or less contemporary. Among Lady Wilbraham's papers is a list from a London painter called Spurling in 1691: he wanted 1/- for walnuttree, cedar and olive, 10d. for oak wainscot, 2d. for stonework and 18d. for white and veined marble. Crisp Burton of Nantwich, on the other hand, seems to have been more expensive: he wanted 1/8 for marble and stone colour, 1/4 for walnut, 1/6 for olive and 1/4 for cedar and oak.[26]

Graining and marbling were by no means confined to large and fashionable houses, and often it seems different rooms in a house might be painted in different ways. For variety perhaps the best example is Great Hundridge Manor, Buckinghamshire (Fig. 176), where no less than three rooms retain this kind of decoration. In the parlour the fields of the panels simulate walnut, the pilasters and mouldings are marbled and the stiles and rails are decorated to simulate Japan. In one bedroom the fields of the panels are marbled and the stiles and rails are japanned; and in another room the fields are "rock stone". The parlour of the Stanton Harcourt Parsonage is even more elaborate (Fig. 177): the fields of the panels imitate walnut veneer; the mouldings are marbled green; the stiles imitate porphyry; the skirting and chimneypiece imitate purple marble. Another successful scheme using marbling and chinoiserie decoration is in the upper room at Swangrove, a house on the Badminton estate in Gloucestershire (Fig. 178); and at Old Battersea House, London (Fig. 179), the surrounds of the panels in Lady St. John's Parlour are decorated in a chinoiserie style.

Of work on a grander scale some of the best examples are at Dyrham. The Balcony Room (Plate XXXVII) has an elaborate wainscot, which, fortunately,

176. THE PARLOUR AT GREAT HUNDRIDGE MANOR, BUCKINGHAMSHIRE. The fields of the panels simulate walnut, the pilasters and mouldings are marbled and the stiles and rails are decorated to simulate japan.

177. THE PARLOUR AT STANTON
HARCOURT PARSONAGE, OXFORDSHIRE.
The fields of the panels simulate
walnut veneer, the mouldings are
marbled green, the stiles imitate
porphyry, and the skirting and
the chimneypiece are marbled.

preserves its original grained and marbled decoration, albeit darkened by time
and coats of linseed oil and varnish. The pine panelling is grained to simulate
walnut, the pilasters simulate porphyry and the mouldings are picked out in
gold (Plate XXXVIII). If restored, it would be possible to get a clearer idea
of the original balance and also of the medium used. On the walls of the
staircase there is excellent marbled decoration, with the blocks picked out.

The fashion for graining went out during the Palladian period, partly
because illusionism as such went out of fashion, partly because woodwork was
reduced to a subsidiary role and partly because the range of colours changed.
And it remained out of fashion until the late 1780s, when Henry Holland
introduced a form of the Louis XVI style to the circle of the Prince of Wales
(Figs. 180, 181).

Associated with marbling was the neo-classical fashion for scagliola, a technique known in England when the Lauderdales were decorating Ham House
but not widely used in architectural decoration as opposed to decorative panels
until the late 18th century (Plate XXXIX). It consisted of plaster of Paris
coloured and mixed with pieces of marble, flint etc., to simulate various
marbles. It was often used for columns and the best known scagliola worker
was Bartoli, who was frequently employed by the Wyatts. Sometimes as in
the Saloon at Shugborough in Staffordshire the scagliola was overpainted later,
only to be revealed once more in recent years; but a typical use of scagliola can

178. EARLY 18TH CENTURY
DECORATION IN THE UPPER ROOM
AT SWANGROVE, BADMINTON,
GLOUCESTERSHIRE. Chinoiserie
decoration on the stiles and doors
with grey marbling on the panels
of the doors and dado.

179. CHINOISERIE DECORATION ON
THE BATTENS IN LADY ST. JOHN'S
PARLOUR AT OLD BATTERSEA HOUSE,
LONDON, ABOUT 1700.

180. GRAINING IN THE LIBRARY AT
BELMONT, KENT. An interior by
Samuel Wyatt, about 1795, with
contemporary graining.

181. A DETAIL OF THE GRAINING
IN THE LIBRARY AT BELMONT.

be seen in Malton's drawing of the Great Room at Portman House, Mrs Montagu's house in Portman Square begun by James Stuart and completed by Bonomi (Plate XXXIX).

However today it is often only the scagliola columns that survive from a complete scheme of decoration of this date and they have to be imagined in combination with areas of marbling, not only of white-marbling but siena or the darker reds and porphyry. They were part of the richer style of the last years of the 18th century that favoured elaborate drapery and plenty of gilding, which tended to get out of control when Walsh Porter succeeded Holland as the Prince of Wales's mentor at Carlton House.

At Attingham in Shropshire, there is an excellent example of how this kind of taste was worked out. Steuart's original hall of the 1780s had scagliola columns and pilasters, and presumably under Nash's direction the walls were marbled about 1806 (Fig. 182). Three types were simulated, but all were related to the cool green-grey of the scagliola and the inlay of the chimneypiece and the grisaille reliefs over the doors by Fagan. Beyond lies Nash's Picture Gallery painted dark red with porphyry scagliola columns, gilt capitals and a gilt fillet. At Downton Castle the 1780-ish decoration in the dining room received a somewhat similar Regency enrichment, the walls being marbled green and yellow with red borders to tone with the porphyry scagliola columns. The dining room at Dodington Park, Gloucestershire, was equally sombre: the pilasters were of yellow scagliola, the chimneypiece was *porto venere*, the frieze marbled porphyry and the entablature siena with bronze enrichment. The skirting, the dado and the dado rail, and the side tables were marbled and bronzed to match. Unfortunately the room has been divided, and another elaborate example, the Egyptian dining room at Goodwood, has lost most of the decoration described by Jacques in the guide to the house published in 1822. Now to get the full effect of this kind of scheme one has to go to the

182. THE ENTRANCE HALL AT ATTINGHAM. Three kinds of marbling done about 1806 in a room of the late 1780s to complement the original scagliola pilasters, the grisaille reliefs and inlaid chimney-piece. The scheme was completed with a fitted oil cloth imitating a Roman pavement.

Soane Museum or to the Reform Club where it exists on a much grander scale and in scagliola rather than paint.

Late 18th and early 19th century graining tends to be lighter in tone than late 17th century work, and less fanciful and vigorous than that at Ham. Few complete schemes have survived, but in the Library at Belmont in Kent, a house designed by Samuel Wyatt in 1792 there is excellent walnut graining of the period. Apart from lighter oak colours, maple and satinwood were particularly fashionable woods to imitate, but it was seldom that a complete room was grained. One of the rare survivors is the Music Room at Pencarrow (Fig. 183), an 18th century room painted to simulate maple about 1830. It was more usual to confine the graining to the dado and skirting and doorcases, as can be seen in the library at Barnsley Park, Gloucestershire, decorated about 1810 (Fig. 31).

When Porden was decorating Gloucester House for Lord Grosvenor in 1807, he wrote to his patron on November 26 proposing: "a tint of satinwood for the woodwork at Grosvenor House for the dado and plinth and the greatest part of the mouldings which harmonizes with the mahogany doors, the hangings and the pictures."[27]

The balance of graining and the rich dark coloured patterns fashionable in the 1830s and 40s was an effective one, but the craze for light and for white and pale colours in the 1920s and 1930s led to the destruction or at least modification of many early 19th century schemes; and even now people are often tempted to try to "lighten" a room with dark walls by painting the doors and doorcases white. Similarly few people intending to use dark patterns would consider setting them off with grained woodwork.

183. THE MUSIC ROOM AT PENCARROW, CORNWALL. A rare example of simulated maple graining, about 1830, in a mid 18th century room.

197

The Hazards of Scrapes

If one is planning the restoration of a room, one of the most obvious needs is to discover its original colour, and although accounts and inventories may give a clue, they almost never describe it accurately, and so one has to look for visual evidence for confirmation. Architect's drawings can be a great help, but it has to be faced that the largest collection of English interior designs surviving from the 18th century are a somewhat dangerous guide. Robert Adam made elegant drawings for his clients, and people often attempt to copy the colours shown on them when restoring the rooms; but not only do the schemes often not work out satisfactorily, but often they bear little relationship to what is revealed by scraping.

The traditional method of doing a scrape is to test two or three areas of about a foot square in several parts of the room, checking and comparing dado with dado, chair rail with chair rail and panel with panel, if they exist, rather than relying on one scrape of each element. With a blunt knife or similar tool it is usually not difficult to remove the top coat to reveal a coat probably applied some time in the last 100 years, and the same process is carefully repeated layer by layer. But there are certain points to be remembered: for instance, the larger the house and the grander the room, the less over-painting is likely to have been done; whereas in smaller houses and in the smaller rooms of a large house that were the ones usually lived in, the chances are that more painting will have been done; and in such cases it is not surprising to find as many as 10 coats applied in the course of a century. Only practice and experience will help one to distinguish the first colour from its priming and undercoats. Butcher's description of painting a room white, quoted above, bears out the general experience of finding two or three undercoats.

Sometimes in an early 18th century room in a middling house like those in Lord North Street, Westminster, scrapes reveal that the simple panelling was grounded in a colour that corresponds to the grey or red lead used today. The use of the latter is confirmed by the 1723 edition of Smith, in which he describes Spanish Brown (one of his reds) as "a dark, dull red, of a Horse-flesh Colour" that "is of great use among Painters, being generally used as the first and priming colour, that they lay upon any kind of timber work".

Making scrapes in rooms that were painted in glazes is particularly tricky, because the glazes were often damaged in the past and are easily scraped away without one realising what is happening.

If it proves impossible to scrape a paint, the same results can be obtained by dissolving each coat with a paint solvent, but great care has to be taken for it may stain or discolour the lower layers of old paint.

Sometimes scrapes produce contradictory evidence, and when this happens, slices of paint down to the plaster have to be taken and sent to the scientific department of a museum for analysis.

Even if one finds a colour of the date one is looking for, it is still hard to relate the small area that has been revealed to a whole room. Here imagination and experience are just as necessary as science, because of the difficulty of interpretation: colour not only alters in the light but also in the dark, as can be seen when a picture is taken down to reveal a darkened square that stands out against the faded colour of the exposed wall. So it is with paints that have been covered over for many years: it is reasonable to presume that the paint had faded or discoloured before it was painted over, and then the oils in the subsequent coats may have sunk into the colour and caused more dis-colouration. All this has to be weighed up and interpreted to get an accurate approximation to what was originally intended. In the Harrison Gray Otis House in Boston there was a vivid illustration of the problem: one of the main rooms was painted on the basis of scrapes and all seemed well, but after 10 years not only did the new colour fade, but the one scrape that was left visible for visitors changed as the oils in the paint "cleared" in the light. Thus that scrape became quite different from those that remained covered over.

In the same house various tests and experiments have been made and the process of "clearing" has been carried out artificially with a fluorescent lamp, achieving the same results in a matter of a few months. The same light test had been done on lumps of paint gathered from dark corners of a room: in these the pigments had not faded when the paint was exposed, and, after the oil is bleached in the light, the paint will recover much of its original brilliance. Work like this is of great value, but it does not avoid the need for skilled interpretation in the mixing and application of the new colour.

With the aid of new microscopes and research on the history of paints and colours, no doubt it will be possible to get more scientific results, but, all the same, areas of old paint should always be left by restorers under their coat of paint so that future generations will be able to make their own assessment of the history of a room.

Uniformity of Colour

Recently the concept of matching fabrics and wall paper has been promoted as a new idea, but it is one certainly 240 years old, and, indeed, it goes back even further, for the concept of uniformity of colour was the basis of interior decoration as we understand it; and it remained the basic concept right through the 18th century and was generally accepted at least until the 1860s.

Probably the earliest surviving example of this concept of unity in England is the Queen's Closet at Ham decorated about 1675 (Fig. 17). There the walls are of "crimson and gold stuff bordered with green, gold and silver stuff," the borders being richly brocaded silk and the same material is used on the pair of sleeping chairs. Just over 20 years later the Boughton inventory (1697) describes the Blue Damask Drawing Room, now the 2nd State Room, as having hangings of blue damask "with mouldings all round," the 8 walnut chairs having blue damask cases and gold fringe and the curtains also being of the same stuff. A few years later Lady Grisell Baillie paid £36 for 6 pieces of green damask for hangings, chairs and window curtains.[28]

The one exception to this rule was that sometimes people had curtains of white damask that did not match the main fabric used. At Kensington Palace, for instance in 1697, the hangings and upholstery in the King's Gallery were of green velvet, but the curtains were white damask; and there were also white curtains in the King's Low Bed chamber. However this was not a purely royal practice for the 1701 inventory of Longnor Hall, a manor house in Shropshire built in the 1670s, describes the Summer Parlour as having chairs in green damask and curtains in white.[29]

In Kent's interiors he or his patrons always insisted on uniformity, as we know. Thus at Houghton the seat furniture and the walls of the saloon are both covered with the same crimson cut velvet (and *porto venere* marble is used for the chimneypiece and tabletops), and originally both the Drawing Room and the State Bedroom were done in green velvet (Plate XII). Now this velvet only survives on the magnificent bed and on a particularly large set of walnut and parcel gilt chairs. Perhaps it was Kent's suggestion that certain damask patterns were adapted for wallpaper for one particular pattern that he used in the Treasury is known in other colours and damask.

As an added refinement to this concept of uniformity the case curtains of a bed sometimes were of the same colour as the upholstery or they matched the lining. The bed at Hampton Court that was made for George II when Prince of Wales originally had case curtains of crimson taffeta to match the crimson damask hangings; and the Chandos inventory records buff coloured mantua silk curtains and covers that matched the lining of an embroidered bed. At

Clandon the state bed is lined with satin that matched the window curtains, and the same idea is recorded at Erthig in 1726, where not only did the linings of the bed curtains match the window curtains, but so did the counterpanes, some of the latter being quilted.[30]

In a sense this insistence on uniformity was a form of conspicuous consumption, but it was not confined to the houses of the richest people. In 1744 Mrs Delany bought crimson damask for bed hangings, curtains and chairs and green damask for another room. And when Benjamin Franklin bought material in London for his wife in 1758, he was reproved by an English acquaintance for getting different material for chairs and bed hangings and curtains.[31]

Quite how long the idea lasted and whether it was rigidly adhered to in more intimate rooms is difficult to discover, but certainly when new State Rooms were created at Northumberland House in the 1820s, crimson silk damask was used in the Saloon and Drawing Room and French grey damask in a third room. An even later example is the pair of drawing rooms at Brodsworth Hall, Yorkshire, which were entirely done in red damask by Lapworth Brothers of 22 Old Bond Street in the early 1860s.[32]

One result of this ordered, or perhaps we should say stereotyped, approach, was that rooms tended to have a very set character, and, instead of creating variety within a room as is done today, the contrasts had to be made between rooms. Perhaps this helps to explain the long surviving fashion for tapestry particularly in bedrooms, although this was partly dictated by warmth, and why there was such a vogue for chinese rooms and gothick rooms as well as the tapestry rooms of the type found at Mereworth and West Wycombe. Rococo taste, in particular, favoured variety, and thus one gets the kind of eclecticism seen at Chesterfield House, where the ante-room and drawing room were decorated in quite a different style from both the library and the Great Room where Lord Chesterfield hung his finest pictures. Variety of colour was also evidently a Rococo fashion, for one of the things that struck William Farington about Norfolk House in 1756 was this novelty. Invited to the opening of what he called the Grand Appartment, he said "there were in all eleven rooms open, three below, the rest above, every room was furnished with a different colour, which used to be reckon'd absurd, but this I suppose is to be the standard, as the immense Grandure of the Furniture is scarce to be conceiv'd." By the middle of the next decade, when the same Duchess of Norfolk was thinking about the decoration of Worksop, the idea was much more usual, but all the same it is interesting to see how she tried to create variety even in the bedrooms by using chinese wallpaper with different themes and different coloured grounds.[33]

Fashion in Colour and Pattern

Colours and patterns are difficult enough to describe when they are new and fresh, but when they are 100 or 200 years old the task is doubly difficult, for then they have inevitably changed through the effects of light and wear. And it is not really satisfactory to attempt to separate them or to classify them solely in accordance with changes in architectural style. Consequently the only way to get a general perspective of developments is to relate them also to changes in social practice, the increasing control of the architect and the decorator, to technical advances and to changes in architectural and ornament design. As one would expect, the increasing sophistication of taste becomes very marked as the 18th century develops, and with this went an emphasis on line and form rather than on ornament and enrichment. One may feel that what follows is a gross simplification, but at least it provides a basis for looking at changes in colour and pattern making.

The baroque style favoured a combination of elaborate line and movement with rich colour and texture, a combination that is apparent not only in the design of state beds, but also in pelmet cornices and valances and some seat furniture, which were all made en suite.

The principal development contemporary with the establishment of the Palladian style was a tendency to simplify not only the line but also to reduce the reliance on lustre and texture. Patterns tended to become less *mouvementé* and more static, and the range of colours was more or less limited to the three primaries and green. However this impression may need modification, for the textiles and wallpapers that survive in situ tend to be in state rooms with bold architectural ornament that call for bold formal patterns; and also state rooms, because of their nature, tend to be treated in a traditional rather than a progressive and inventive way. In our present state of knowledge this view can only be surmise, but it would appear to be supported by the way some designs constantly re-occur. For instance there is one that exists both in damask and wallpaper, but in different colours, at the Treasury, Withepole House, Ipswich, Clandon (Plate XXI) and elsewhere. It is still produced in damask and paper, the latter being known as Amberley.

Whether less important rooms were treated with more freedom before the mid 1740s is simply not known. Insufficient evidence has been collected from documents, and little remains in situ.

Another problem when trying to study colour and pattern for a restoration is that whereas one may develop a feeling for the date of a colour and a pattern, the natural tendency now is to see it in isolation and to lose sight of contemporary attitudes to series of colours and textures in a house. The fabrics at Houghton and Holkham are justly famous, but they need to be considered not only individually but in relation to the general scheme worked out for the parade rooms. At Houghton, for instance, the original cut velvet with its bold pattern contrasted with the ground survives in the Saloon, but what has been lost is the intentional contrast with the plain green velvet used in the drawing room and the state bedroom. At Holkham the contrasts are not so strong for the richly patterned cut velvet in the Saloon is shaded down to a *ton-sur-ton* damask in the cabinet.

The Stowe guide books, which describe the house in detail from 1763 to 1838, provide a great deal of information of this kind, and, what is more, they also enable us to see not only what was used, but what was kept and what was altered. For instance, in the time of the 1st Earl Temple the state apartment consisted of the gallery, dressing room, bedroom and closet, the first two rooms being done in blue damask and the second two in crimson damask. No change was made here, apart from tapestries being moved into the dressing room, until some time between 1797 and 1817, when the closet was rehung with yellow damask; the state bedroom and dressing room were only redone for Queen Victoria's visit in 1845.

Against the lack of change in these rooms, Lady Temple's dressing room and bedroom were altered fairly regularly. In 1763 they were both done with fine printed cotton, but in 1773 it is stated that tapestry was to be put up; the latter was evidently hung by 1777, but two years later Lord Temple was succeeded by his nephew, the future 1st Marquess of Buckingham. His wife was an heiress, and so, not surprisingly, the tapestry was immediately taken down and replaced by blue damask in the bedroom and white damask in the dressing room, the bedroom being redone in white by 1788.

This is more or less what one would expect, for it is obvious that the most expensive stuffs used in a house would be kept for the most magnificent rooms. It was natural for Lady Lincoln to choose crimson damask for her Great Apartment in London and less formal and more feminine painted taffeta in her own rooms; but whereas one appreciates the sense of order in the uniformity of colour in a single room or even a complete apartment, to our eyes there would have been an arguable lack of imagination shown in the reds used

201

at Holkham, the blue damask at Woburn and Kedleston, and the reds at old Fonthill. At the latter the saloon was red damask, the bedchamber red velvet and gold, and the dressing room crimson damask. If and when it comes to the restoration of such rooms today, the natural temptation is to introduce more variety of colour.[34]

However colours, patterns and fabrics cannot be looked at in isolation for another reason. They were also related to the kind of pictures and the number that were to be hung in a room. As we will show later, there was an evident shortage of large pictures in English houses throughout the first half of the 18th century, and as virtually no one was able to hang a large room as closely as an Italian princely collector, more reliance had to be placed on the pattern of the wall covering. Again to cite Holkham, Lord Leicester hung the huge Rubens and the Van Dyck at either end of the Saloon, and over the chimney-piece were later placed two full length family portraits; and the hangings always made a positive contribution to the unity of the room. In the adjoining drawing room cut velvet is used and more of the wall is covered with pictures, and in the cabinet with the more delicate classical landscapes a much more subdued damask is used.

At Ditchley a particularly exotic cut velvet after an Indian design was used in the state bedroom in 1738, and it is obvious that it could never have been combined with pictures of any importance.

Plain fabrics with a pile like velvet and plush are particularly liable to damage if the arrangement of pictures is changed, and one of the few houses where pictures are still shown against a background of old plain red velvet is Saltram.

As collections increased in size during the century, the tendency was to use quieter backgrounds for pictures, with more frequent use of plain colours and particularly green. Occasionally one finds yellow chosen, as in one of the drawing rooms at Hopetoun which was partly re-hung in the mid 19th century, but evidently there was always a school of opinion that considered that yellow conflicted with the gilding of the frames and killed pictures. The most famous example of this is Mrs Arbuthnot's outburst against her friend, the Duke of Wellington, when he was completing the Waterloo Gallery at Apsley House: "He is going to hang it with *yellow* damask, which is just the very worst colour he can have for pictures and will kill the effect of the gilding. However he *will* have it." Evidently Sir Thomas Lawrence shared her view, for in 1813 he wrote to Farington: "Instead of the yellow paper that I knew would be harmful to my pictures . . . it is now a rich crimson paper with a Border, one gold moulding of this size fix'd to an Inch flat of Black."[35]

However there is another aspect of colour to be considered, at least at the end of the 17th and beginning of the 18th century, the association and attributes of colour as set down by Randle Holme, a Midland genealogist who produced the first edition of his *Academy of Armoury* in Chester in 1688. It is difficult to tell how important this curious book was at that time, and later, and whether the ideas it contains enjoyed wide currency, but his remarks on colour are in keeping with contemporary attitudes to planning and allegory, and a parallel to them still survives in the Church's use of colours. In Book I, Chapter II he wrote of the *Significations of the Colours Used in Arms*. For red, for instance, he gives its heraldic name, Gules, its stone as Ruby, and Mars as its planet, and then continues: "This colour Vermilion, or Red, is the chief amongst colours, for as much as it representeth the Fire, which of all the other Elements is the most lightsome, and approaches nearest to the quality of the Sun: in regard whereof it was ordered, that none should bear this Colour but Persons of Noble Birth and Rank, and Men of Special desent; for it signifyeth Dignity."

He calls Blue the colour of Jupiter and says that it "signifieth Piety and Sincerity". Green is the colour of Venus and is associated with Felicity and Pleasure. Purple is Mercury's colour and represents Honour and Dignity.

This thinking is as far removed from modern attitudes as from those of the second half of the 18th century, but at least an element of it could have survived into Kent's day, and it gives a particular point to the State Bedroom at Houghton where the velvet is green and the tapestries depict the loves of Venus and Adonis. Of course, this may be just coincidence, but at the same time it is tempting to see Randle Holme's interpretation as one reason why so much crimson was used.

Crimson was the conventional colour both for parade rooms and picture galleries, being chosen by Reynolds for the Royal Academy and later used in the galleries at Petworth and Attingham. It never went out of favour, but it was rivalled by green, the use of which possibly tended to increase in the late 1730s. The surviving shades from this period tend to be fairly strong, as can be seen in the green velvet at Houghton, the cut velvet in the Round Drawing Room at Longford Castle and in the Victorian copy of the original green damask in the Gallery in the same house. The green velvet recorded in the Grenville Room at Stowe in 1763 and the green damask seen in the Saloon at Redlinch by Horace Walpole were probably of much the same intensity.

However round about 1760, when the secondary colours became more fashionable, the shades tended to lighten. Probably one of the first big rooms to be hung with light green damask was the Saloon at Buckingham House redecorated by Chambers in the early 1760s, and it is followed by an increasing number of references to pea-greens and light greens. For instance, Chippendale supplied plain green paper for Sir Rowland Winn's dressing room at Nostell in 1767 as well as green lacquer furniture for the state bedroom. In 1759 Lady Caroline Fox had her dressing room painted pea-green colour to match some china and also mentioned carving in her London drawing room being painted in two greens and varnished. The gallery at Osterley was painted "pea green" by 1772, and at Luton Hoo Lady Mary Coke was struck that almost all the rooms were "hung with light green papers, which shews the pictures to great advantage." In 1771 William Chambers wrote to Robert Gregory in Berners Street: "If you have any particular fancy about the painting your principal rooms, my intention is to finish the whole of a fine stone colour . . . excepting the parlour which I propose to finish pea green with white mouldings ornaments."[36]

Today only the paler blues are widely used in decoration, and most people avoid such strong blues as found in the saloon at Clandon and the ceiling of the state dressing room at Houghton. However once the weight of references to decoration start, it is obvious that blue was quite common, and often the choice seems to have been for quite strong shades, particularly in wallpapers. Blue and gold is as splendid a combination as any, and so not only was the Gallery at Fonthill hung with blue damask, but a decade earlier in 1759 Lady Caroline Fox wrote to Lady Kildare: "I have fitted up the gallery with blue paper, gilt borders, and a few good pictures",[37] a description that could almost be taken to be of Sir Lawrence Dundas's room in Arlington Street as painted by Zoffany (Plate XV). And just as there were light greens in the 70s and 80s, there were light blues, light blue paper, for instance, being used in the breakfast room at Heveningham.

There are a surprising number of references to plain papers, among them to one in the Duchess of Portland's dressing room in 1759, but it is not clear whether they were bought complete from the paper stainer or completed in situ. The evidence for the latter comes in correspondence from Elwick, a York upholsterer, to John Grimston. "They was to begin up on the Drawing Room," he wrote, "& the Library & the plane Buff, that is they was to put on the Paper as this is always put up & colour'd after." And ". . . I am sure it is much for the advantage of the wall to have a paper upon it to do it in oil or size which you will, & as to the Drawing Room I do assure you, you can't have so fine a colour as you may have in the way do those plane colours, Indeed nothing to

Compare with it, & if you chouse to do your library in oil you will see the Difference . . ." Elwick's letter appears to be confirmed by a bill of 1822 from Morant which lists "8½ pieces of fine stampt Elephant hung pommiced and coloured in distemper fine blue."[38]

Yellow seems to have been the least used of the primary colours, but rooms hung with gold-coloured damask are recorded in Mrs Clayton's house in Dublin in 1731 and in yellow caffoy at Houghton. As one would expect the earlier examples tended to be stronger in tone, but few would expect one as strong as the satin embroidered with red that occurs on a set of chairs at Ham House (Plate II). Softer shades probably became more fashionable in the late 1730s and 40s under French influence, but the French combinations of pale yellow with sky blue or lilac are not recorded here at that time. As we have already said, there was a prejudice against hanging pictures against a yellow ground, because of the effect on the gilt frames, but it is interesting that on at least two occasions in the 1760s and 70s yellow damask was combined with silver, in the Yellow Drawing Room at Harewood and in an apartment at Stowe, where the 1763 guide describes yellow silk damask hangings trimmed with silver. On the other hand yellow or straw colour appears to have been a fashionable colour for print rooms, and one of Linnell's designs for a room is shown with a good mid yellow ground.[39]

In the 1760s and 1770s lilacs and greys came into fashion along with pea greens and pale blues. By that time purple seems to have lost its connotation as a colour of royal mourning—purple rather than black was used for the funeral of Queen Mary II—and it became fashionable in paler shades of violet and lilac. We have not encountered examples of their use in architectural decoration in the 1750s except possibly in the dining room at Felbrigg. But a pale lilac combined with paler green appears as the colour scheme for one of the rooms in Hardwick's drawing of 1763 (Fig. 12) and it is mentioned by the Duchess of Northumberland in her description of the dining room ceiling at Kedleston two or three years later.[40]

The references to Paris grey and French grey are not to what is often called *gris trianon*. The latter is a rather dead colour that seems to have been used in the second quarter of the 19th century with particularly unfortunate results at the Petit Trianon where it is much more evocative of the period of Louis Philippe than of Louis XVI. A true French grey is a paler and livelier colour with pink and blue in it but no yellow. It seems to have come into fashion in England in the late 1760s. Chambers mentions it, so does Mrs Lybbe Powys in her description of Fawley in 1771, and traces of it have been found in Garrick's villa at Hampton. However perhaps the most interesting example is the hall at Osterley, where the painting bill specifies that it was done in white and French grey with the trophy panels "minutely pick'd in with three tints of grey."[41]

It might be assumed that white would be the easiest colour to comment on, but in fact it is perhaps the one with the most complex history. Today it is quite usual to paint the mouldings and the woodwork of a room white, and there are many 18th century precedents for this, among them a letter from Sarah Duchess of Marlborough to her daughter Diana, in 1732, when she wrote: "Though several people have larger rooms, what you have is as much as is of any real use to any body, and the white painting with so much damask looks mightily handsome."[42] All the same it seems that the use of white may not have been quite so common as is presumed today. Indeed it may even have had definite connotations of grandeur and stateliness in some 17th and early 18th century houses. At Ham, for instance, the rooms that are white or marbled white are in the Duchess's apartment on the ground floor, the first floor Drawing Room and two of the rooms in the State Apartment. And at Marble Hill, scrapes revealed that most of the house was painted stone colour and only the Saloon was white and gold.[43]

Today stone colour, drab and olive are seldom used, but from 18th century documents and pictures it seems that they have been quite often chosen instead of white. Stone was frequently used to set off Baroque painted decorations as at Hanbury Hall in Worcestershire, where the walls of the staircase are decorated with splendid gold grisaille trophies, and drab is used for the wainscot of all the state rooms at Boughton, which were painted by Dandridge in the late 1680s or early 1690s. The hall at old Buckingham House was originally painted stone colour and the picture frames were marbled. And the fashion continued, for not only was the saloon at Ditchley originally olive, but so was the ball room at Wanstead, the setting of Philips's group of the *Duke of Somerset and His Family*, the saloon at Eastbury and evidently many of the rooms at Houghton. Mrs Lybbe Powys, who went there in 1756, noted "the rooms are, instead of white, painted dark green olive; but this most likely will be soon altered."[44] Unfortunately she does not specify which rooms.

The main reason for the fashion was presumably to avoid overstrong contrasts that would detract from the impact of pictures or painted decorations. In the staircase hall at King's Weston, for instance, original painted decoration survives in the niches, but the walls are now white, and so there is an uneasy clash between architecture and decoration, whereas surely the drab colour that appears out of the shadow at the edge of the niche with the Farnese Hercules should be the colour of the hall as a whole?

On a smaller scale Mrs Delany records having her English room "painted a sort of olive for the sake of my pictures," but changed the colour to dove-coloured flock in 1750. Another reason was evidently economy, for in 1770 Chambers wrote to a friend "with regard to the painting of your Parlours if they are for Common Use Stone Colour will last best and cheepest, but if you mean them to be very neat pea-green and white, Buff-colour and white, a pearl or what is called Paris grey and white is the Handsomest."[45]

Obviously there was a considerable variation in shade ranging from the fairly dark colours at Boughton to the pale tinted white of the entablature of the Speaker's Parlour at Clandon. The scrapes at Marble Hill revealed a tinge of green in the stone colour. It is an old trick to add black and raw umber to break white, but it is conceivable that the subtleties of tone that we associate with the Baroque period went out of fashion together with other aspects of Baroque house painting and that the fashion for dead colour was accompanied by one for cleaner whites. However until more research is done we cannot know the answer.

Recently when the halls at Clandon and Syon were repainted, a series of different whites were used in each case, and it is interesting to compare the effects with those evidently achieved in the hall at Bowood in the 1760s. At Clandon the contrast between the slightly rough textured plaster of the walls and the harder and smoother plaster of the entablature and other architectural detail was emphasised by a slight variation in the whites used; and at Syon three tones of white were used, a grey white for the dado, main wall and upper wall above the entablature, a broken white for the columns, cornice, triglyphs and other ornaments and a darker white for the background of the ornaments in the coffering. Two hundred years ago Spinnage must have achieved a somewhat similar variation of tone at Bowood by using distemper on the ceiling and on the walls, which were given four rather than three coats and finished dead stone at an extra 1d. a yard, and for the entablature five coats in oil and sanded (at 1/- a yard).[46]

These three examples all relate to important rooms in large houses, and it is worth remembering that when such rooms were first painted, or even more likely when they were repainted, that they were not done necessarily by the Spinnages of the time: they are just as likely to have been done by local painters with less sophisticated ideas. This is brought out in a point made by Wyatt Papworth in his 1857 lecture, when he quoted a friend then in his 85th year, who said "The plastered walls of houses were coloured, the sashes painted white, the doors, skirtings and other parts generally black. Several present can no doubt recall houses in the country still exhibiting this ancient style of ornamentation."[47] If it was unusual in 1857, such a survival would be so rare today that it would be misunderstood, but at least one example should be mentioned, the gothick chapel at Milton Manor, Berkshire, where the walls are white and the doors appear always to have been painted black. A variant on this practice is provided by Philip Yorke of Erthig in 1772 when he instructed: "The colour of the Paint a dead white as to the skirting board, and shutters, but the door of a chocolate colour."

In the 1760s and 1770s the role of white and colours was often reversed, and one finds references to rooms hung with white material and with coloured woodwork. The Duchess of Leinster, for instance, "being the Great Lady, has no less than three white damask rooms" in 1772, and at Castletown, Co. Kildare, her sister Lady Louisa Conolly had her dressing room "fitted up in ye French taste hung with white damask. Portraits tyed with knots of Purple and Silver Ribband." A few years later, in 1775, her sister, Lady Sarah Bunbury, was suggesting to the Duchess having white hangings and coloured woodwork or coloured hangings with white woodwork; and she took the colour of her china also into account. (So did another of the sisters, Lady Holland, who had her dressing room done pea-green colour to go with pea-green china.) Occasionally beds were hung with white satin. At Luton Hoo in 1774 Mrs Delany noticed that most of the rooms were done with plain papers to match the beds, but her bed was white satin and the paper was green. Naturally this use of white was a great extravagance because it was bound to get dirty, and no contemporary rooms have survived. However at Powderham Castle there is a set of white and gold furniture made about 1790 of which some pieces are still covered in the original white silk; and at Audley End the state bed has a white ground.[48]

Paper was naturally cheaper than hangings, and it is not surprising to find the fashion copied a few years later. At Cossey in 1785, the parlour looked "very neat" as it had been "new painted" and had "the white paper in it with a green border."[49]

Related to this use of white was the popularity of painted furniture from the 1760s onwards. This must have been produced in very large quantities, but it is rare today to see a neo-classical room surviving intact with its painted furniture. The Etruscan Room at Osterley and the Etruscan Room and Library at Heveningham immediately come to mind. However it is not known which room in England was the first to have specially designed painted furniture made for it; nor is it known which was the first drawing room or saloon in a house of pretension to have painted furniture.

However it is probably safe to relate the fashion for it to the decline in the use of gilding, but again this relationship should not be seen in isolation, because it is necessary also to relate it to the materials used for the upholstery. Again little has been written about this, but a clue lies in Sheraton's remarks about sofa beds: "The frames of these beds are sometimes painted in ornaments to suit the furniture. But when the furniture is of rich silk, they are done in white and gold, and the ornaments carved."[50]

One of the attractions of painted furniture was that it could be used to carry through the element of uniformity in a room. Instead of contrasts of mahogany and gilding, the furniture could be painted to match the upholstery. At Mersham-le-Hatch the Ante-Room had blue damask window curtains and blue leather seats; and the oval glass and girandoles were painted blue and white. Similarly in the Front Bed-chamber in 1769 a purple and white striped wallpaper was used and the large pier glass was Japanned purple and white.[51] In the library at Heveningham the chairs are picked out in purple-brown to match the porphyry scagliola of the chimneypiece and the colour used for the skirting and picking out of the woodwork and ceiling.

Much of the charm and elegance of schemes like these lay in the planning of the whole, and the results must have been very different from the faded and fragmented ones that survive. The skill of the painters was considerable, but it is seldom that anything as fine as a bed from Alnwick Castle comes to light. Apparently undocumented, it is more likely to have been acquired by the wife of the 2nd Duke of Northumberland rather than of the 1st, for it is close in style and detail to the bed at Inveraray (Fig. 227) provided in the 1780s. At the time of writing only some of the later overpainting had been removed, but the detail (Plate XL) shows not only the extremely high quality of the carving but the delicacy of the painting in tempera. Fortunately the painting has survived remarkably well, and its freshness helps one to appreciate other aspects of taste in the last quarter of the 18th century.

It was a fashion that contributed to light and gay interiors and introduced a new freshness into houses. A much greater variety of colours was used, and the effect of a complete scheme is admirably conveyed by Mrs Powys in her description of Fawley in 1771. The hall was stuccoed French grey and the Saloon was hung with paper to match it and finished with a light blue & gold cord instead of a fillet. The dining room was stucco and painted Quaker brown; the billiard room had a pink Indian paper with prints; the breakfast parlour was pea-green stucco with a gilt border and the chimneypiece was also green marble. And in that room Mrs Freeman had worked the sofa and chairs in pink, green and grey, and the curtains were pea-green lustring.[52]

Of course many of the motifs used in pattern making had altered, and both the Rococo and the neo-classical styles evolved new vocabularies of ornament and also new proportional relationships of motifs to backgrounds. But the neo-classical victory did not come overnight, and just as Rococo forms and details survived in furniture-making through the 1760s, they continued to be used by textile and wallpaper designers. The crimson silk used in the Red Drawing Room at Syon, for instance, has nothing neo-classical about it and yet that dates from about 1769.

At the same time two other sources of influence should be borne in mind, the impact of archaeology that not only provided new forms to copy but also new colours, and the scientific study of colour that enabled artists and decorators to work out a more precisely calculated palette, with an increased emphasis on secondary colours and on subtler tones.

Here it is interesting to compare, let us say, James Stuart's Painted Room at Spencer House with an Adam interior of several years later. Stuart's is a pioneer room and as such has all the staccato effects that tend to go with a scheme that is not fully digested. With Adam there is a better balance of architectural elements and painted ornament, and the two are held together by the skilful use of colour. Unfortunately he nowhere gives us his theory of colour, and all he mentions in his *Works* is his use of "light tints of pink and green, so as to take off the glare of white, so common in every ceiling, till of late" and so create "a harmony between ceiling and side walls with their hangings, pictures and other decorations." Elsewhere he says that he first used colour in this way at Kedleston.[53]

There is little evidence about the colouring of ceilings before Adam's day, but it was not entirely unknown. At Clandon for instance the original pale blue and biscuit has recently been revealed in the saloon (Plate XXVII). And in 1752 Lady Luxborough wrote to William Shenstone: "I must now beg the favour of you to instruct me about the ceiling, which I would have adorned a little with papier mache and the ground painted a colour; . . ."[54]

Inspired by Adam's ideas, the painting of earlier ceilings became fashionable. At Castletown, for instance, Lady Louisa Conolly kept the original ceiling of the 1730s, when she redecorated the Gallery in the 1770s, and recorded painting it in "scarlet & grey & white & gold & it really looks much better than I expected."[55]

An interesting later example is the dining room at Attingham. In 1806 Steuart's original cool colouring was replaced, and both the walls and ceiling of the room were painted Pompeian red.

Towards the end of the century, under French influence, fashionable taste went in two directions at once: one taste was for richer and darker effects and for a greater range of textures (but not cut patterns). This is apparent not only in the increased use of scagliola, marbling and gilding but in a return to favour of velvet and heavy trimmings. The style became increasingly linear in its emphasis and patterns more closely toned, with self-stripes and self-stripes with sprigs or medallions set in a geometrical but isolated pattern on a plain ground. In 1802 when the younger Chippendale was working at Stourhead, he supplied a yellow and black satin for the curtains for the Picture Room at a cost of 13/6 a yard, and blue satin with black spots for the curtains in the Cabinet, and yellow satin for the ante-room. Indeed, much more use was made of satin in decoration than might be assumed today, and its sheen made it particularly popular about 1800. In 1803 Mrs Powys went to see a Miss Heathcote in Bath: "she has an elegant house in the Crescent, and he (Mr Whaley) has one in St James's Square, Bath, which, tho' most elegantly furnished, after he returned from Paris, finding paper hangings were there call'd vulgar, immediately took all down and hung all with satins."[56]

Writing of fashions a few years later George Smith says: "In elegant Drawing Rooms, plain coloured satin or figured damask assumes the first rank, as well as for use as richness: lustring and tabareys are next; the latter, however, makes but indifferent drapery."[57]

It is tempting to see Thomas Hope as the prime mover in this change of direction, but there are signs that fashionable taste had been moving towards a richer style before his book came out. Lord Grosvenor, for instance, acquired Old Gloucester House, Park Lane, in 1806 and had it remodelled by Porden, and judging by comments on its opening, its effect seemed novel. Hope, however, was both more imaginative and more influential, and he must have been gratified when Britton wrote of his *Household Furniture* in 1827 that it "has not only improved the taste of cabinet-makers and upholsterers, but also that of their employers." It is hard to judge the effect of his colour schemes from descriptions and from the arid plates in his book, but it seems that they would strike most people today as hard. Writing of his Indian Room (Fig. 184), he said "As the colours of this room in compliance with the oriental taste, are everywhere very vivid, and very strongly contrasted due attention has been paid to their gradual lightening, as the eye rose from the skirting to the cornice. The tint of the sofa is deep crimson; that of the walls sky blue; and that of the ceiling pale yellow, intermixed with azure and with sea-green. Ornaments of gold, in various shades, relieve and harmonize these colours." However before recoiling from such a scheme, it is important to remember that the room was for parade and for demonstrating Hope's theories rather than for daily living.[58]

One of the houses of which Hope evidently approved was White Knights, a house near Reading that had been acquired in 1798 by the Duke of Marlborough. In 1819 he wrote a preface to Mrs Holland's account of it that gives a good idea of the eccentricity of contemporary taste. The Drawing Room was hung with peachblossom coloured cloth and had curtains of rich purple silk mixed with peach-blossom coloured sarcenet and trimmed with most splendid fringe, lacings, and tassels of gold-coloured silk; the upholstery was of purple satin woven to represent embroidery.

The Prince Regent's Carlton House and Beckford's Fonthill are both equally atypical, but from the contemporary descriptions and illustrations one gets a strong sense of the increasing heaviness of early 19th century taste.

In this respect Sir John Soane's house is a much better illustration, for although the concept is eccentric, the scale is domestic. Here one finds plenty

of dark tones, a porphyry dado and marbled walls in the hall and on the staircase, walls painted dark red and picked out in green in the Parlour, and yellow picked out in green in the drawing room. In another room recently restored the doors are painted a stone colour and picked out in black.

This appearance of black is at first slightly surprising, but it seems likely that it was introduced into the decorator's palette by Sir William Hamilton, in his plates of Etruscan antiquities and was occasionally used for picking out. At Bridewell in Devonshire the drawing room appears to have been painted in the early 1790s, and there the walls are cane, and lines of black are used to pick out the skirting, dado rail and the door architrave. In upholstery a deep black silk fringe was used on the new state bed at Burghley House in 1789: the bed itself was of striped coloured velvet and lined with white satin. And rather later in the Wainscot Library at Goodwood, the wallpaper was scarlet flock and there was a drapery of black velvet edged with gold coloured silk.[59]

Such schemes required a great deal of control and we do not know how widely they were copied. However it is not without interest that Hay, writing in 1828, said: "In my search for examples of harmonious colouring in interior decorations, I found the most perfect were generally to be met with in the houses of amateurs, or lovers of the higher branches of the art of painting, whose knowledge of the qualities which constitute the excelling of colouring in pictures, had enabled them to impart a degree of the same excellence to the decorations of their mansions."[60]

However, the whole history of fashionable taste at the end of the 18th century and the beginning of the 19th century cannot be written in terms of rich dark colours and florid patterns. Indeed the aspect of this period that has aroused greatest interest in recent years has been its simpler patterns and lighter fabrics, its linens, cottons and chintzes and its wallpapers that are closer in feeling to the delightful clear designs found on fine earthenware produced at that time.

209

Chapter 6
The treatment of floors

Recently when Sudbury Hall was restored, there was an outcry that the "beautiful polished oak boards" had been "stripped" and that generations of loving work on them had been swept away. This criticism was understandable in that it has been almost entirely forgotten how floors were treated in the past. And so rather than attempt an all-too-abbreviated account of carpet making in England, which is anyway a poorly documented subject, this chapter concentrates on the background to the use of carpets and on dry scrubbing.

One of the surprising details that emerges from a study of documents relating to housekeeping is the rarity of references to polished floors. Indeed we seem to have got our attitudes to panelling and floors oddly reversed: whereas pine panelling was almost never left in its natural state and there has been a regrettable 20th century fashion for making it look like a cigar box, hours are spent on getting a high polish on a floor which 200 years ago would have been left unpolished.

Hannah Glass in her *Servants Directory* of 1760 never mentions polishing a floor, but says in her instructions to the Housemaid: "be sure always to have very clean Feet, that you may not dirty your Rooms as soon as clean'd, nor make any Noise, but learn to walk softly, and not disturb the Family;" and having described the sweeping of a carpet, she continues: "take some sand, pretty damp, but not too wet, and strew all over the Room, throwing it out of your Hand hard, and it will fly about the Floor and lick up all the Dust and Flew." And again: "Take Tanzy, Mint, and Balm; first sweep the Room, then strew the Herbs on the Floor, and with a long hard Brush rub them well all over the Boards, till you have scrubb'd the Floor clean. When the Boards are quite dry, sweep off the greens, and with a dry Rubbing brush dry-rub them well, and they will look like mahogany, of a fine brown, and never want any other washing, and give a sweet smell to the Room," "Sope is not proper for boards," she wrote, "and sand and water shews the grain, which is the beauty of a Board."[1]

Mrs Whatman's MSS[2] notes might almost be culled from Hannah Glass's book: "To use as little soap as possible (if any)" she wrote, "in scowring rooms, Fuller's earth and fine sand preserves the colour of the boards, and does not leave a white appearance as soap does. All the rooms to be dry scrubbed with white sand." And Mrs Boscawen would have agreed with her; in 1787 she talks of scouring the floor and dry rubbing it after taking up the carpet.[3] When Grosley came to England in 1772, he was struck by the floors in houses being "washed and rubbed almost daily, have a whitish appearance, and an air of freshness and cleanliness, which the finest inlaid floor has not always."[4]

Washing, of course, made a room damp, and this no doubt encouraged the habit of dry scrubbing. Almost inevitably Sarah Duchess of Marlborough was fussy about damp and wrote to Lord and Lady John Russell: "But what I apprehend most, and which is the chief reason of my writing to you, is that the bed won't be finished time enough to have the room thoroughly cleaned and dry to be rubbed before you come to town. And if you come into a room that is but just washed you will get a cold, which will be very troublesome to you at this time. I do not doubt but you will take care not to lie upon a new feather bed and to have all the quilts well aired."[5]

Today one seldom sees a dry scrubbed floor in a house, but it is of interest that a number exist in country houses usually where specially ordered 18th century carpets have survived. This suggests that these floors have never been polished and that the effect is not a 20th century revival of the old habit. Among the rooms where such a floor can be seen is the Saloon at Uppark and the Red Drawing Room at Syon, but there are others including rooms at Bridewell in Devonshire and various rooms both at Boughton and Drumlanrig. To our eyes the soft look of the floor throws up the colours in the carpets and tones with the mellow paintwork in a pleasing way.

Of course inlaid floors must have always been polished to bring out the contrasts of grain and colour, and it is doubtful whether they would have stood up to dry scrubbing. Although now a great rarity, at the end of the 17th and beginning of the early 18th century there must have been a considerable number of them. The idea seems to have been introduced by Queen Henrietta Maria when she returned at the Restoration, for Evelyn in his *Account of Architects & Architecture* says "In the mean time not to be forgotten are the *Floorings* of *Wood* which Her Majesty the Queen *Mother* has just brought into use in *England* at her *Palace* of *Somerset-House*, the like whereof I directed to be made in a Bed-Chamber at *Berkeley House*: the *French* call it *Parquetage*, a kind of *Segmentatum opus*, and which has some resemblance to these Magnificencies . . ."[6]

Celia Fiennes mentions several: at Stowe in 1694 "Some of the ground floors are inlaid fine pictures;" at Nottingham Castle in the Chamber of State "the floors of the roome was inlay'd with cyphers & the Coronet;" and at Ashtead she saw "some closets with inlaid floors."[7]

Of these early inlaid floors only fragments have survived. At Ham the remains of the dais exist in the original state bedroom, now the Queen's Drawing Room, and there is more work in the adjoining closet. In the Duchess of Norfolk's Closet at Drayton there are the remains of a marquetry floor, and at Boughton there is a late 17th century table with a marquetry top that may have been part of a floor. Some late 17th century staircases including those at Powis Castle and Longnor Hall, Shropshire, are inlaid, but they are much simpler than the half landing from the staircase bearing Lord Carpenter's arms that comes from 22 Hanover Square and is now in the Victoria and Albert Museum (Fig. 185).[8] Much the finest and best preserved inlaid floor of the early 18th century is the one in the Drawing Room at Mawley Hall, Shropshire, a room of extraordinary virtuosity and probably the work of a rather old fashioned cabinet-maker.

With the increasing use of carpets in the second quarter of the 18th century, the fashion for inlay declined, just as it did in furniture making, and this was noticed by Isaac Ware, who wrote in 1756: "The use of carpeting at this time has set aside the ornamenting of floors in a great measure."[9] There were, of course, exceptions like the staircase at Claydon (Fig. 186), installed in the late 1760s, which is inlaid with ebony, holly and ivory, and must be by the same man who did the saloon doors. However nothing to match it has survived, and all we have are bare references like that of Mrs Powys in 1767 to the floors at Buckingham House being "all inlaid in a most expensive manner."[10]

Towards the end of the century, again presumably under Holland's influence, the use of inlay was revived to give an extra border to a carpet. This occurs

185. THE INLAID LANDING FROM
22 HANOVER SQUARE, LONDON.

186. THE STAIRCASE AT CLAYDON
HOUSE, BUCKINGHAMSHIRE.
It is inlaid with ebony, holly and
ivory.

212

in Nash's gallery at Attingham of 1806 and on a much more extravagant scale in the saloon at Ballyfin, Morrison's great house in Co. Leix done for Sir Charles Coote in the 1820s (Figs. 187, 188).

In Elizabethan and Stuart portraits oriental carpets are to be seen, and a few contemporary ones like those bearing Sir Edward Montagu's arms and the dates 1584 and 1585 still survive, but even information about early 18th century carpets is very scanty. A few fine carpets made by Passavant of Exeter in the late 1750s, or a little later by Moorfields and by Whitty of Axminster still exist, but of the more ordinary carpets there is virtually nothing known: the first Kidderminster factory began to make pileless carpets similar to what were called Scotch (a form of floor covering still to be seen on a set of chairs at Traquair House, Peebleshire) carpets about 1735, and five years later Wilton produced carpets with a looped pile, but of their early production nothing seems to have survived.

Both made carpeting by the yard, and this was then sewn together and finished off with a border. Benjamin Franklin, for instance, bought carpeting for "a best Room floor," and he wrote to his wife: "There is enough for one large and two small ones,—it is to be sew'd together, the Edges being first pull'd down, and care taken to make the Figures meet exactly: there is Bordering of the same."[11] According to Lady Shelburne, the best Kidderminster carpets in 1768 cost 5/6 a yard,[12] and in 1752–53 Vile and Cobb supplied carpet border for the Vyne at 5/6 a yard.[13]

The fashion for this kind of carpeting was related to the fashion for fitted carpets and carpets planned to a room, and it started surprisingly early. Mazarin, for instance, had a moquette carpet of three widths listed in his inventory of 1654. It is not known when they first appeared in England, but they were apparently quite usual by the 1750s, for Ware, having commented on the decline in the use of inlay, continued "it is the custom almost universally to cover a room entirely."[14] The Felbrigg inventory taken in the 1760s lists a fitted Wilton in the Drawing Room, and the Clandon inventory of 1778 lists fitted carpets in both the Palladio Room and the Green Drawing Room.

However there were some surprising exceptions to this, notably at Bucking-

187. A DETAIL OF THE FLOOR IN
THE SALOON AT BALLYFIN, CO. LEIX.

188. THE FLOOR IN THE ROTUNDA
AT BALLYFIN.

ham House, where "The cold and hard-rubbed floor (of the Japan Room) is
without a carpet, a luxury of which His Majesty deprives himself in almost
every apartment, for the opinion that carpets and other means of great warmth
are injurious to health . . ." And the account continues "on this western side
of the house are the King's and Queen's warm-rooms, apartments so called
because they have the distinction of carpets, of which there are only four in
the house, though not less than twenty of the rooms are in frequent use by the
Royal Family; the others are in the Dining Room and the Queen's bedroom;
but none of these complete cover the floor."[15] If with George III the reason
was a health fad, in other houses an element of the mobile tradition lingered
on. At Stowe, for instance, not all the state rooms had permanent carpets. The
1845 account,[16] from which we have already quoted, says: "The two apartments
opening from the Salon, viz the State Drawing Room on one hand, and the
music room opposite had formerly no carpets on the floor in general—the
carpets were laid down occasionally if required. These floors were bare and
of highly polished oak."

The carpets designed by Robert Adam are justly famous, and as can be seen
at Syon, Osterley, Saltram and Audley End, they are specially woven to complement the ceiling decoration but they do not cover the whole floor. The
reason for this was that he did not want the design spoilt by being broken into

214

by pieces of furniture ranged round the wall, a point made by Smith in 1812, when he recommended a rich border with a plain centre, and the whole carpet set in two feet from the wall to clear the furniture. This idea carried out on the grandest scale could be seen at Eaton Hall, where fitted carpets were used in all the principal rooms (Fig. 189). Today we tend to dislike the look of empty floorspace and show these very formal carpets in a way that would be quite contrary to Adam's intention.

However, by 1812, when Smith wrote,[17] the formality of 18th century rooms had already started to break up, and the combination of chairs permanently drawn out into a room and the taste for strip carpeting favoured the kind of design that Smith had in mind. It was obviously considered fashionable at the end of the 18th century, for when the White Drawing Room at Houghton was redecorated about 1797, a carpet was made up of geometrically patterned strips sewn together on the dropped pattern principal (Fig. 190) to form a very grand looking design that is finished off with a handsome border. This is much the best preserved carpet of its type and date, but in a number of country houses there are fragments of slightly later Brussels carpets of a somewhat similar type; and some of these are in production once again. Probably the earliest is the Rocksavage carpet from Cholmondeley Castle, designed about 1807; a rose and ribbon design made about 1830 and formerly in a bedroom at Ashburnham Place is also available; and simple medallion and quatrefoil designs based on early 19th century carpets at Attingham, and in the later state coach at Tatton, have also been copied.

In inventories there are frequent references to mats of different kinds, and most fine carpets seem to have had hearth rugs to match, but usually these have disappeared. The survivors, even when the carpet is of Brussels weave, have a pile. Beds also had their own carpets, but most have disappeared too. Indeed possibly the only survivors are the Moorfields carpet specially designed and woven to go round the state bed at Osterley and the Axminster carpet round the state bed at Blickling (Fig. 191). Presumably the one "of red cloth brocaded with gold and silver & red and blue velvet" listed in the state bed-room in the Chandos inventory[18] and the "very pretty Exeter carpet, with sprigs of flowers," which the Duchess of Northumberland saw at Bulstrode in the early 1750s were of a similar shape.

Among the aspects of the uses of carpets about which we know little are seasonal changes. It is more than likely that it was a more common practice in France than England, for Repton in his Red Book for Sheringham in Norfolk says: "In France the furniture is always changed with the season, from Chintz & silk or muslin, to cloth or Velvet, & carpets are substituted for mats and floor

189. GILLOWS' CARPET PLAN FOR EATON HALL, CHESHIRE.

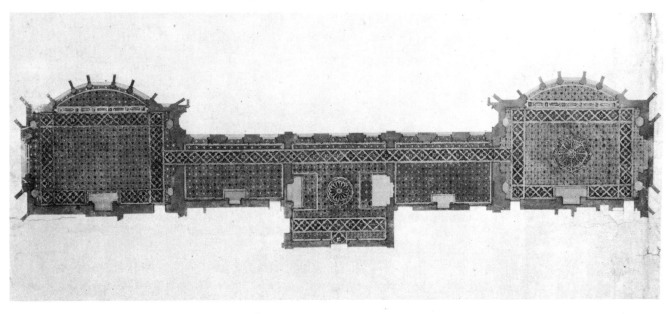

190. THE CARPET IN THE WHITE
DRAWING ROOM AT HOUGHTON. It is
a strip carpet with a border, but,
as with hangings, the pattern is
"dropped" to give a more subtle
effect.

XXIX. THE ENTABLATURE OF THE
GREEN DRAWING ROOM AT CLANDON.
All the gilding is original, except
for the ribbons in the frieze that
were painted white to contrast with
the bay leaves when the room
was restored.

XXX. THE ENTABLATURE IN THE
SALOON AT CLANDON.

XXXI. THE MARBLE PARLOUR AT
HOUGHTON. Kent's choice of colour
in the marbles and their cutting
complements his architectural
design.

cloth." The only reference to this happening in England is in one of Mrs Boscawen's letters in which she gave instructions for a carpet to be taken up for cleaning and for it not to be put down again "for when I come I shall bring mats, for I hate a carpet in Summer." However she writes as if this was a quite normal attitude, and so perhaps it was done in a number of houses.[19]

Repton's reference to floor cloth might easily slip by unnoticed, but in fact what is remarkable is the number of occasions on which floor cloth or oil cloth was used in the 18th century. The earliest reference known to us is in 1736 when "a large floor cloth" is listed in the Dining Room at Denham Hall.[20] Three years later a set of designs were published under the title "*Various kinds of Floor Decorations represented both in Plane and Perspective being Useful Designs for Ornamenting the Floors of Halls Rooms Summer Houses etc Whiether in Pavements of Stone or Marble or With Painted Floor Cloths. In Twenty four Copper Plates. Designed and Engraved by John Carwithen.*"[21]

The best known maker was evidently the firm of Smith whose name altered on several occasions in the course of the 18th century. As Nathan Smith it is recorded in Knightsbridge in 1754, three years after a composition of india rubber and gum mastic was first used; and payments to it occur in the Longford Castle accounts in 1768, in the Northumberland House accounts in 1783 and in Lord Berwick's accounts in 1798. His bill headed Smith, Baber & Downing is for a Mess room costing £103–9–0, and it is apparent from their bill head that they did "Trelliswork, Temples, Garden-Seats, Cover'd Ways, Portable Rooms and all kinds of temporary erections." The only survivor of this kind of building is the Chinese tent at Boughton, which is stamped with their name.

216

However they still did floor cloth at that date, for there is a letter among Matthew Boulton's papers that described one that they were making for him: "The pattern to complete requires much time but when executed will be the grandest ever laid on a floor. The size of our pattern is 8ft square which makes a charming centre, and with the addition of appropriate brick pavement as in the original, and to that according to size of floor, may be added a verde-antique, seina marble etc to a variety of designs."[22] The idea of reproducing a pavement was not a new one, for when Horace Walpole visited Painshill in 1761, he wrote "the tesselated pavement unluckily resembles a painted oil-cloth;"[23] and in a letter to Lady Upper Ossory he said that Mr Lysons had some copied from Roman pavements at Woodchester. And at Attingham until the sale in 1826 there was an unusually large one in the hall: it measured 7 yds. by $6\frac{3}{4}$ yds. and had 4 extra pieces to go in the doorways and was "stone and slate colour octagon panelled."

As well as being used on their own in halls, in corridors and lesser rooms, floor cloths were also used in dining rooms where they were painted to match the carpet. At Attingham in the dining room there was a Turkey carpet and pieces of Turkey-pattern floor cloth under both sideboards, two pieces each side of the fireplace and four in the window embrasures. There was a similar and presumably contemporary arrangement in the dining room at Stourhead, for a bill for 1802 specified an Axminster India Carpet costing £43–12–0, a hearth rug and an oil cloth £6–4–8.[24]

As far as we know no complete 18th century floor cloth survives, but there are two fragments at Winterthur, in the 1762 Dutch Room and in the Hardenburgh Parlour.

XXXII. A SERVING NICHE IN THE
MARBLE PARLOUR. The use of
the different colours of marble to
express the architectural design
should be compared with a colour
scheme like that in the saloon
at Clandon.

A variant on a floor cloth, and indeed its probable origin, was a painted floor. Of these only two old ones exist in England, at Crowcombe Court, in Somerset, and at Belton House, Lincolnshire (Figs. 192, 193). The Crowcombe floor, which is in the dining room, is apparently mid 18th century in date; the centre of the floor is decorated with the arms of the Carews and the outer border is of white outlined in black. The floor of the Tyrconnel Room at Belton appears to be pre-1750 in date for it displays the Brownlow arms. No other references to them in England appear to be recorded, but as simple stencilled decorations still survive in New England[25] and an elaborate marbled floor has been recently restored in a garden pavilion in The Hague, they may be part of the Dutch tradition.

192. THE PAINTED FLOOR IN THE DINING ROOM AT CROWCOMBE COURT, SOMERSET, ABOUT 1760.

193. THE PAINTED FLOOR IN THE TYRCONNEL ROOM AT BELTON HOUSE, LINCOLNSHIRE.

Chapter 7

Light and heating

Methods of lighting and heating in the past play little part in modern restorations, and both tend to be ignored in histories of the English house and the English interior, but, like the uses of houses, an understanding of them is helpful in appreciating how houses seemed to the people who lived in them. We are not concerned with the stylistic development of chandelier design or chimneypiece and grate design: instead we have tried to examine the contrast between private life and gala days as regards lighting and to give a sense of the intense cold and damp of winter, both of which are alluded to in 18th century letters and memoirs.

It is unrealistic to compare a single electric light bulb with a single candle, for, as Mr William O'Dea, has shown, one candle may only be equal to 1/100 part of a 60 watt lamp bulb, but 100 candles will give a totally different light from the bulb. And this, too, is an unsatisfactory comparison, because virtually no one would have used 100 candles at a time except at some great entertainment. Leaving aside the rush light, as it would not have been used in the houses with which we are concerned, let us turn to the tallow candle and the beeswax candle. The former, which was much cheaper, Mr O'Dea found an infuriating device, because it gave less and less light as it burnt down and needed snuffing more frequently than the 30 minutes he expected. In the course of time snuffing has come to mean extinguishing, but before 1825 when Cambaceres improved wick design so that it did not smoke, snuffing meant trimming a wick and removing the burnt fragments. Hence a snuffer-stand was fitted not only with an extinguisher, but with a pair of scissors with an open box on one blade.[1]

Beeswax candles, if well made, had relatively few disadvantages and needed less snuffing. The only drawback was their cost, which was three times that of tallow. They were also much more heavily taxed—4d. a lb. in 1710 as opposed to ½d. on tallow. It was their cost that caused Sarah Duchess of Marlborough to step in and stop a maid selling candle ends to the tallow chandler. Later however the ends became a recognised perquisite of the servants, and indeed in the Adams' book, *The Complete Servant*, published in 1825, they say that the butler "gets the pieces of wax candles." A generation later Prince Albert stopped the practice in the Royal Palaces, where it was the custom to light candles only once and for the remains to be a perquisite of one of the servants.[2] This may not have been as extravagant as it sounds for evidently when a

194. TWO GIRLS DECORATING A
KITTEN BY JOSEPH WRIGHT. Wright's
interest in painting candlelit
subjects evokes the darkness that
generally pervaded 18th century
interiors at night.

reception was planned, it had to be decided what size of candle should be used.
To us the length is a matter of visual proportion, but, according to the *Servants
Guide* of 1830 (p. 67), "wax candles, four in the pound, will last about eleven
hours and should be used when the evening is expected to be five hours, as, in
that case, each candle will serve two nights. Shorter candles, of six to the
pound, are preferable when required to burn six or seven hours."[3]

Today it is very difficult to visualise the dimness of houses most of the time
or the cost of light that forced almost everyone to economise. This affected
not only the Brontes at Haworth, the poet Crabbe and Anthony Trollope's
parents,[4] but even George III and Queen Charlotte. When the Duchess of
Northumberland went to see the Queen in her dressing room in 1772, she
recorded her impressions of the gloom: the room "being very large and hung
with crimson damask, was very dark, there being only 4 candles on the Toilet
& these being in Branches, and the King, wanting to shew us some improvement he had made in the stove, was obliged to carry one of them about in the
nossell of the candlestick in his fingers."[5] At Castle Howard lighting like heating might be expected to have been a problem, and no doubt Vanbrugh was
relieved when Lord Carlisle "finds, that all his Rooms, with moderate fires
are Ovens, And that this Great House do's not require above one pound of
wax, and two of tallow candles to light it, more than his house at London did.

221

Nor in short, is he at any expense more, whatsoever than he was in the Remnent of an old house . . ."[6]

The difference in cost between wax and tallow led to the development of niceties of social distinction of the kind recorded by Brian FitzGerald in his life of *Emily Duchess of Leinster*. When the arrival of the new tutor, Mr Ogilvie, was announced by the Groom of the Chambers, he asked whether he was to have wax or tallow candles. To this Lady Leitrim interjected "Oh, moulds [i.e. tallow] will do, till we see a little."[7] No doubt Mr Ogilvie was given wax, for he was soon accepted and years later the widowed Duchess married him.

Not only were there these distinctions that are now quite forgotten, but problems of lighting led ladies to do different work in the evening. Mrs Delany, for instance, writes of her "candlelight work" "finishing a carpet in double-cross-stitch, on very coarse canvas, to go round my bed." And when she was at Holkham in 1774, she was surprised to find "my Lady Leicester works at a tent-stitch frame every night by *one candle* that she sets upon it, and *no spectacles*."[8] A single candle, however, gives a bright light if correctly placed, and there are several references to the use of shades.

Some idea of the attention given to candles can be gained from the Cannons accounts. There ordinary candles were made on the place, as was soap, first under the direction of the brewer and later of the housekeeper, but the best candles were sometimes imported from Holland or Portugal. The Duke of Chandos also imported myrtlewax and green wax from America and Barbadoes. Myrtlewax from Carolina cost 7d. a lb., and in 1739 he was prepared to pay 10d. a lb. for 4 or 5 cwt. of New England wax. This seems an enormous quantity, but he expected the housekeeper to have 2,400 lb. always in stock; this was sufficient for two candlemaking sessions in the house. It was reckoned that 140 lbs. of wax was needed for 700 candles, and as 5 candles took 1 lb. of wax, each candle used less than 1d. worth of wax.[9]

It is particularly interesting to have the reference to coloured candles. The green he liked was evidently an almost transparent lime green. The white candles had a tendency to yellow, and so they had to be bleached in the air. The myrtle candles gave off a delicate smell.

Unfortunately his records do not tell us how many candles were used on any one occasion or what it cost to light the house, but, as Ware points out, the number of candles was partly conditioned by the decoration of a room. He says that six candles in a wainscot room are the equivalent of eight in a stucco room and ten in a room with hangings.[10]

Lighting was evidently not just a matter of seeing adequately and of cost, but it was also a matter of prestige and a symbol of hospitality. At Versailles, for instance, Louis XIV used to order lighting in accordance with the importance he attached to the occasion.[11] In England customs tended to be less formalized, but when Sir Robert Walpole entertained the Duke of Lorraine at Houghton in 1731 before the house was quite complete, the degree of lighting must have been intended as a compliment to his guest. Sir Thomas Robinson described how "They dined in the hall which was lighted by 130 wax candles, and the saloon with 50; the whole expense in that article being computed at fifteen pounds a night."[12] Three years later Decker mentioned a lantern with 18 candlesticks in the hall and this was obviously taken as a symbol of Walpole's extravagance.[13]

When George III visited the Dowager Duchess of Portland at Bulstrode in 1779, Mrs Delany says "Her Grace had the house lighted up in a most magnificent manner; the chandelier in the great hall was not lighted before for *twenty years*."[14] The phrase "lighted up" crops up quite frequently in 18th century letters describing entertainments, people tending to record not only the remnent of guests but the number of candles. When Shelburne House, for instance, was nearly finished in 1769, the young Lady Shelburne was obviously very excited when she saw it lit up for the first time: "The House look'd very fine

as it was very much lighted up."[15] Lady Cowper's letter to Miss Dewes written the same year gives a similar expression: "I had an assembly in my great room, with above five dozen wax lights in the room. Three quadrille tables, and a table for Prince Ernest for vingt-un."[16] When the Duke and Duchess of Northumberland entertained in London in the 1760s, there were four large glass chandeliers each of 25 lights in the Great Gallery; and Count Kielmansegge, who was one of the 600 guests at an assembly there, commented that they "light the room even more brilliantly than is necessary."[17]

Such extravagance was widely recognised, and when Maria Edgeworth

195. THE TEA PARTY BY HENRY SARGENT, ABOUT 1820. This picture of an early 19th century New York interior is a rare illustration of characteristic lighting in a house at that time and how guests used a formally arranged room.

wanted to give an impression of Lord Glenthorn's prodigality in *Ennui*, she wrote: "The London winter commenced; and the young earl of Glenthorn, and his entertainments, and his equipages and extravagances, were the conversation of all the world, and the joy of the newspapers . . . the hundreds of waxlights, which burned nightly in his house, were numbered by the idle admirers of folly; and it was known by everybody that Lord Glenthorn suffered nothing but wax to be burned in his stables, . . ."[18]

And just as light was to do with prestige, chandeliers of glass were objects of what Veblen would have called conspicuous consumption. The earliest ones in England are those made of rock crystal at Hampton Court and Penshurst, all dating from the late 17th century. They were obviously a great rarity then, for when Charles II dined with the Grand Duke Cosimo on his visit to England in 1669 it was thought worth mentioning that "From the ceiling was suspended a chandelier of rock crystal with lighted tapers."[19] Others are mentioned in the Queen's closet, but it is not said whether they were brass, glass or silver. Silver ones were also objects of great prestige, but the only two 17th century examples that survive are the one at Chatsworth made in 1694 and the one at Drumlanrig made about 1680.

By the 1730s it was usual to light a very large room with a series of chandeliers. The Assembly Room at York has 8 each with 14 lights (copies made in 1951 of the original one now in Treasurer's House). But as far as we know no country house interior had more than the five now in the hall at Grimsthorpe, and throughout the 18th century a chandelier was a symbol of extravagance. At Woburn, for instance, there is a very fine one of carved and gilded wood in the Saloon that cost £86 in 1760. It has 18 lights and was apparently the first one in the house.[20] For ease of replacement and snuffing the chandeliers were often hung with a counter balance that could be disguised with a tassel as happens with the pair of George II chandliers in the Saloon at Sudbury.

To add extra light and to give greater spread torchères with candelabra were often placed in the corners of a room. They have always stood in that position in the Saloon at Saltram and recently the Victoria and Albert Museum have put them back in a similar position in the Drawing Room at Osterley. Marble or alabaster vases were also adapted to take candles inside them, and examples of this kind of lighting are recorded at Newby, Audley End and in Porden's drawing room at Eaton Hall (Plate XVIII).[21]

For a particularly large party extra lights might be brought in. For instance when there was a ball at Saltram in 1810, patent lamps were placed over the windows in the saloon and a quantity of candles were put over the doors and their sockets concealed by wreaths and festoons of leaves and flowers.[22]

The late 18th century was a period of technical development in lighting as it was in other spheres for it saw the invention of the Argand lamp. Argand placed a tubular wick between inner and outer tubes, on the principal of an *Aladdin* paraffin heater, and protected it by a tubular glass funnel that greatly improved its performance. When he came to England in 1783 he approached Matthew Boulton and the following year patented his invention, but the patent was infringed and in 1786 it was declared invalid. Heavy oil was used and this had to be forced up from a tank below or placed in a reservoir at a higher level, the design depending on whether it was a hanging lamp or of a pedestal type to be placed on a table or a torchère. The lamp did not drive out the candle, for, as Mr O'Dea has shown, a lamp could not provide as economically the same light as a single candle, a but cluster of candles could not compete with a lamp, or with a couple of burners as was often the usage.

When Sophie von la Roche came to England in 1786, she was very impressed by the lamps and records finishing "the evening at tea investigating Argand lamps of all descriptions . . ."[23]

The invention of the Argand lamp, and later developments, made an enormous difference, but still they involved a lot of work, for they created dirt in a room, and a lamp room was a department on its own in a great house. When Mrs Ramsden, the housekeeper at Woburn in 1770, inspected "my Lord Duke's bed," she found "it so very black with burning of oil in the room that she thinks it proper to have it cleaned."[24] And there is a good description of a lamp room in Eller's *History of Belvoir*: there they "are considered to be the most complete in their arrangement. The lamps are filled over cisterns, which receive the unavoidable waste of oil in the operation. The waste thus collected is afterwards used in the offices etc. In the season of his Grace's residence, about 16 or 17 weeks, 400 burners are required, and about 600 gallons of oil consumed." And the accounts for the 18 weeks from December 1839 to April 1840, show that 2330 wax lights and 630 gallons of sperm oil were used. To get this in perspective, 1997 dined at the Duke's table, 2421 at the steward's and 11,312 in the servants' hall and other departments. To light the Elizabeth Saloon, there was a central chandelier, bracket chandeliers and four carved and gilded candelabra on black marble pedestals each with seven burners. The chandelier and the wall-lights are still there but the seven burner lamps have gone.[25]

Just as it is difficult to visualise the darkness of most 18th century parlours and the contrast between them and a room lit up for an assembly, it is hard to imagine the cold and damp of 17th and 18th century houses. However, once one reads old letters for references to discomfort, they appear common enough. There are particularly graphic accounts in Lady Kildare's letters to her husband in the early 1760s. On December 9, 1762 she wrote from Carton: "I have been here these two days and wou'd you believe it? Starved with cold after coming from Castletown, which shews the coldest houses when constantly lived in will be warmer than the warmest when at any time uninhabited, as is the case here. I feel the want of my winter rooms now sadly, and shall set about finishing them directly. You will say, what, was the print room cold? No, but the way to it from the apartment we are in at present perishingly so—those stairs running with wet, as is the passage above and most of the rooms to this back side of the house; which shows, my love, the necessity of having very, very often fires almost all over the house. We must never be sparing in the article of coals, not indeed was it ever our orders they shou'd be spared, but the maids are exceedingly so of their trouble; . . . I have not seen anything here out of these three rooms (for I live in the India paper room chiefly, as 'tis near my own, and that I have no passage or staircase to pass)." In November 1764, her sister Caroline, Lady Holland wrote to her "Your rooms are not large at Carton, but they lie so well together, I think it a comfortable house. Large rooms are I think more necessary in winter than summer; a small room with open windows and no fire does very well, but shut up they are not pleasant, when they open into one another as yours do, a door open answers the purpose of a large room."[26]

Lady Holland felt the cold, for the previous winter she had written to the same sister: "This cold weather prevents my wearing (2 gowns you sent) as I am, you know, apt to clothe warm; it's the only kind of heat I like; at present I live in a wadded gown, which is so warm and so light how I shall ever leave it off I don't know." At Bramshill the cold was so great that Mrs Powys said Sir John Cope used to put on his hat to go from one room to another, and at Eaton Hall in the early 19th century Lady Elizabeth Grosvenor wore flannel underwear, 2 pairs of stockings, washleather insteps to protect her legs from cold indoors, "muffetees" which she knitted for her wrists, and she wrote that "only very close to the fire does one attain the desired object of keeping oneself warm."[27]

It was not just a matter of keeping rooms warm when in use but keeping up a steady temperature through the winter. "Pray take particular care of the house while the family is absent. Let there be a fire *constantly* kept in my brother's chamber and mine." There is a ring of truth about these instructions, but in fact they came from a novel and are Miss Tabitha Bramble's instructions in Smollett's *Humphrey Clinker*. At Hopetoun when Cullen was discussing the hangings for the drawing room he suggested that he might make them up so that they could be taken down when the family went away for any length of time, because he said "the winter damp in large rooms sometimes will milldew the hangings." But for some the cold and damp were quite beyond them.[28]

Barbara Charlton described the discomfort of life at Hesleyside in Northumberland in the mid 19th century: "Coal and firewood they had in great abundance, it is true, but the long passages had no heat, the outside doors were never shut, the hall and corridors were paved with flagstones, while to complete the resemblance of Hesleyside to a refrigerator, the grand staircase, also of stone, and the three large old-fashioned, full-length windows half-way up with their frames warped by the excessive damp . . . contrived to make the downstairs space a cave of icy blasts. Even in my early years at Hesleyside funguses grew on the passage woodwork . . ."[29] So it was at Windsor Castle in George IV's time it was cold, for Hazlitt found "As to physical comfort, one seems to have no more of it in these tapestried halls and on marble floors, than the poor bird driven before the pelting storm . . ."

To combat this in the late 17th and early 18th century the coal burning grate was developed, and it was thought sufficiently interesting by Francois Misson[30] in 1698 to describe in considerable detail. However it did not have an immediate success, and at a house like Dyrham the fireplaces would be equipped both with irons for wood burning and with grates for coal, often called stove grates in inventories and accounts. Grate design had considerable influence on room design, for grates needed a much smaller opening than was required for woodburning, and this meant that the whole chimneypiece was reduced in size. The importance of this is well brought out when one compares 18th century chimneypieces in England and America, where coal was not burnt and so big fireplaces continued to be constructed right through the century. Apart from that, grate design could be adapted to reflect all passing fashions, Rococo, gothick, chinoiserie, Empire, Egyptian and so on, but undoubtedly

196. JAMES WYATT'S DESIGN FOR THE DINING ROOM AT SLANE CASTLE, IRELAND. The alcoves are fitted with stoves supporting figures holding lamps.

226

the finest were the free standing pierced basket grates.

Towards the middle of the 18th century people began to experiment with slow combustion stoves and with central heating. Some of the surviving stoves are splendid-looking affairs designed as part of the decoration of the room, as can be seen in the Saloon at Kedleston. Among Wyatt's designs for Slane Castle (Fig. 196) is a proposal for the dining room with a pair of alcoves at one end fitted with stoves topped by classical figures holding lamps. At Inveraray Faujas de St. Fond was impressed by "large bronze vases, of antique shape, placed on their pedestals, between the columns" of the vestibule. "These

197. THE STOVE AND LAMP AT THE FOOT OF THE MAIN STAIRCASE AT PENCARROW.

vases served, at the same time, as stoves to warm the air of the vestibule and the staircase."[31] A few of these classical vases have survived: there is one at the foot of the basement stairs at Castlecoole and until 1970 one was to be seen as a convincing garden ornament at Kentwell Hall in Suffolk. Of the early 19th century ones there used to be a fine example in the Ante-Room between the Drawing Room and the Library at Dodington in Gloucestershire and at Pencarrow there is one at the foot of the stairs capped by a three light oil lamp (Fig. 197). At Belvoir the stoves were disguised as trophies of arms: "At the end of the entrance passage are banners, and two stands of pikes, one of which is intended to mask an ingenious contrivance, for procuring an effectual draught for the stove, which warms this passage;" and arrangements of arms masked stoves in the Guard Room.[32]

How effective these were is not known. Nor is much known about early forms of central heating. Probably one of the earliest was that in the hall at West Wycombe by Sir Francis Dashwood about 1760. He was interested in all kinds of patent devices and materials, but here he revived a form of hypocaust. At least two systems were patented in the next two years, one by someone called Green and another in 1769 by James Watt, who was interested in warming pipes with steam. Matthew Boulton adopted this system in 1774

198. THE ETRUSCAN ROOM AT OSTERLEY. The fireplace is filled with a painted chimneyboard.

228

and he still recommended the method 20 years later when writing to Lord Lansdowne.

As well as steam, hot air and hot water were also tried. Richard Lovell Edgeworth tried hot air in the hall at Pakenham in 1807 and it was used for the gallery at Lansdowne House as completed by Smirke in 1819 and at Charlecote in the 1830s. Sir Walter Scott preferred steam heating for Abbotsford in 1823. But in the end it was hot water that won the day. The Great Duke of Wellington installed a hot water system at Stratfield Saye in 1823 and a few years later another was installed at Hatfield.[33]

In the summer, when fires were not needed, there were two ways of dealing with the space. Many pictures show vases with or without flowers in them in the grate and this was certainly quite usual practice in the early 18th century. The Dyrham inventory of 1716, for instance, lists delft ware in the chimney of several rooms.

A more effective alternative was a chimney board. These are virtually never seen in England now, but a considerable number have survived in America. Possibly the earliest evidence for one in England is the survival of the knobs for securing one in the Duchess of Lauderdale's bedroom at Ham, but we have only come across references to them shortly before the middle of the 18th century. When Dr Pococke went to Longford Castle in 1754, he said "the chimney boards through the house are made of Chinese pictures, which show several of their customs;" and one of presumably similar type can be seen at Osterley where it is en suite with the furnishings of the Taffeta Bedroom.

Almost inevitably both Mrs Delany and Horace Walpole went in for them, and in 1757 Walpole wrote to Chute: "Muntz has absolutely done nothing this whole summer but paste two chimney boards. In short, instead of Claude Lorraine, he is only one of Bromwich's men."[34]

And the most sophisticated survivors are those from Osterley and Audley End. At Osterley apart from the one for the Taffeta Bedroom, there is one in the Etruscan Room (Fig. 198), but rather oddly it is not listed in that room in 1782 but in the State Bedchamber. Recently four have been discovered for the Adam rooms at Audley End (Fig. 199).

Chapter 8
Attitudes to pictures and picture hanging

Any discussion of attitudes to pictures in a book on decoration might sound like the tail wagging the dog, but as the history of decoration is a part of the history of taste, it must be bound up with attitudes to works of art and ideas of how they should be arranged; moreover fashions in collecting were one factor that determined the planning of great houses, and occasionally to this day the dominant date in a house may be set by the choice of works of art and their arrangement rather than by the style of decoration. And it is even arguable that the whole concept of decoration was only capable of development when appreciation of works of art had reached a certain stage.

In England there was little understanding of European painting and sculpture until the circle round Charles I began to collect on a considerable scale. The names of many of those interested in the arts at that time are known, and so are the contents of some of their collections, but unfortunately we know virtually nothing about how they were arranged. Inigo Jones designed a picture room for Henry Prince of Wales in 1611, and in 1630 Gerbier designed another for the Duke of Buckingham, but the earliest impressions of galleries are those in the backgrounds of Mytens's portraits of the Earl and Countess of Arundel. The most interesting piece of contemporary advice is that given by Sir Henry Wotton in 1624: "Lastly that they bee as properly bestowed for their quality as fitly for their grace: that is, cheerful Paintings in Feesting and Banqueting Roomes: Graver Stories in Galleries: Landscaips and Boscage, and such wilder works, in open Terraces, or in Summer Houses."[1] Here, as in other aspects of architecture and decoration, is reflected a very ordered approach to life, with everything having its correct place just as everyone had his or her precise place in society. Today the only 17th century house where there is any sense of this is at Wilton: there in the Double Cube Room are the full length Van Dyck portraits installed in 1654; in the Hunting Room, arranged in the two orders of the panelling that is presumably based on a French engraving, are the scenes of sporting life by the elder Pierce, and in the Corner Room is a modern re-arrangement of cabinet pictures acquired later but not untypical of the taste of Charles I's circle.

Wotton's view was also paralleled by the concept of a picture painted for a particular position and being part of a decorative scheme. Van Dyck's portrait of *Charles I on Horseback with M de St. Antoine in Attendance* was designed to be hung at the end of the Long Gallery at St James's Palace, a dramatic piece of Baroque illusionism; and it is conceivable that others of his full lengths were intended to be illusionistic. However one of the few places where this can be experienced now is in the hall at Lamport constructed in the 1650s, where a copy of the *Charles on Horseback*, which was acquired in 1655, has been rehung in recent years to face a copy of the Louvre portrait of Charles I as a country gentleman; both are hung only just above ground level.

This illusionism was related to the concept of a portrait as a kind of moral lesson, for the idea was widely held that one could learn the lessons of history by studying portraits: as Peacham wrote of reliefs on coins, "their lively presence is able to persuade a man he now seeth two thousand years ago." Or, as John Duke of Buckingham wrote in 1704: "I have so many portraits of famous persons in several kinds, as are enough to excite ambition in any man less lazy, or less at ease than myself." It was for this reason that people liked the idea of sets of portraits, whether they were of ancestors, kinsmen, notables or beauties: they were a very positive reminder of the past to the present and particularly suitable in galleries where one could walk up and down studying them on days when the weather was too inclement to take exercise out of doors.[2]

Pictures other than portraits were frequently regarded as curiosities and to be admired for their ingenuity, their accuracy of detail and their ability to deceive the eye. Hence the taste for still life and for perspective pictures like the *View Down the Corridor* painted by Samuel Hoogstraeten about 1668 that belonged to Thomas Povey and is now at Dyrham (Fig. 19).

However, apart from Van Dyck who knew how to exploit architectural design in his images of Kingship, the relationship between painting and decoration does not seem to have been satisfactorily worked out until after the Restoration. It was only then that pictures began to occupy a more definite place in the total scheme for a room and were related to the patterns of panelling. Perhaps under the influence of contemporary French engravings, which tended to be of door and chimneypiece units rather than of complete rooms, pictures were used to create definite vertical emphases in a room, being placed over doors and chimneypieces, the complete unit contrasting with areas of plain panelling or tapestry or some other hanging Plates XX, XXXVII). In most cases such pictures were only of moderate quality, being vaguely classical landscapes, ruin pieces, or sets of lesser relations by minor painters. Usually the top of the overdoor picture was level with the top of the overmantel picture, and sometimes towards the end of the century a panel of looking glass was introduced between the top of the chimneypiece and the bottom of the picture to reflect light and to build up the composition. There are many examples showing variations on this idea of balance, among them the Blue Drawing Room at Ham; there the overdoors are much larger than the overmantel picture and the latter is enriched and set off by carved and gilt swags, and the main panels are covered with richly worked hangings. In the Balcony Room at Dyrham the Hondecoeter overmantel placed above a horizontal glass is balanced by overdoors by Jean Baptiste Monnoyer; but the modern arrangement of the looking glasses and flower piece on the inner wall contradicts the original rhythm. *The Tea Party at Lord Harrington's* by Charles Philips (Fig. 118) is another excellent illustration of how ideas have changed: today most people would find the verticality of the room unrelaxed, and choose a smaller overmantel picture; also instead of having overdoors they would hang pictures on the panelling flanking the chimneypiece. But by so doing they would deny the original balance of the room.

However it is surprising to find that in late 17th century and early 18th century panelled rooms although there might be a sense of the total effect as we have suggested, pictures that were not actually incorporated in the decoration were often hung with little regard for the pattern of the panelling. Frequently they seem to have over-ridden the mouldings and were tipped forward to avoid the top moulding. This is seen not only in Hogarth's *The Indian Emperor*, but in such sophisticated rooms as those depicted on the Duc de Choiseul's box. The tilting was done to reduce reflections and to make smaller pictures hung high up more visible, as can be seen in Leslie's picture of Lady Holland in the

Gallery at Holland House.

Some late 17th century engravings, particularly those by Marot, show how cords could be made part of the decoration of the room, with bows, sleeves and tassels added, but how usual this was in England is not known. However it could not have been so rare for otherwise it would not have been considered a suitable detail for Pugh to include in his satirical picture of Lord Granard having his hair powdered (Fig. 200). The only documented examples we have come across are rather later: when Buckingham House was being decorated in 1763, Edward Parker, a silk laceman, supplied "crimson silk cordoon and large crimson tassells" to hang pictures in a bed chamber and two rooms adjoining. Lady Louisa Conolly used purple and silver cords in her white damask room at Castletown in the late 1760s, and when Chippendale was working for Sir Lawrence Dundas in Arlington Street, he charged for 40 large tassels of the bellindine silk at 4/10d each "to hang the girandolas, and all the pictures in long Room, and making Ornaments even Do."[3]

Comparatively few English collections of pictures other than portraits date back to the 17th century: the nucleus of the Alnwick, Syon and Petworth collections all belonged to the 10th Earl of Northumberland before the Civil War; while the Althorp, Lamport and Burghley collections all date from after the Restoration. However, from quite early in the 18th century the combination of the increase in European travel and the development of the picture trade led to pictures making a more important contribution to the appearance of English houses: not only did their number increase, but their quality improved,

200. *LORD GRANARD HAVING HIS WIG POWDERED* BY HERBERT PUGH, ABOUT 1770. Although a caricature, it is a good illustration of the decorative use of cords for picture hanging.

and some of the more ambitious collectors began to think in terms of galleries and cabinets. King William III, for instance, added a gallery at Kensington Palace in 1695 and he told Huygens to hang the pictures on cords so that he could rearrange them himself more easily.[4] Burlington's addition of his villa to his house at Chiswick was primarily done to take his collections, and both at Houghton and Holkham considerable provision had to be made for their owners' collections.

Unfortunately we have no visual record of how Houghton looked in Sir Robert's time, although we know what each room contained, but probably the effect was not unlike that of the gallery at Corsham, which Brown designed in 1762 (Figs. 201, 202). Over the years the hanging there has been altered partly to make room for pictures inherited from the Rev. John Sandford in 1855, but the basic idea has been kept: that is to say the whole of the wall from the dado to the entablature is used, each group of pictures forming a satisfactory arrangement on its own and carefully matched by another group where appropriate to create a totally balanced and harmonious effect. And the hanging is related to the equally carefully thought-out arrangement of pier glasses, tables and seat furniture. All the parts add up to a splendid whole.

However, it is worthy of notice that the picture that is the key to the room is not autograph: the overmantel is a studio replica of Rubens's *A Wolf and Fox Hunt* and it is set in a superb frame that matches the pier glasses. This was not an isolated case of using a picture of lesser importance for such a position, for there was a great shortage of large pictures in England throughout the 18th century. At Kedleston, for instance, where the collection survives more or less intact, Horace Walpole commented: "There are many and large pictures, but most copies or sadly repaired, bought for the house in Italy".[5] It is this shortage

201. THE GALLERY AT CORSHAM. The balance achieved through the grouping of the pictures complements the architectural design of the room.

that partly explains the high price of £2200 paid by John Spencer in 1758 for Reni's *Liberality and Modesty* and Sacchi's *Apollo rewarding Merit and punishing Arrogance*, both of which hung in the Great Room at Spencer House (Fig. 203). And schemes like that at Kedleston which depended on large canvases usually forced a patron to choose between commissioning a series from a decorative painter, acquiring copies or making do with a set of portraits adapted to fit. At Shugborough Thomas Anson chose to order from Dahl a set of architectural pieces for his Great Room, now the dining room, and later Adam usually relied on Zucchi, as in the Music Room at Harewood, the Saloon at Nostell and the Dining Room at Osterley. These were essentially undemanding pictures, for Adam's patrons no doubt shared Gilpin's view that "If a picture does not please the sight, it is fitter for a painter's chamber, or a curious cabinet, than for a saloon or a drawing room."[6] On the other hand Campbell's Saloon at Stourhead was fitted with a series of copies (Figs. 204, 205). The grandest scheme of this type was the Gallery at Northumberland House, for which Mengs was commissioned to copy Raphael's *School of Athens*, Batoni to do the *Feast of the Gods*, Constanzi to do Annibale Carracci's *Bacchus and Ariadne* and Mesuccio to do Guido Reni's *Aurora*. At Woburn there was always a problem and it has never been satisfactorily solved by 18th century standards: in the Saloon Walpole mentions copies of Van Dyck's portraits of the 10th Earl of Northumberland and of Lord Bedford and Lord Digby, which presumably hung over the two chimneypieces, and he goes on to say that the pictures in the Dressing Room and Drawing Room were too small for state rooms.[7] The copies were no doubt removed from the Saloon later, probably because they were thought not important enough artistically, and two of the splendid Mortlake Raphael tapestries put up instead, but they do not answer the architectural needs of the room.

202. THE REVERSE VIEW IN THE GALLERY AT CORSHAM.

203. THE GREAT ROOM AT SPENCER
HOUSE, ABOUT 1890. Although the
furniture is arranged in a late
19th century way, the large pictures
by Reni and Sacchi are hung in
their original positions.

204. THE SALOON AT STOURHEAD,
WILTSHIRE. Buckler's watercolour,
done about 1820 shows the formal
arrangement of the room with
the furniture in case covers.

205. THE SALOON AT STOURHEAD
BEFORE THE FIRE OF 1902. This
shows some of the copies
commissioned for the room.

Among the rooms decorated with sets of earlier portraits are the drawing
room at Ditchley and Rousham and the dining room at Drayton, in all three
cases a feeling for history combined with a need for economy. However, harmony and balance were achieved, and to most 18th century owners that was
the chief consideration. Today we are primarily concerned with questions of
feeling and originality in individual pictures, but this is a post-Romantic view:
we no longer "read" pictures, nor do we choose them for their ideas, and so
copies are despised. And yet to an 18th century owner "a copy of a very good
picture is preferable to an indifferent original; for there the invention is seen
almost intire, and great deal of the expression, and disposition, and many times
good hints of the colouring, drawing and other qualities".[8] Given that view
of a copy and that approach to pictures, it was quite logical to hang large
pictures high because they could still be "read" and to hang them in relation
to the wall space rather than in relation to the spectator.

This is little understood today and rows of pictures in gilt frames against
crimson damask or flock are thought to be oppressive rather than grand; but
if one looks at Adam's design for the drawing room at Kedleston, Atkinson's
design for the drawing room at Burton Constable, or Sir Richard Colt
Hoare's Gallery at Stourhead (Figs. 206, 207), or on a more moderate scale,

206. THE GALLERY AT STOURHEAD,
ABOUT 1900.

207. THE GALLERY AS IT IS TODAY.

208. THE CABINET AT FELBRIGG HALL, NORFOLK. A 17th century room refitted by Paine in the 1750s to take part of William Windham's collection of pictures. The hangings are of the original wool damask.

209. ONE OF A SERIES OF DRAWINGS TO SHOW THE PROPOSED HANGING OF THE PICTURES.

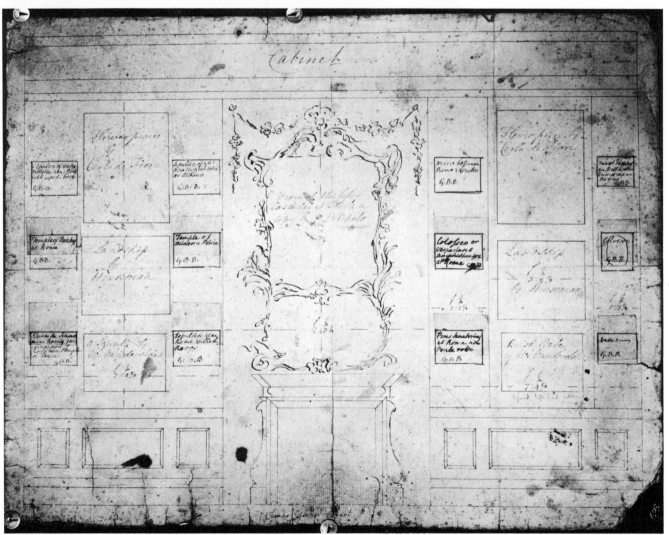

the Cabinet at Felbrigg, the dining room at Farnborough Hall (Fig. 210) with its Canalettos and Paninis in stucco frames, or the portraits in the Cordel Room at Long Melford, the Breakfast Room at Saltram (Fig. 211) or the cut out panels of wallpaper in the Chinese room at Erthig (Fig. 212), the success of the 18th century system becomes apparent. A modest recent example that bears this out is to be seen in the reconstructed drawing room at the Soane Museum, where the portraits on the chimneypiece wall have been hung as they appear in Soane's watercolour and not in relation to modern taste.[9]

Of course the ideal situation of the right number of pictures of appropriate size for any particular room probably seldom existed, and anyway a living collection by its very nature is always in a state of growth. Moreover a collector's interest in particular artists or pictures is quite likely to conflict with his feeling for the design of a room. So, as in any theory involving decoration, there are more exceptions to "rule" than text book examples.

As yet we have not sufficient evidence to comment at all precisely on changing attitudes to the close hanging of pictures, although this needs to be considered in relation to the choice of colour, pattern and texture for the background against which they are hung. But a move away from the Corsham kind of idea probably began about 1790, for in the early 19th century it became fashionable to hang pictures less thickly in rooms other than galleries. At Carlton House, for instance, the Prince Regent tended to have a single picture on a wall if it was a recognised masterpiece and to set it off with false panels or drapery (Fig. 213). There is a similar clarity in the drawing room at Attingham: although the room was finished in the mid 1780s, the pictures were acquired in the 1790s and the pier glasses added in 1806 when the room was repainted. Although the hanging has had to be altered, the uncrowded simplicity recalls

210. PART OF THE DINING ROOM AT FARNBOROUGH HALL, WARWICKSHIRE. The elaborate panes are placed in relation to the proportions of the wall rather than to the viewpoint of the spectator.

XXXIII. PART OF A DOORCASE IN
THE TAPESTRY ROOM AT WEST
WYCOMBE PARK, BUCKINGHAMSHIRE.
The painting, which is a most
unusual survival, gives an idea of
the skill in planning as well as
execution required for fine 18th
century decoration: all the
architectural details are in *trompe
l'oeil*.

XXXIV. A DETAIL OF A DOORCASE
IN THE STATE BEDROOM AT
BLICKLING HALL, NORFOLK. Here
alternate leaves are picked out.

XXXV. A SECTION OF THE
ENTABLATURE AND A CAPITAL IN THE
STATE BEDROOM AT BLICKLING.
The gilding of the flutes should be
compared with an alternative
way to be seen in the Boudoir at
Attingham (Plate III).

XXXVI. A DETAIL OF THE DADO
RAIL AT BLICKLING, SHOWING THE
VARIATION IN THE GILDING.

211. THE BREAKFAST ROOM AT SALTRAM. A revised rehanging of an 18th century group of pictures against plain red velvet hangings.

that of the drawing room at Southill, a room completed in the opening years of the 19th century. At Farnley Hall Turner's watercolour of the drawing room (Figs. 214, 215) shows his *View of Dort* overriding the chimneypiece (this was later moved to the wall facing the window) with two sea-scapes hanging to left and right under portraits of Kit-Kat size: it is obvious that none of the pictures were hung in relation to the cornice, but in relation to the spectator, a step recommended by Sheraton. In his *Cabinet Dictionary* he says: "The largest pictures should be placed so high only as to bring their centres nearly as may be perpendicular to the eye of the spectator;" and he goes on to say that if they have to be hung higher, they should be made to hang forward.[10]

So far we have only considered the element of pattern making in picture hanging and not commented on what was thought appropriate to a particular room, but this was probably of equal importance. For instance, we have already seen that the hall was regarded not only as the room of entry but the waiting place for servants, and so it was obvious not to hang it with old masters. Kent frequently used no pictures at all, but relied on sculpture, busts and reliefs. Many Palladian halls were treated in this way, and Adam continued the idea at Syon and Harewood. As an alternative, pictures of horses, sports and country pursuits were acceptable, as can be seen in the halls at Longleat, Althorp and Badminton. At Badminton Kent decorated the hall to take a series of pictures of the 3rd Duke of Beaufort's field sports, a life size canvas over the chimneypiece and four big scenes by Wootton, all specially framed and hung above stucco trophies emblematic of country pursuits. At Althorp, where the 5th Earl of Sunderland's field sports are depicted, the frieze incorporates foxes' masks, hounds and trophies of horns and quivers.

However sometimes portraits were used. At Stourhead they are of the family,

241

212. THE CHINESE ROOM AT ERTHIG.
Cut-out roundels of Chinese
painting and a cut-out border
mounted on yellow wallpaper,
about 1775.

but at Chippenham Park in Celia Fiennes's day the hall was "hung with
pictures at full proportion of the Royal Family, all in their coronation robes
from Charles the First to his Majesty with the Queen also . . ." There is something of the same idea in the Great Hall at Drayton where there are portraits
of the royal benefactors of its owners; Henry V, Henry VII, Henry VIII,
Charles I and William III (Fig. 15); and at Grimsthorpe the recesses in Vanbrugh's hall are filled with images of William I, Edward III, Henry V, Henry
VII, Henry VIII, William III and George I. Another house that had a great
series of royal portraits was Euston, where in 1698 Celia Fiennes saw a "Long
Gallery hung with pictures at length—on the one side the Royal Family from
King Henry 7th by the Scottish race his eldest daughter down to the present
King William and his Queen Mary, the other are foreign princes . . ."[11]

The Drayton, Grimsthorpe and Euston kinds of arrangement are typical of
the Baroque period and are directly comparable with the themes of decorative
painting found on walls and ceilings. Later generations took a much less
thematic view of painting, and, anyway if they collected pictures, they did not

242

place such emphasis on portraits of historical figures. Instead they collected history and subject pictures and, depending on the nature of the house and the collection, generally divided them between gallery, great drawing room and cabinet.

Lord Chesterfield evidently thought in these terms for he wrote to Solomon Dayrolles in 1748, "I do not care for the Teniers you mention, both my picture-rooms being completely filled—the great one with capital pictures, the cabinet with bijoux." At Corsham the Gallery was next to the Cabinet. The corollary to this was that other rooms might have no pictures of any importance. At Stowe, for instance, the gallery always had tapestry, and apart from the Grenville Room, which was hung with portraits, virtually all the pictures hung in the drawing room: the other rooms only had overmantels and overdoors. No doubt this was partly because the collection was a small one, but also it made it possible to introduce an element of variety into a house where the range of colours used was restricted and apartments tended to be uniform in colour. Of course this is supposition, but it is interesting to see, particularly from the 1740s onwards, how the disposition of works of art tended to be worked out in this way.[12]

In most English houses where the pictures are an accumulation rather than a formal collection, the majority will be portraits and will tend to be grouped together in a gallery or dining room. There are many examples of portraits in dining rooms starting with the Double Cube Room at Wilton, and continuing with Compton Place, the former dining rooms at Badminton and Firle, and the Speakers' Parlour at Clandon. One of the last of these must be the (private) Dining Room at Chatsworth fitted up by the Bachelor Duke in 1832. Granted that he was not seriously interested in pictures, it is odd that he selected such

243

244

a miscellany and got Wyatville to design the lozenge fillings to the panels so that it would not be obvious that they were not all of the same size or, as he put it, that "the short and long" portraits sent from Devonshire House would be "swallowed at the same time."[13]

The literary approach to painting is also apparent in the old tradition of library portraits that dates from before the frieze in the Upper Reading Room of the Bodleian Library at Oxford painted by John Clarke about 1618 and revived at the Restoration by Bishop Cosin in his choice of heads for his library at Durham. The most famous 18th century set was in Lord Chesterfield's library (Fig. 216) starting with Chaucer and Shakespeare and going up to his own day with Pope, Swift and Johnson, but it was by no means the only one. At Clandon in 1778 there were portraits of Chaucer, Milton, Shakespeare, Spencer, Dryden, Richardson and Hobbes. In Holland's library at Woburn there is another set, and there are two rows of portraits above the books in the libraries at Badminton and Petworth. At that height one cannot judge their quality but one has the suggestion of presence of great figures.

This attitude is also implicit in the fashion for library busts which developed in the 1740s. Dr Delany, for instance, "bought four portraits and bespoke two more for his library—Seneca, Aristotle, Galen and Horace: they are done in plaster of Paris, and varnished so well that they look like polished marble at a proper distance."[14] Later the idea was developed by Wedgwood.

It is both ironical and an exaggeration to say that it seems that as the literary approach gave way to a visual one and the quality of pictures in English collections improved in the late 18th and early 19th century, felicitous hanging became rarer and rarer. This would certainly apply to the finest of all English collections, the Bridgwater collection, if the Edwardian photograph of Fig. 217 can be relied on. This shows a reasonably effective pattern on the left wall,

214. TURNER'S WATERCOLOUR OF THE DRAWING ROOM AT FARNLEY HALL, YORKSHIRE.

215. THE SAME ROOM AS IT WAS IN 1946. Over the chimneypiece is Turner's *View of Dort*, hung in relation to the spectator rather than in relation to the wall. The chimneypiece was moved in the mid 19th century.

216. THE LIBRARY AT CHESTERFIELD HOUSE. It contained the most famous 18th century set of portraits of literary men.

217. THE GALLERY AT BRIDGEWATER
HOUSE, LONDON (NOW DESTROYED)
AS IT WAS ABOUT 1900.

but on the lower part of the right wall there is a double and even triple row of very fine cabinet pictures hung below larger pictures that makes no architectual sense at all.

Against this inharmonious arrangement must be set a room like the gallery at Adare (Fig. 218) that was crowded with pictures in the mid 19th century. The aim was not to create classical order, but to convey a sense of antiquity and continuity through the massing of old English portraits, many of which were bought from dealers to supplement the inherited possessions of the Dunravens.

It is not easy to explain why an arrangement of pictures is evocative of an epoch, particularly if the history of frame design and mounting is not discussed. However they are both too complicated subjects to embark on here.

Occasionally one comes across a house where not only the pictures but the arrangement gives pleasure, though few are as successful as Meols Hall, Lancashire. There the arrangement of the pictures was worked out even before the reconstruction of the house was begun in 1960, but the result is a harmony of pictures and architecture that seems to capture exactly the feeling of an 18th century house.[15]

218. THE GALLERY AT ADARE MANOR, CO. LIMERICK. The massing of the pictures, partly inherited and partly bought, was intended to give a sense of the antiquity of the family.

Chapter 9
Ladies' amusements

The idea for the title of this chapter is taken from a book of designs published in 1763 by Robert Sayer called *The Ladies Amusement*, but the most vivid example of 18th century ladies' skills is to be found in an eccentric hexadecagonal house at Exmouth. Called À la Ronde it was built in 1795 for the Miss Parminsters, two spinsters who had travelled extensively in Europe and who returned to Devonshire to build a house inspired by S. Vitale in Ravenna. This eccentric cottage ornée still retains most of its original contents and gives a good idea of the varied skill and patience of Georgian ladies. In the centre of the house is an octagonal hall that rises the full height of the house with a gallery round it at first floor level. All the upper walls are encrusted with patterns of shellwork, as is the staircase up to it, which combines shells with pieces of looking glass, and let into the gallery walls are feather pictures of birds (Figs. 219, 220). In the drawing room the cornice is of feathers and the chimneypiece is made into a grotto with more shells. Elsewhere in the house hang pictures made of sand and seaweed.[1]

The total effect is quite extraordinary, but it does not give a complete idea of the variety of arts and crafts practised by ladies. Some like Mrs Lybbe Powis and Mrs Delany were very versatile, for the former not only collected china, fossils, shells and coins, but painted on silk and paper, did embroidery and feather work, plaited straw, made pillow lace, paper mosaic, and dried flowers. And Mrs Delany constantly mentions what she and her friends were making. Unfortunately her chimney boards and shellwork garlands and lustre have all disappeared, but some of her embroidery still exists, and so do her cut paper flowers in the British Museum.

Sewing of some sort was the most useful skill to acquire, and this young ladies began very early as can be seen from a casket now in the Whitworth Art Gallery. A girl started it at the age of 12 when in Oxford in 1654–56 and it was made up by a London cabinet maker. Among the more ambitious survivors are the needlework hangings from the state bedroom at Stoke Edith that are now at Montacute: according to family tradition they were worked by the five wives of Thomas Foley. And at Aston Hall are panels worked by Mary Holte, the 3rd daughter of Sir Charles Holte, who was 60 in 1744. At Wallington in an upstairs room there are a series of panels in wool and tent stitch done by Julia, Lady Calverley. One panel is dated 1717, the set being brought to Wallington in 1755 by her son Sir Walter Calverley Blackett. Probably the most elaborate neo-classical needlework decorations by an amateur are those done by Lady Mary Hogg for the drawing room at Newliston: designed by Adam, they are in wool appliqué with details partly stitched and partly painted in watercolour.[2]

219. THE DRAWING ROOM AT À LA RONDE, DEVON. The cornice is of feathers.

220. THE GALLERY TO THE OCTAGONAL HALL AT À LA RONDE. It is decorated with mosaics in shells and feathers.

248

A considerable number of needlework carpets of the kind collected by Mrs Gubbay and now to be seen at Clandon must have been made by ladies, but their identities have been lost. However the tradition has been maintained, notably by the late Queen Mary and by the Gladstone family at Hawarden Castle; where after the war all the family collaborated in copying in needlework a Savonnerie carpet, a complicated feat planned by Mrs Gladstone. Among historic examples there are two signed ones at Milton, Northamptonshire, one a carpet and the other a rug and both by Mary, wife of the 2nd Marquess of Rockingham, who died in 1761.[3]

There are rather more sets of needlework covers for furniture, but among the most interesting is a set of settees and six chairs done in gros point and petit point, traditionally made by a member of the Chester family from Chicheley Hall, and a settee cover in 1723 by Elizabeth Drax, later the wife of the 4th Earl of Berkeley.[4] As a touching human story the stools at Arbury should also be mentioned: they were the work of Sophia Conyers, the first wife of Sir Roger Newdigate and are supposed to show objects that she left lying about.[5]

Hours of work were put into such achievements, but sometimes the reasons were not creative, as Liselotte explains. Writing of knotting in 1718, she says it "is more *à la mode* than ever, and for a good reason. When ladies who arn't entitled to a tabouret do needlework, they are allowed to sit in the presence of Madame de Berry and myself, and knotting counts as needlework, so when ladies come to call they knot . . ."[6]

As a change from needlework for upholstery some ladies specialised in picture making either in wool, silk or felt. Among the most celebrated of these was Anne Eliza Morritt who died in 1797 and whose work still exists at Rokeby. Lady Caroline Campbell, according to Horace Walpole, made good worsted and chenille pictures, and at Gwsaney in North Wales there is a series of pictures of flowers (Fig. 221) done in cloth by Helena Countess of Mountcashel, who died in 1792. It is conceivable that they were inspired by Mrs Delany's paper mosaics.[7]

Other ladies, including naturally Sarah Duchess of Marlborough, preferred more useful tasks like fringe making. Today it is impossible to tell how many of the elaborate late 17th century fringes were made by amateurs, but it is worth remarking that the Duchess of Beaufort had "divers gentlewomen commonly at work embroidering and fringe making, for all the beds of state were made and finished in the house." Even Queen Charlotte had a frame for fringe making that she showed Mrs Delany.[8] Probably one of the few now in working order is the early 19th century hand loom at Traquair House, Peebleshire.

221. FELT PICTURES BY HELENA, COUNTESS OF MOUNT CASHEL AT GWSANEY, NORTH WALES.

Probably Mrs Montagu was the best known person to work in feathers, but unfortunately her feather tapestries have disappeared.

The shell workers included Lady Anne Coventry,[9] who did a shell parlour at Snitterfield, and the 3rd Duchess of Richmond, who is said to be responsible for Carné's seat at Goodwood, a work of such sophistication that it is hard to believe it was not professionally done. And in this context perhaps Elizabeth Radcliffe[10] should be mentioned: apparently well known in her own time as the best maid in England, she was a member of the Yorke household at Erthig, and there remain examples not only of her embroidery but also of her work in crushed mica and mother-of-pearl, table tops done with chinoiserie scenes, the ruins of Palmyra in a glass case, and the chinese pagoda (Fig. 222).

222. A PAGODA AT ERDIG DECORATED WITH CRUSHED MICA AND MOTHER OF PEARL BY ELIZABETH RADCLIFFE.

A considerable number of people decorated furniture in other ways. Japanning, for instance, became popular in the late 17th century and in 1689 Sir Edmund Verney[11] wanted his daughter to learn how to do it. Rather later both Lady Sunderland, the wife of the 5th Earl who died in 1728, and Princess Elizabeth, one of George III's daughters, took it up. Indeed the Princess's decoration of the Japan room at Frogmore is illustrated in Pyne's *Royal Residences* (Fig. 223).

Some *arte povere* was probably done in English houses but we have not come across references to it. However Princess Elizabeth did cut paper work and others did quill work. Making print rooms was another occupation and we know that Lady Louisa Conolly played an active part in making the Print Room at Castletown. She also painted materials, for in 1768 she wrote: "I am at present busy with a new work, its painting flowers with the stamps I got at Paris on a white satten with which I intend to hang a little closet."[12]

Ladies even took up turning, lead carving and gilding. Mrs Delany describes the Duchess of Portland turning amber and Lady Luxborough mentions an urn turned by the Duchess of Somerset. Lady Luxborough also gives an account of lead carving in 1748: "Miss Merediths write that the present fashion, is all lead carving, which ladies do themselves, by cutting India, or other thin lead themselves with scissors, and shaping it into flowers, knots, etc, and fixing it to a wire, which is afterwards nailed on in the form designed; and the carving is either gilt or else painted the colour of the stucco or wainscot, according as suits the place." The most enthusiastic gilder was evidently Lady Hertford, for she wrote to Lady Pomfret in 1741: "Within doors, we amuse ourselves (at the hours we are together) in gilding picture frames, and other small things:

223. THE JAPAN ROOM AT FROGMORE. A plate from Pyne's *Royal Residences* showing the decoration carried out by Princess Elizabeth, one of the daughters of George III.

this is so much in fashion with us at present, that I believe, if our patience and pockets hold out, we should gild all the cornices, tables, chairs and stools about the house."[13]

If at times one is surprised at some of these activities, they are interesting not only individually but collectively as evidence of the increasing home-making instincts of 18th century ladies. It is probably right to attribute to them that indefinable thing called the English Style and also much of the charm of the English Country House as well.

Chapter 10
Care and housekeeping

When one goes to a great house and marvels at the state of preservation of the hangings of a room, the needlework on a bed, the unfaded colour of walnut or mahogany and the brilliance of the gilding, there are two reasons that are very closely related: houses were very carefully looked after, and the splendid things were seldom used and subjected to light. And so it is a very sobering thought that it is seldom possible nowadays to look after a house as well as it was a hundred years ago, and that the opening of country houses to the public for six months of the year or more is likely to do more damage in ten years than used to happen in a hundred. This is not fantasy, and several disturbing examples could be quoted, but it is sufficient to take one from the 1930s that is near enough to the present but by no means too remote to be historical. Among the records of *Country Life* on Castlecoole (Fig. 224), which Christopher Hussey described in December 1936, is a letter from Miss Viola Lowry Cory about the upholstery of the saloon furniture; this, she says, "is a rather crimson shade of red and the striped silk on the settees is in very good condition, it has always been covered, except when the family were entertaining; the two 'tabourets' which stand in the windows used not to have any covers when I was a child, and the silk in consequence is much worn, the curtains are in a bad state and terribly rotten from the light."

Such care was logical when the furniture was so expensive, but few visitors to houses understand this today. Presumably there were a number of printed manuals to advise the young mistress of a house on the right procedure, but the interest of a book like Hannah Glass's *Servants Directory* of 1760 lies in other directions. It is not known how widely it was read, but it seems more than likely that it was used by Susannah Whatman, who compiled a housekeeping book in 1776, the first year of her marriage to James Whatman of Turkey Court in Kent. This MSS, which was published in 1956, is particularly fascinating because it gives details that enable one to envisage the scale on which the Whatmans lived.

Among the notes are instructions to the housemaid for dry scrubbing a room, already quoted in an earlier section on the Treatment of Floors.

And she continues: "To use a painter's brush to all the ledges, window frames and furniture, and then the duster. Never to dust pictures, nor the frames or anything that has a gilt edge." Hannah Glass would have agreed with her for she said "with a pair of bellows blow the dust off your Pictures and Frames, for you must not touch a Picture with a Broom or Brush of any sort."[1] And she recommended buying large bellows from the turners to blow dust out of stucco.

224. THE SALOON AT CASTLECOOLE. Except for the stool in the windows all the seat furniture had case covers, and these were in regular use until the late 1930s; only the stools did not have them, and their upholstery rotted.

Mrs Whatman was well aware that light was the great destroyer and these were her notes:

"The sun comes into the Library very early. The window on that side of the bow window must have the blind let down. The painted chairs must not be knocked against anything, or against one another.

"The books are not to be meddled with, but they may be dusted as far as a wing of a goose will go.

"The Drawing Room. The blinds always closed in the morning and the window up . . . The girandoles Mrs Whatman always cleans herself. They should never be touched: nor the pictures.

"The Eating Parlour. The sun never comes in.

"Mrs Whatman's Dressing Room. The sun must always be kept out, or it will spoil the carpet, chairs and mahogany cabinet.

"The Bedchamber. The sun must be kept out of this room, as it shines full on the bed early and on the mahogany press at one o'clock."

And so on.

Mrs Glass adds one point here about festoon curtains: "If you draw up the Curtains, let them down every Morning & whisk them with a long whisk or Soft brush . . . Nothing gathers dust more than drawn up curtains."

The mistress of a house was expected to be skilled and energetic and it is interesting to see how much Mrs Whatman did herself. In a larger house these jobs would probably have been done by the housekeeper, but still the mistress had considerable responsibilities, as Lady Betty Germaine told Swift in 1725: writing to him from London on her return from Drayton and telling him how she could not take exercise outside because of the weather, she said "but as that house is large the necessary steps the mistress must make is some . . ."

However to return to Miss Lowry-Cory's letter, the greatest protection lay in covers, whose use goes back to the earliest days of cabinet making. The steps taken to protect chairs have already been discussed in an earlier section, but they were made for a surprising range of objects. Probably the earliest ones to survive are the scorched and gilded leather covers made about 1670 for a pair of globes at Ham and now on show there (Fig. 225). In accounts and inventories there are many references to covers of leather or cloth, and here we can only suggest their widespread and long continued use. Leather covers are listed for walnut and Japan furniture at Dyrham in 1716; when George Lucy bought carved and gilt mirrors for Charlecote about 1760, he had holland cases made for them; among the Dundas accounts in 1765 is a charge of £1 15s. od. for a cover for a semi-circular table, "For a Brown leather cover lin'd with flannel with a fall to hang quite to the floor welted & bound with gilt leather;" and as late as 1806 the tables in the Gallery at Attingham were supplied with covers of baize and leather.[2] Where a leather cover was inappropriate as with some chairs, "shamey stockings for the feet" were provided as was the case with a set of seat furniture made by Charles Smith for Shugborough in 1794. And at Norfolk House there was even an oil cloth to cover the marble hearth in the Music Room.

Beds, tapestries and carpets were also protected. Marot in his designs shows metal rods coming out in front of his state beds, but in those houses where the beds of the period survive, they have usually been taken down. However in the Green Velvet Bedroom at Houghton cantilevered rods appear in old photographs. These rods were for case curtains, and they too make a regular appearance in inventories, including that for Dyrham inventory in 1716 and for

225. COVERS OF SCORCHED AND GILDED LEATHER ON GLOBES AT HAM HOUSE, ABOUT 1670.

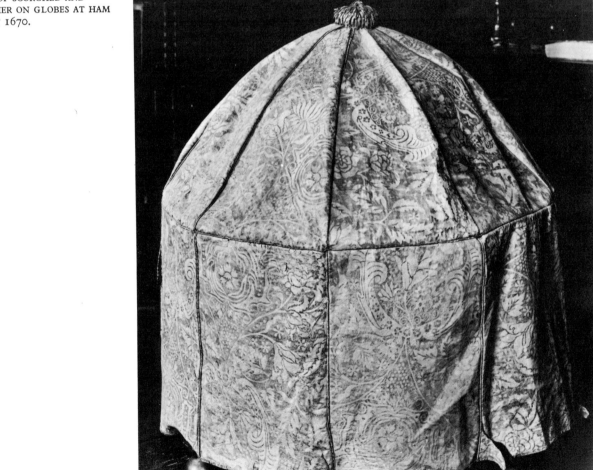

XXXVII. THE BALCONY ROOM AT
DYRHAM. Although much darkened,
the original scheme of graining
and marbling survives here as
does the gilding, which gives an
excellent idea of how a well-carved
room was picked out in 1700.

XXXVIII. A DETAIL OF A CAPITAL
AND THE ENTABLATURE IN THE
BALCONY ROOM AT DYRHAM.

Clandon in 1782. And they are shown *in situ* in the view of Queen Mary's bed at Hampton Court in Pyne's *Royal Residences* (Fig. 226). The canopies of beds were sometimes protected with sheets of paper, for Mrs Whatman notes that they should be changed twice a year.[3]

How early tapestries were protected we do not know, but the 1697 inventory for Kensington Palace lists "white stufe curtains for before ye hangings" in the King's Great Closet. Various sets of tapestries put up in the third quarter of the 18th century had covers. The Croome Court set of Neilson Gobelin panels originally had paper covers and later chamois ones, and fabric covers appear in an old *Country Life* photograph of the State Bedroom at Inveraray Castle (Fig. 227) in 1927.[4]

Probably the only carpets that are now regularly covered up are those at Waddesdon, where traditional standards of housekeeping are maintained with scrupulous care, but again many used to have covers of baize. The Moorfields carpets in the Drawing Room and State Bedroom at Osterley both had green baize covers according to the 1782 inventory, and Sheraton in his *Cabinet Dictionary* mentions the practice.[5]

XXXIX. THE GREAT ROOM AT PORTMAN HOUSE, LONDON. Malton's drawing shows an interior in a house designed by Stuart and completed by Bonomi that is now destroyed: it shows the effect of scagliola columns in a painted room of the 1770s and 80s.

XL. A DETAIL OF A BED FROM ALNWICK CASTLE, ABOUT 1780. Later overpainting has been removed to show the high quality of the painting in tempera.

226. CASE CURTAINS IN USE ROUND QUEEN MARY'S BED AT HAMPTON COURT PALACE. From Pyne's *Royal Residences*.

227. THE STATE BEDROOM AT INVERARAY CASTLE, ARGYLL, AS IT WAS IN 1927. This shows covers for the tapestries still *in situ*.

Of course, despite all the precautions, houses did get dirty with constant fires, candles and lamps. Thus in 1770 Mrs Ramsden, the housekeeper at Woburn, inspected the Duke's bed and "finds it so very black with burning of oil in the room that she thinks it proper to have it cleaned." This kind of work would probably have been done by professional upholsterers, for there are many references to it in accounts. At Hatfield, for instance, Beckwith and France charged for "taking down all the window curtains, brushing them and cleaning them very well with bread and cloths and putting by—cleaning and papering up all the window cornices, chimney glass, gerandoles, sconces, etc & taking up all the Carpets."[6]

Chapter 11
A matter of balance

At the beginning we said that we do not believe in the possibility of restorations of decoration that are authentic down to the last detail, for virtually never does all the evidence as to original colours, materials and contents exist. Research can provide many answers and obviously will produce more, but as yet so little has been done that one is often in the dark for lack of even comparative examples. However it is important to realise that research cannot provide all the answers, and so a great deal has to be left to the restorer's knowledge and disciplined imagination. The trouble is that experts whose knowledge is based to a large extent on documentary research find this the hardest part of the process of restoration to accept. But it surely must be so if rooms and houses are to have a quality of life and balance. In each case the balance will have to be struck in a different way, but it seemed a good idea to end this book with comments on a few places where John Fowler has worked in recent years.

In choosing four rooms the idea is to bring out the differences in intention and approach between restoration and fashionable decoration. Two of the rooms were decorated with Mrs Lancaster, one in London and the other at Haseley Court in Oxfordshire. The other three, at Clandon Park near Guildford and Sudbury Hall near Derby, were restored for the National Trust. The London room dates from 1821, the Haseley room from 1770 and the Clandon rooms from 1735, and as all five are large, handsome rooms, it might be presumed that they presented more or less similar problems. However this was not so.

The London room (Fig. 228) was designed by Wyatville for his gallery office in 1821 and is tucked away at the back of an older Mayfair house overlooking a courtyard, hence its unusual proportions. Architecturally it is simply, even austerely, detailed and basically cold in feeling. This was not the right kind of atmosphere for Mrs Lancaster or her way of life, and so the challenge was to transform it into a room that was stimulating and relaxed at the same time. This meant keeping its masculinity and carrying it through in comfortable chairs, sofas and banquettes that in type would not be out of place in the sitting room of a country house. They are arranged so that groups for conversation develop naturally, and yet the atmosphere is stimulated by the decoration. This is quite the opposite of what might be expected in a room of that type and date, for it creates a dramatic, almost baroque air with huge chandeliers from Venice, glazed and varnished yellow walls reflecting the background in the Bessarabian carpet, marbled skirting and cornice, and large Elizabethan portraits. The curtains, although elaborately headed, do not stand out for they are of a yellow taffeta that "lives" with the walls and thus avoid drawing attention

228. DECORATION OF A LONDON
DRAWING ROOM. Wyatville's gallery
office of 1821 as decorated for
Mrs Lancaster by John Fowler
in 1959.

to the relative narrowness of the room. At the time the room was decorated shiny paint was still frowned on by most people of pretention to fashion, and Elizabethan portraits had a limited number of admirers, and so there was a greater element of shock than exists today.

In Mrs Lancaster's Oxfordshire drawing room (Figs. 229, 230), which no longer exists in the form shown in the illustrations, the architectural decoration was not only more sympathetic in itself but created an atmosphere that it was desirable to play up rather than play down. Consequently the whole approach was more deferential and, also partly because of the basic difference between an all purpose living room in a London *pied à terre* and a drawing room in a country house, there was less need to provoke. Whereas in London it was the

260

carpet that suggested the yellow walls, here it was the 18th century silk curtains from Ditchley that suggested the acquamarine blue silk for the walls: the carpets were 18th century Aubusson, rather naif in feeling. The long Kentian table had apparently always been at the end of the room, and it was just luck that scraping revealed picking out in white and a blue slightly deeper than the one chosen for the walls. Here was that valuable element of surprise already present, and this was continued in the new treatment of the Wyattesque ceiling. The bolder relief ornament was painted darker than the ground, instead of the more usual white, and the elements that were gilded were done in two colours of gold rather than one, a detail that gave an added and surprising sparkle to the decoration. The combination of the exotic Rococo carvings from Ditchley, the Elizabethan portraits originally also from Ditchley that Mrs Lancaster bought back later, and the magnificent chandelier from Clumber was certainly one of many objects that were individually superb, but it was also eclectic and so suited to a country house like Haseley that had grown over the centuries: it had that timeless quality that is one of the most appealing aspects of an undisturbed house and so difficult to recreate.

What is significant about both rooms is not only what was done but what was not done. Chintzes and silk were freely mixed; and there was an avoidance of materials and colours matching and of sets of furniture that would give a static character, or indeed of a "period" feeling in the normal meaning of the term. And yet none of the original decoration of either room was disturbed. Indeed at Haseley the plasterwork was most carefully restored. Thus history was respected but re-interpreted to meet the needs and tastes of a particular person.

In the case of restoration, as at Clandon and Sudbury, certain elements that were influential in the London and Oxfordshire rooms are of course not present. The restored rooms are not intended for use, and consequently the creation of a sense of comfort and the desire to be stimulating do not exist; and as a result those means of giving life to a room and creating a background for people also do not exist. The rooms are just to be looked at. This brings one to the paradox of restoration: one is having to treat a room as authentically as possible, but without giving it a proper function. Thus all too easily it can turn out to be lifeless looking and so unconvincing. This explains why so many restorations are dead, and even when passably authentic, displeasing to most people.

At Clandon in particular the rooms on the main floor are rooms of parade, and any serious restoration must emphasise this aspect of them. Theirs is a formal, not to say formidable character, and it is doubly difficult to keep a sense of life and reality in them once they have passed out of even occasional use.

Secondly, and this one would expect, most of the rooms at Clandon and Sudbury have been altered in some way or other since they were formed, and so one has to decide how far back to put the clock or whether to try to put it back at all, again questions that are not so pressing in decoration. Presuming that one decides not to alter the dominant features in any way, there remains the problem of how to do justice to them and to tie them together to establish a sense of unity. Compromises have to be accepted as well as made, and there has to be a playing up as well as a playing down. There can be nothing absolute about the synthesis achieved, and it must be a matter of opinion whether it is successful and harmonious or not; and, as we said at the beginning, the synthesis will be a reflection of its own time just as much as the drawing room at Haseley.

The problem of linking work of two periods is particularly well illustrated in the Palladio Room at Clandon (Figs. 231, 232). About 1765, some thirty to thirty-five years after it was completed, the room was considerably remodelled, as was discovered when the Reveillon wallpaper was taken down for restora-

229. RESTORATION AND DECORATION:
"A MORE DEFERENTIAL APPROACH".
The drawing Room at Haseley
Court as it was in 1960.

230. THE DRAWING ROOM AT
HASELEY COURT.

231. THE PALLADIO ROOM AT
CLANDON STRIPPED DOWN. When
the 1780 wallpaper was taken down,
the original arrangement of the
fireplaces and doors was discovered.

tion five years ago: the two original facing chimneypieces were replaced by
one in the centre of the long wall facing the windows; this took the place of a
big door; and two other dummy doors that balanced the existing ones on the
shorter walls were also suppressed. These alterations were disguised by the
silk flock paper. This is perhaps the finest of its type still *in situ* in an English
house, but it is not particularly happily related to the more monumental
character of the original decoration either in colour or weight of design; nor,
as the room was painted in the 1960s, was it related to it tonally for all the
woodwork and plasterwork was plain white. It was this disturbing lack of unity
that suggested that the pale blue ground colour of the paper should be the key
to the room and that related shades should be used for the woodwork of the
dado and in limited areas of the ceiling. The use of several tones is an authentic
practice as we have seen and the Saloon at Clandon provides a precedent for
using different tones on early 18th century plasterwork, but it would be wrong
to claim that the room appears today precisely as it did nearly 200 years ago.
The furniture is once more ranged round the walls in the 18th century fashion,
a piece of authenticity that becomes pedantry in a house like Haseley, but the
use of different colours of material on the seat furniture is contrary to 18th
century practice; it survives from the arrangement of the room in the early
1960s before there was such stress on authenticity in furniture arrangement.

264

In restorations such as these it is usually impossible to buy or introduce objects of the quality and scale of those available at Haseley, for historical as well as financial reasons, and there has to be much more make do and mend. Other rooms at Clandon illustrate this point admirably, for much of the furniture left to the National Trust by Mrs Gubbay is of superb quality, but few pieces are of a scale that is really suitable for such a house. At Sudbury the same problem arose for there is little furniture of a quality comparable with the house. Even the bed in the Queen's Room (Fig. 233) is made up from 18th century bits, but there was no question of changing it. Instead its hangings were repaired with material salvaged from the old wall hangings, and new damask for the walls was specially woven after the old design. The rest of the furniture is not convincing state bedroom furniture, but had to be arranged as effectively as possible. A minor but interesting change was the removal of the whitewash from the cornice of the alabaster entablature to the overmantel.

In the Saloon (Fig. 234) even fewer changes and replacements were made and only a little gilding was added to improve the balance of the wainscot where it had been over painted in touching up at some time. No attempt was made to furnish the room, which has been virtually empty for 50 years, and so the row of portraits inserted in the 17th century panelling in the mid 18th century or later was left to gaze out on the room. One positive change was to use different tones of white to bring out the magnificent richness and elaboration of the ceiling ornament. No 17th century precedents for this can be given for

232. THE PALLADIO ROOM TODAY. Here restoration involved the use of colour to create a unity out of the 1730 conception of the room and its ceiling and the late 18th century flock wallpaper.

233. THE QUEEN'S ROOM AT SUDBURY. The walls have been hung with a new copy of the old damask and the bed hangings have been remade out of the old damask. The restoration of the overmantel is illustrated in Figures 170 and 171.

234. THE SALOON AT SUDBURY. Here restoration involved repairing the ceiling and repainting it in different hues, cleaning the wainscot and the addition of a little gilding to improve the balance of the design.

all ceilings have been cleaned and repainted many times to get rid of the deposit from earlier forms of lighting, and it was done here for purely visual reasons. A less significant alteration, which caused criticism and misunderstandings at the time, was the removal of the dark varnish from the floorboards to give an effect similar to that of a dry scrubbed floor. There was more than ample historical justification for this, but again the reason was also visual: the lightening of the colour of the floor enormously helped the unity of the room.

Of course all attempt to play up the character of the decoration could have been resisted, and the whole place could have been frozen, but particularly in a sparsely furnished house like Sudbury, whose sole use is to be shown to visitors, the impact on those visitors must be considered and they must be given an experience that is as rich and enjoyable as possible. It is a matter of degree how far one goes in this, but there must be some compensation for the loss of contents over the years and that living feeling that inevitably goes when the family moves out. However, at the same time whatever is done must not lose touch with either reality or credibility. There can be no absolute and timeless answer to such problems, and each generation will restore country houses in different ways just as they will decorate them in different ways. Indeed it is to be hoped that the element of decoration will continue to influence approaches to restoration. Then at least there will be a striving after a sense of life and not just slavish renewal of the misguided taste of the day before yesterday.

Selective bibliography

There are few books devoted to the history of interior decoration in England, and those that exist are mostly concerned with its architectural aspects. All the authorities from which we have quoted are cited in the notes, but it was thought that a selected bibliography might be helpful, and this is given in four sections: basic modern books; a selection of diaries, letters, memoirs and biographies; a selection of recent books and articles with full quotations from contemporary documents; and a short list of books containing technical material mainly relating to paint and colour.

All books were originally published in Great Britain unless otherwise stated.

Modern Publications with Quotations from Contemporary Documents

ASKE AND THE COLLECTIONS OF SIR LAWRENCE DUNDAS see various authors in *Apollo*, September 1967.

CARLTON HOUSE Geoffrey de Bellaigue, 'The Furnishings of the Chinese Drawing Room', *Burlington Magazine*, September 1967.

CHIPPENDALE Anthony Coleridge, *Chippendale Furniture* (1968). See also various authors in *Furniture History*, 1968.

CROOME COURT TAPESTRY ROOM *Decorative Art from the S. H. Kress Collection* (1964).

DAYLESFORD Lindsay Boynton, 'The Furniture of Warren Hastings', *Burlington Magazine*, August 1970.

DUMFRIES HOUSE Christopher Gilbert, 'Thomas Chippendale at Dumfries House', *Burlington Magazine*, 1969.

HAREWOOD Anthea Stephenson, 'Chippendale Furniture at Harewood', *Furniture History*, 1968.

HATFIELD Anthony Coleridge, 'English Furniture and Cabinet-Makers at Hatfield House', *Burlington Magazine*, February, April 1967.

THOMAS HOPE David Watkin, *Thomas Hope* (1968).

HOPETOUN Anthony Coleridge, 'James Cullen, Cabinet-Maker at Hopetoun House', *Connoisseur*, November, December, 1966.

KENSINGTON PALACE Th. H. Lunsingh Scheurleer, 'Documents on the Furnishings of Kensington Palace', *Walpole Society*, XXXVIII 1960–62.

LINNELL Helena Hayward, 'The Drawings of John Linnell in the Victoria and Albert Museum', *Furniture History*, 1969.

MERSHAM-LE-HATCH Lindsay Boynton, 'Thomas Chippendale at Mersham-le-Hatch', *Furniture History*, 1968.

NOSTELL PRIORY Lindsay Boynton and Nicholas Goodison, 'Thomas Chippendale at Nostell Priory', *Furniture History*, 1968.

STRAWBERRY HILL Ed. Paget Toynbee, *Strawberry Hill Accounts* (1927).

Diaries, Letters and Memoirs

HARRIET ARBUTHNOT *Journal* 1820–32. Ed. Francis Bamford and the Duke of Wellington (1950).

C. H. ASPINALL-OGLANDER *Mary Boscawen, Admiral's Wife* (1940). *Admiral's Widow* (1942).

THE LETTERS OF THE EARL OF CHESTERFIELD Ed. John Bradshaw (1892).

LADY MARY COKE *Letters and Journals*, 4 Vols. (1889–1896).

AUTOBIOGRAPHY AND CORRESPONDENCE OF MRS DELANY Ed. by Lady Llanover (1861–62).

MARIA EDGEWORTH *Letters from England* 1813–44. Ed. Christina Colvin (1971).

JOURNEYS OF CELIA FIENNES Ed. Christopher Morris (1947).

THE MARCHIONESS GREY OF WREST PARK Joyce Godber. Bedfordshire Historical Society, XLVII (1968).

THE CORRESPONDENCE OF EMILY, DUCHESS OF LEINSTER Ed. Brian FitzGerald, Vol. I (1949); Vol. II (1953); Vol. III (1957).

PASSAGES FROM THE DIARIES OF MRS PHILIP LYBBE POWYS Ed. Emily J. Climenson (1899).

HORACE WALPOLE   *The Letters of Horace Walpole*, Ed. Mrs Paget Toynbee,
   Walpole Society, Vol. XVI.
   The Yale Edition of Horace Walpole's Correspondence, Ed. W. S. Lewis.
   Strawberry Hill Accounts, Ed. Paget Toynbee (1927).

WOBURN AND THE RUSSELLS   Gladys Scott Thomson, *Family Background*
   (1949).
   Russells in Bloomsbury (1940).

Basic Modern Books

EDWARD CROFT-MURRAY   *Decorative painting in England*, Vol. I (1962); Vol.
   II (1970).

RALPH EDWARDS   *Shorter Dictionary of English Furniture* (1964).

E. A. ENTWISLE   *The Book of Wallpaper* (1954 and 1970).
   A Literary History of Wallpaper (1960).

MARGARET JOURDAIN   *English Interior Decoration* (1950).

PERCY MACQUOID AND RALPH EDWARDS   *Dictionary of English Furniture*. Revised ed. (1954).

FLORENCE MONTGOMERY   *Printed Textiles, English and American Cottons and
   Linens 1700–1850* (1970).

PETER THORNTON   *Baroque and Rococo Silks* (1965).

JOHN WATERER   *Spanish Leather* (1971).

PETER WARD-JACKSON   *English Furniture Designs of the 18th Century* (1958).

References

REFERENCES   CHAPTER 1

1   *A Backward Glance*, reprinted 1972.

2   *Left Hand Right Hand*, p. 218.

3   Martin Battersby, *The Decorative Twenties* (1969) and *The Decorative Thirties* (1971); Madge Garland, *The Indecisive Decade* (1968).

4   *The Edwardians*, p. 113.

5   Christopher Hussey, *English Country Houses. Late Georgian* (1958), p. 211.

6   ex inf. Peter Howell.

7   Michel Gallet, *Paris Domestic Architecture of the 18th Century* (1972), p. 33.

8   C. H. C. and M. I. Baker, *The Life of James Brydges 1st Duke of Chandos* (1949), p. 116.

9   *The Letters of the Earl of Chesterfield* I, ed. John Bradshaw (1892), pp. 258-9.

10   *The Letters of the Earl of Chesterfield* II, p. 879.

11   Unpublished letter, Collection: The Hon. Desmond Guinness.

12   J. D. Williams, *Audley End, The Restoration of 1762-1797* (1966), p. 3.

13   Harriet Arbuthnot, *Journal 1820-32*, ed. Francis Bamford and Duke of Wellington (1950), Vol. II, p. 150.

14   R. Campbell, *The London Tradesman* (1747, reprinted 1969), p. 170.

15   Malcolm Elwin, *The Noels and the Milbankes 1767-1792* (1967), p. 54.

16   Lady Elizabeth Cust, *Records of the Cust Family* II (1909), p. 251.

17   Anthony Coleridge, 'English Furniture and Cabinet-Makers at Hatfield House I', *Burlington Magazine*, February 1967, p. 67.

18   Geoffrey de Bellaigue, 'The Furnishings of the Chinese Drawing Room, Carlton House', *Burlington Magazine*, September 1967, p. 518.

19   Gladys Scott Thomson, *Family Background* (1949), p. 63.

20   *The London Tradesman*, p. 171.

21   E. A. Entwisle, *A Literary History of Wallpaper* (1960), Plate 22.

22   *Passages From the Diaries of Mrs Philip Lybbe Powys*, ed. Emily J. Climenson (1899), p. 146.

23   *A Collection of Household Designs* (1808), text to Plates 152 and 153.

24   Peter Ward-Jackson, *English Furniture Designs of the 18th Century* (1958), Plate 2.

25   Marot designs preserved at Kasteel Duivenvoorde, near the Hague, and illustrated in *De Geschiedenis Van Het Kasteel Duivenvoorde En Zijn Bewoners* by E. A. Canneman and L. J. Van der Klooster (1967), pp. 61, 63, 65.

26   Geoffrey Beard, *Georgian Craftsmen and Their Work* (1966), p. 91.

27   Margaret Jourdain, *The Work of William Kent* (1948), pp. 48, 61.

28   Derek Linstrum, *Sir Jeffry Wyatville Architect to the King* (1972), p. 185.

29   *The Absentee*, Chapter II.

30   Duke of Devonshire, *Handbook of Chatsworth and Hardwick* (1845), p. 53.

1   *The Selected Letters of Josiah Wedgwood*, ed. Finer and Savage (1965), p. 55.

2   *Ibid.*, p. 131.

3   Grosvenor MSS, 5 September 1805, 12 November 1807.

4   Eric Robinson and Keith R. Thompson, 'Matthew Boulton's Mechanical Paintings', *Burlington Magazine*, August 1970, p. 497.

5   *The Complete Works of Sir John Vanbrugh*, Vol. 4 (1928), p. 45.

6   *Country Life* CXLV, 27 March 1969, p. 724.

7   Drayton, *Country Life* CXXXVII, 27 May 1965, p. 1288; Boughton, *Country Life* CXLIX, 25 February 1971, p. 420; Aston Hall, *Country Life* CXIV, 20 August 1953, p. 554.

8   E. F. Carritt, *A Calendar of British Taste 1600–1800*, p. 219.

9   *The Correspondence Between the Countess of Hartford and the Countess of Pomfret* (1805), Vol. III, p. 292.

10 C. Willet Cunnington and Phillis Cunnington, *Handbook of English Costume in the 18th Century* (1957, revised 1972).

11 *The Correspondence of Emily, Duchess of Leinster* (subsequently referred to as *Leinster Letters*), ed. Brian Fitz-Gerald I, p. 425 (Vol. 1, 1949; 2, 1953; 3, 1957).

12 Oliver Millar, 'The Inventories and Valuations of the Kings Goods 1649–51', *Walpole Society* XLIII. (1972).

13 Reprinted Gregg Press, 1968.

14 Walter Houghton, 'The English Virtuoso in the 17th Century', *Journal of the History of Ideas* III (1942).

15 *Journeys of Celia Fiennes*, ed. Christopher Morris (1947), pp. 69, 100.

16 Gervase Jackson-Stops, 'William III and French Furniture', *Furniture History*, 1971.

17 'The Classical Country House in the 18th Century', *Journal of The Royal Society o Arts*, 19 July 1959.

18 A. L. Rowse, *The Later Churchills* (1958), p. 89.

19 Percy Macquoid, *A History of English Furniture*, Vol. III, *The Age of Mahogany* (1906), p. 101.

20 *Country Life* CXXXIX, 13 January 1966, p. 58; 27 January 1966, p. 188; 3 February 1966, p. 224.

21 Desmond Fitz-Gerald, *The Norfolk House Music Room* (1973).

22 *The Letters of Horace Walpole*, edited by Mrs Paget Toynbee, Vol. 6 (1904), pp. 376, 379, 399, 426.

23 *Decorative Art from the S. H. Kress Collection. Tapestry Room from Croome Court* (1964).

24 *Leinster Letters* I, p. 431.

25 Carritt, p. 252.

26 *Leinster Letters* II, p. 152.

27 *The Yale Edition of Horace Walpole's Correspondence*, ed. W. S. Lewis, Vol. 28 (1955), p. 101.

28 Wyatt Papworth, *John B. Papworth* (1879); see also E. A. Entwisle, *The Book of Wallpaper* (1970), pp. 78, 81; George Smith, *The Cabinet Maker and Upholsterer's Guide* (1826) caption to Plate CLIII, p. 194. H. Clifford Smith, *Buckingham Palace* (1931), p. 109 says that John James Boileau of Sloane Square and Louis André Delabrière both worked at Carlton House.

29 Birmingham Assay Office, Boulton Letters MSS, Vol. IV, p. 469.

30 *Country Life* CXLIX, 4 February 1971, p. 248.

31 D. Jacques, *A Visit to Goodwood* (1822).

32 *George IV and The Arts of France*, catalogue to exhibition in The Queen's Gallery, Buckingham Palace, 1966.

33 Caroline Grosvenor, *The First Lady Wharncliffe* I (1927), p. 163.

34 *Country Life* CXLVII, 25 June 1970, p. 1250; *Country Life* CXLVIII, 2 July 1970, p. 18. George Smith (1826), Plate CLII.

35 Desmond Fitz-Gerald, 'A history of the interior of Stowe', *Apollo*, June 1973, pp. 581–3.

1   *Country Life* CXLVII, 18 June, 25 June 1970, pp. 1164, 1258.

2   Jean-Pierre Babelon, *Demeures Parisiennes Sous Henri IV et Louis XIII* (Paris, 1965); ‚Hugh Murray-Baillie, 'Etiquette and the Planning of the State Apartments in Baroque Palaces', *Archaeologia*, Vol. CI (1967), p. 169.

3   *Horace Walpole's Journals of Visits to Country Seats*, ed. by Paget Toynbee, *Walpole Society* XVI, p. 58.

4   John Kenworthy-Browne, *Dyrham Park*, National Trust Guidebook, 1971, p. 40.

5   Joyce Godber, 'The Marchioness Grey of Wrest Park', *Bedfordshire Historical Society* XLVII (1968), p. 162.

6   *Walpole Society* XVI, p. 28.

7   *Journal of the Royal Society of Arts*, 19 July 1959.

8   *Autobiography and Correspondence of Mrs Delany*, ed. Lady Llanover, (1861–62). Series II, Vol. III, p. 108.

9   C. H. Aspinall-Oglander, *Admiral's Widow* (1942), p. 54.

10 Carola Oman, *The Gascoyne Heiress* (1968), p. 106.

11 Caroline Grosvenor II, pp. 55, 57.

12 Joyce Godber, p. 142.

13 *Country Life* XCCII, 18 July 1957, p. 116.

14 MSS at Bowood.

15 *Lord Hervey and His Friends*, ed. Earl of Ilchester (1950), p. 71.

16 Joyce Godber, pp. 25, 30.

17 *Leinster Letters* I, p. 59.

18 *Mrs Powys*, p. 6.

19 *Mrs Delany*, Series I, Vol. III, p. 306.

20 *Strawberry Hill Accounts*, ed. Paget Toynbee (1927), p. 61.

21 Collection of The Dowager Marchioness of Cholmondeley.

22 *Leinster Letters* I, p. 59.

23 Brian Fitz-Gerald, *Emily Duchess of Leinster* (1949), p. 166.

24 See letters of the Rev. Thomas Talbot quoted in *Country Life* CXLI, 11 May 1967, p. 1160.

25 *A Complete Body of Architecture* (1768), p. 335.

26 *Mrs Delany*, Series I, Vol. I, p. 405.

27 *Works in Architecture of Robert and James Adam I* (1773), Plate V.

28 *Tour in England, Ireland and France in the years 1828 and 1829 by a German Prince* (1832), Vol. I, p. 44.

29 *Mrs Delany*, Series I, Vol III, p. 385.

30 Oliver Hill and John Cornforth, *English Country Houses. Caroline* (1966), Plate 227.

31 L. Magalotti, *Travels of Cosimo III Through England* (1821), pp. 150, 249.

32 Lady Elizabeth Cust, Vol. II (1909), p. 160.

33 Diary of Sir Matthew Decker. Typescript of a manuscript belonging to the Earl of Pembroke.

34 Peter Muilman, *A New and Complete History of Essex* (1770–72), Vol. 4, pp. 229–230.

35 Francois de La Rochefoucauld, *A Frenchman in England*, 1784 (1933), p. 151.

36 *Country Life* CXLI, 11 May 1967, p. 1161.

37 *Mrs Delany*, Series I, Vol. III, p. 158.

38 Emily J. Climenson, *Elizabeth Montagu Queen of the Blue Stockings* (1906), Vol. I, p. 49.

39 Joyce Godber, p. 90.

40 Joyce Godber, p. 120.

41 *Farington Diary*, ed. James Greig, Vol. III (1924), pp. 244, 258.

42 *Maria Edgeworth, Letters From England 1813–44*, ed. Christina Colvin (1971), p. 194.

43 *Works*, Vol. I, Plate V.

44 Collins Baker, p. 175.

45 *Mrs Delany*, Series I, Vol. III, p. 158.

46 *Memoirs of Madame de La Tour du Pin*, ed. Felice Harcourt (1969), p. 17.

47 Robert Kerr, *The Gentleman's House* (1864), p. 104.

48 *Mrs Delany*, Series II, Vol. III, p. 152.

49 Ralph Edwards, *Shorter Dictionary of English Furniture* (1964), p. 311.

50 Fanny Kemble, *Records of a Later Life* II (1882), p. 185.

51 Clare Williams, *Sophie in London being the Diary of Sophie la Roche* (1933) p. 199.

52 *The Age of Mahogany*, p. 88.

53 Ware, p. 433.

54 Ware (1768), p. 33.

55 *Mrs Delany*, Series II, Vol. I, p. 455.

56 *Mrs Delany*, Series II, Vol. III, p. 149.

57 *Mrs Delany*, Series II, Vol. III, p. 444.

58 Louis Simond, *Journal of a Tour and Residence in Great Britain During the Years 1810, 1811*, Vol. II (1815), p. 219, quoted in *Country Life* CXLVII, 18 June 1970, p. 1167.

59 Mrs Hugh Wyndham, *The Correspondence of Sarah Spencer, Lady Lyttleton* (1912), p. 75.

60 Caroline Grosvenor I, p. 140.

61 *Journals of Miss Elizabeth George*. We are indebted to Mr Colin Anson for bringing them to our attention (subsequently quoted in *Apollo*, June 1973, pp. 581–3).

62 *Memoirs*, ed. W. H. Dixon, Vol. I (1862), p. 172.

63 *Mrs Delany*, Series II, Vol. III, p. 308.

64 Gillow drawings, V & A, E. 400–1955.

65 *Leinster Letters* III, pp. 169, 181.

66 *Fragments on the Theory and Practice of Landscape Gardening* (1816).

67 Drawing in the collection of Mr and Mrs Paul Mellon, John Harris, *A Catalogue of British Drawings from Architecture, Decoration, Sculpture and Landscape Gardening in American Collections* (1971), Plate 121.

68 *Country Life* CXXI, 31 January 1957, p. 195.

69 Repton, p. 52.

70 *Maria Edgeworth, Letters From England*, p. 227.

71 George Smith (1808), Caption to Plate 79.

72 *Maria Edgeworth, Letters From England*, p. 335.

73 Pembroke MSS.

74 MSS at Bowood.

75 *Leinster Letters* III, p. 2.

76 *Travels Through England* I, Camden Society, 1888, p. 63.

77 Grosvenor MSS, 12 November 1803.

78 A. T. Bolton, *The Architecture of Robert and James Adam*, Vol. II (1922), p. 3.

79 H. Clifford Smith, 'The Countess of Ashburnham's Dressing Table'. *Connoisseur*, 1953. Supplement in memory of Queen Mary, to June, p. 8.

80 *Mrs Delany*, Series I, Vol. III, p. 308.

81 *Leinster Letters*, Vol. I, p. 151.

82 *Maria Edgeworth, Letters From England*, p. 84.

83 *Maria Edgeworth, Letters From England*, p. 25.

84 C. H. Aspinall-Oglander, *Admiral's Wife* (1940), p. 68.

85 *Mrs Delany*, Series II, Vol. I, p. 174.

86 Henry Meister, *Letters During Residence in England 1791* (1799), pp. 283–4.

REFERENCES   CHAPTER 4

1   MSS at Bowood.

2   *London Tradesman*, p. 169–70.

3   New information is likely to emerge with the publication of the researches of Gervase
    Jackson-Stops.

4   *Walpole Society*, Vol. XLIII, pp. xxx, 57, 119.

5   Percy Macquoid, *Age of Walnut*, p. 36.

6   Marot reprint, *Das Ornamentwerk des Daniel Marot . . . nach Gebildet* (1892).

7   Sir Thomas Robinson to Lord Carlisle, Hist. MSS Comm. Carlisle 15th Report.
    Appendix, Part VI (1897), p. 85.

8   MSS at Bowood. See also Journal of the Duchess of Northumberland, 7 September
    1762. MSS at Ahwick Castle.

9   *Apollo*, June 1973, pp. 581–3.

10 Lapierre. Francis Thompson, *A History of Chatsworth* (1949), p. 156; Feathers,
    Wardrobe Accounts; Houghton lace bill, quoted *Country Life Annual*, 1963, p. 37.

11 *Furniture History*, 1971, p. 121.

12 John Vardy, *Some Designs of Mr. Inigo Jones and Mr. William Kent* (1744), Plate 4;
    Celia Fiennes, p. 72; MSS Elizabeth George, *Apollo*, June 1973, pp. 581–3. See
    also for Bretby, *Celia Fiennes*, p. 171; for Cassidonry Journal of the Duchess of
    Northumberland 1752; for Norfolk House, London in 1756, see *The Norfolk House
    Music Room*, p. 48. William Farington noted a brass rail round the bed in the
    State Bedroom "to prevent people coming too near".

13 *Age of Walnut*, p. 5. The "buttons and loopes" are the linking pieces at the corners
    of the Valances, made of lace or braid.
    Dalemain, *Country Life* CXL, 21 March 1952, p. 820.

14 See also *Celia Fiennes*, p. 277.

15 *English Furniture Designs of the 18th Century*, Plate 44. Journal of the Duchess of
    Northumberland records that the bed was made by Vile and Cobb. Country Life
    CLV, 7 February 1974, p. 251.

16 David Green, *Blenheim Palace*, 1951, p. 169; *Apollo*, June 1973, 581–3.

17 *Etchings of Burghley* by Lady Sophia Pierrepont 1813–1822.

18 Ex. inf. Mr Peter Thornton.

19 Le Concert: The Louvre.

20 Lapierre, *Duke of Montagu's Executors' Accounts at Houghton House*, Christopher Gil-
    bert; The Temple Museum Furniture Bills. *Furniture History* (1967), p. 23. It is
    interesting to compare this reference with one in *The Servants Directory* by Hannah
    Glass (1760): "Shake your window curtains, and pin them up smooth; but you
    should have little Rings to the bottom, three to each curtain, fold them smooth,
    and hang the Rings on a Hook for that purpose."

21 *Printed Textiles. English and American Cottons and Linens 1700–1850* (1970).

22 John Harris, *Sir William Chambers* (1970), p. 179; Anthony Coleridge, *Chippendale
    Furniture* (1968), p. 28.

23 Lindsay Boynton, *Thomes Chippendale at Mersham-le-Hatch*; *Furniture History* (1968),
    p. 91; Chandos, typescript in V & A Woodwork Department; David Green,
    Blenheim Palace (1951), p. 190; Hatfield, *Burlington Magazine*, April 1967, p. 209;
    Hampton Court, ex. inf. Peter Thornton; Lapierre, MSS at Boughton.

24 Alice Fairfax-Lucy, *Charlecote and the Lucys* (1958), p. 228.

25 *The Director*, Plates XLII, XLIII.

26. Many of the contents were removed to Beningbrough by the Earl of Chesterfield.

27 Townshend, BM Add MSS 41656 f. 273; Christopher Gilbert, 'Thomas Chippendale at Dumfries House', *Burlington Magazine* (1969), p. 676.

28 Croome, *Decorative Art from the S. H. Kress Collection*, p. 32; Packington, *Country Life* CXLVIII, 16 July 1970, p. 165; Bridewell, Accounts in the house.

29 *The Cabinet Dictionary* (1803), p. 208.

30 *The Cabinet-Maker and Upholsterer's Drawing Book* (1793), p. 408; see also *Cabinet Dictionary*, p. 185.

31 *Country Life* LIII, 7 April 1923, p. 473.

32 *Memoirs*, Vol. I (1862).

33 *A Collection of Designs*, p. XI; Porden, Grosvenor MSS, December 1807.

34 *Designs for the Private Apartments at Windsor Castle*, sold Sothebys, 9 April 1970; John Rutter, *Illustrated History and Description of Fonthill Abbey* (1823), p. 11.

35 Photostat of letter sent by CR St. Q Wall to JBF; *Blenheim*, p. 190; Woburn, *Family Background*, p. 74.

36 Smith (1808), p. XII.

37 MSS at Boughton.

38 Felbrigg MSS, letter of 5 January 1752 from W. Wyndham to his steward.

39 Abbott Lowell Cummings, *Bed Hangings* (SPNEA, Boston, 1961); Ambrose Heal, *London Tradesman's Cards of the 18th Century*, Plate VIII; trade card lent to JBF.

40 Ex. inf. Gervase Jackson Stops; see *Country Life* CLIII, 22 March 1973, pp. 752–3 where extracts from *System Proposed for Furnishing the New Building May, 1766* are quoted.

41 *Apollo*, June 1973, pp. 581–3.

42 *Coleridge, Chippendale*, p. 26; see also *Family Background* (1949), p. 64.

43 *Mrs Delany*, Series I, Vol. II, pp. 561–2.

44 *A Literary History of Wallpaper*, Plate 19.

45 Anthony Coleridge, 'Hanging Chinese Wallpaper' *Furniture History*, 1966; p. 65.

46 *Letters of Sarah Byng Osborn 1721–1773*, ed. John McClelland (1930), p. 36.

47 For other instructions about hanging wallpapers see *Charlecote and the Lucys*, p. 279.

48 *Country Life* LXXXII, 27 November 1937, p. 551.

49 Anthea Stephenson, 'Chippendale Furniture at Harewood', *Furniture History*, 1968, pp. 72, 73; Hatfield, *Burlington Magazine*, April 1967, p. 206; Attingham, MSS in the house.

50 *Leinster Letters*, Vol. II, p. 155.

51 *Furniture History*, 1968, p. 94; *Family Background*, p. 60.

52 *Family Background*, p. 52.

53 Charlotte Fermor, *History of Burley-on-the-Hill*, Catalogue II, p. 62.

54 Anthony Coleridge. 'James Cullen Cabinet-Maker at Hopetoun House', *Connoisseur*, Nov.–Dec. 1966,

55 Grosvenor MSS, 3 September 1806.

56 Anthony Coleridge, *Some Rococo Cabinet-Makers and Sir Lawrence Dundas. Apollo*, September 1967, p. 217,

57 Chippenham, *Celia Fiennes*, p. 153; Ivy House, *The Book of Wallpaper*, Plate 17.

58 Grand Duke Cosimo, Lorenzo Magalotti, p. 177; Windsor, *Celia Fiennes*, p. 280.

59 John Waterer, *Spanish Leather* (1971).

60 Kensington velvet, ex. inf. Gervase Jackson-Stops; Victoria and Albert Museum. Queen's Loan 978; *Longford Country Life* LXX, 26 December 1931, p. 715.

61 Peter Thornton, *Baroque and Rococo Silks* (1965), p. 82; Duke of Bedford, Gladys Scott Thomson, *Russells in Bloomsbury* (1940), p. 265.

62 Caffoy at Houghton, Ripley, *Houghton Hall* (1760); *Mrs Delany*, Series I, Vol. II, p. 308; Stowe, see *Guidebook*, 1763 edition.

63 Caffoy wallpapers, *A Literary History of Wallpaper*, Fig. 20; *Mrs Delany*, Series I, Vol. III, p. 385; *Strawberry Hill Accounts*, p. 42.

64 Carton, *Leinster Letters* I, p. 158; Manchester, *Age of Walnut*, p. 24.

65 Longford damask, see *Country Life* LXX, 12 December 1931, p. 680; Hopetoun, Coleridge *Chippendale*, p. 167; Lady Sarah Bunbury, *Leinster Letters* II, p. 153; *Buckingham Palace*, p. 77.

66 Lady Holland, *Leinster Letters* I, p. 425; Lady Holdernesse, Lady Shelburne's Journal, MSS at Bowood.

67 Christopher Hussey, *English Country Houses. Mid Georgian*, Figure 200.

68 *Burlington Magazine*, 1967, p. 66.

69 Dumfries, *Burlington Magazine*, 1969, p. 676; Mersham, *Furniture History*, 1968, p. 91; Lindsay Boynton and Nicholas Goodison, *Thomas Chippendale at Nostell Priory*, *Furniture History*, 1968, p. 17; Ashstead, *Celia Fiennes*, p. 339; Bedford House, *Russells in Bloomsbury*, p. 344.

70 Lady Kildare, *Leinster Letters* I, p. 93; Wyatt, National Library of Ireland; Houghton, *Aedes Walpolianae* (1752); *Strawberry Hill Accounts*, p. 108.

71 Houghton, *Aedes Walpolianae*; Lady Kildare, *Leinster Letters* I, p. 93.

72 *Mrs Powys*, p. 144; Journal of the Duchess of Northumberland. *Country Life* CLV, 7 February 1974, p. 252.

73 Nostell, *Furniture History*, 1968, p. 46; Lady Holdernesse, Lady Shelburne's Journal MSS at Bowood; Lady Sarah Bunbury, *Leinster Letters* II, p. 153.

74 Luton Hoo, *Lady Mary Coke*, IV, p. 390; *Mrs Powys*, p. 353; Chippendale, Photostats of bills at the V & A.

75 Lady Holland, *Leinster Letters* I, p. 263; Nostell, *Furniture History*, 1968, pp. 17, 44.

76 Anthony Coleridge, 'Some Mid-Georgian Cabinet-Makers At Holkham,' *Apollo*, February 1964, p. 122.

77 Francis W. Steer, 'A Sussex Mansion in the Eighteenth Century', *Sussex Archaeological Society*, Vol. 94, p. 13.

78 *The Book of Wallpaper. A Literary History of Wallpaper*.

79 Duke of Bedford, *Family Background*, p. 60; Grey to Walpole, *Strawberry Hill Accounts*, p. 42; Chippendale, *Furniture History*, 1968, p. 47; Chambers, BM Add MS 41, 133.

80 V & A T268–1960, 474–1882, T57a–1954; John A. H. Sweeney, *Winterthur Illustrated* (1969), pp. 27, 43.

81 *Literary History of Wallpaper*, Plate 22.

82 Peter Thornton, Plate 114A.

83 *The Correspondence between the Countess of Hartford and the Countess of Pomfret, III*, p. 280.

84 Aubert, *Literary History of Wallpaper*, pp. 31, 32; Madame de Pompadour, Nancy McClelland, *Historic Wallpaper* (1924), p. 55; Lady de Grey, Joyce Godber, p. 53; Walpole, *Strawberry Hill Accounts*, p. 39.

85 *Walpole Society* XVI, p. 14.

86 Mrs Powys, p. 146.

87 Sophie Von La Roche, p. 276.

88 V & A T357–1960.

89 *Country Life* CXIII, 16 January 1953, p. 152.

90 Longford wallpaper, *The Book of Wallpaper*, Plate 35.

91 Southill, *A Regency House* (1951); F. J. B. Watson, *The Furniture and Decoration of Southill*, p. 19; Woburn, *Guide*, 1818.

92 Houghton fragments in V & A. Chinese Drawing Room, 'The Room Furnished with silk made in Spitalfields', see *Burlington Magazine*, September 1967, p. 518.

93 Shugborough, *Country Life* CXV, 4 March 1954, p. 593; Townley, *Country Life* CIV, 23 July, 30 July, 1948, Fig. 8, p. 230.

94 Lindsay Boynton, 'The Furniture of Warren Hastings', *Burlington Magazine*, August 1970.

95 Bagatelle, Michel Gallet, Plate 175; Shrublands, *Late Georgian*, Fig. 407; Cranbury, *Late Georgian*, Fig. 33.

96 Mrs Fitzherbert, *The Journal of Mary Frampton*, ed. Harriot Georgiana Mundy (1885), p. 15; Sheraton, *Cabinet Maker's Drawing Book*, p. 379.

97 Smith (1808), Fig. 151; Attingham, Crace, E. Maurice Bloch, 'Regency Styling. The Prince and the Decorator', *Connoisseur*, 1953, p. 131; Mid Georgian, Fig. 396.

98 Lord Fitzwilliam, *Country Life* CXXIX, 1 June 1961, p. 1272; Lady Sarah Bunting, *Leinster Letters*, II, p. 153.

99 Heythrop, *Mrs Powys*, p. 199; Lady Mary Coke, *Age of Mahogany*, p. 101.

100 Clandon chairs, *Country Life* LXII, 17 September 1972, Plate 11, p. 402.

101 Cushions at V & A, T95–97–1912; set lent by R. L. C. Bridgeman, T48 to E–1967.

102 Lyme, Evelyn Lady Newton, *House of Lyme* (1917), p. 349; Canons, see copy of inventories in V & A Woodwork Department; Croome, *Decorative Art From the Kvess Collection*, p. 38; Arlington Street, *Apollo*, September 1967, p. 198.

103 *Mrs Delany*, Series I, Vol. II, p. 396.

104 Kimbolton, Francis Lenygon, *Decoration in England*, Plate 228.

105 Augustus Hare, *The Story of Two Noble Lives*, Vol. I (1893), p. 252.

106 Bedford, *Russells in Bloomsbury*, p. 98; Hawarden, MSS at Hawarden.

107 Badminton, Roger North, *Lives of the Norths*; Lyme, *House of Lyme*, p. 308; *Mrs Delany*, Series I, Vol. III, p. 301; Miss Hamilton, *Mrs Delany*, Series I, Vol. III, p. 542.

108 *Country Life* CXLVIII, 10 December 1970, p. 1109.

109 *London Tradesman*, p. 153.

110 *Family Background*, pp. 74, 75.

111 We know of no other illustrations of funeral decorations in English houses, but engravings exist of the lying-in-state of Amelia, widow of Prince Frederick Henry, the Stadholder of the Netherlands, who died in 1675, and the lying-in-state of William IV who died in 1751 and his widow who died in 1759.

112 Marlborough's funeral, David Green, 'Homage to Marlborough', *Country Life* CLI, 15 June 1972, p. 1543; Inf. from David Green, Iris Butler, HIS: SATIS EST MALBURIUS JACET, *Journal of the Royal United Services Institute*, June, 1970, p. 55.

113 Misson, p. 90.

114 *Celia Fiennes*, p. 294.

115 Frances Parthenope Verney and Margaret M. Verney, *Memoirs of the Verney Family During the 17th Century* (1904), Vol. II, p. 501.

116 E. A. B. Barnard, *The Sheldons* (1936), p. 68.

117 Half Mourning, Saint Simon, Lucy Norton, *Duc de Saint-Simon Historical Memoirs*, Vol. I (1967), p. 63; Kensington, Th. H. Lunsingh Scheuvleer *Documents on the Furnishing of Kensington Palace*, *Walpole Society* XXXVIII, p. 24; Harcourt, *Harcourt Papers*, Vol. II, p. 124 (14 vols. 1880–1905).

118 Mourning beds 1624, *Shorter Dictionary of Furniture*, p. 37; Evelyn, 5 March 1685.

119 Liselotte, p. 98.

120 Lady Bute, *Age of Mahogany* (1906), p. 95.

121 Hiring, Bedford, *Russells in Bloomsbury*, p. 148; Marlborough, Iris Butler; Trade Card, *London Tradesmen's Cards of the 18th Century*, Plate XCVII.

122 *The House of Lyme*, p. 350.

Chapter 5.

1   F. Schmid, 'The Painter's Implements in Eighteenth Century Art', *Burlington Magazine*, 1966, p. 519.

2   Moses Harris, *Natural System of Colours*, reprinted 1963.

3   *The London Tradesman*, p. 103.

4   Smith, *The Art of Painting in Oyle*, 1676.

5   *Old-Time New England*, Vol. LXII, No. 1, Summer 1971.

6   Quoted by Margaret Jourdain, *English Interior Decoration* (1950), p. 68.

7   Butcher's 1821 edition of Smith's *Art of Painting in Oyle*.

8   Michel Gallet, p. 124.

9   Wyatt Papworth lecture, *Papers Read at the RIBA Season 1857-58*.

10   *Workshop Receipts* (1883), Table of the Composition of the different coats of White Paint.

11   p. 103.

12   See *Caroline*, p. 286.

13   V & A typescript of inventory valuation.

14   Croome, *Decorative Art from the Kress Collection*, p. 39; *The Cabinet Dictionary*, p. 227.

15   Coleridge *Chippendale*, p. 122.

16   *William Constable as a Patron*, Ferens Art Gallery, Hull, 1970, p. 12.

17   Anthony Coleridge, p. 170.

18   *Norfolk House Music Room*, p. 51.

19   *Norfolk House Music Room*, p. 48. Of the State bedroom, he says, "the Carving Gerandoles in this Room are all Gilt with Pale Gold, which was vastly admir'd, but to me look like tarnish'd silver."

20   *Furniture History*, 1968, pp. 76, 77.

21   *Charlecote and the Lucys*, p. 228.

22   p. 108.

23   *Lady Mary Coke* IV, p. 395.

24   p. 153.

25   John Stalker & George Parker, *A Treatise of Japanning and Varnishing*, 1688 (reissued 1960), Preface XV.

26   Stoke Edith, Edward Croft Murray, Decorative Painting in England (1962); Lady Wilbraham, Weston Park MSS.

27   Grosvenor MSS.

28   *The Household Book of Lady Grisel Baillie*, Scottish History Society, Vol. 1 (1911).

29   Kensington, *Walpole Society*, Vol. XXXVIII; Longnor, Shropshire Record Office, Inventory of 1701.

30   V & A typescript.

31   *Mrs Delany*, Series I, Vol. II, pp. 308, 339, *The Papers of Benjamin Franklin*, ed. Leonard Labaree (1963), Vol. 7, p. 382,

32   *Country Life* CXXXIV, 10 October 1963, p. 878.

33   *The Norfolk House Music Room*, p. 48; Worksop, *Country Life* CLIII, 22 March 1973, pp. 752-3.

34   Lady Lincoln, *Mrs Delany*, Series I, Vol. III, p. 416; Fonthill, MSS at Bowood.

35   Mrs Abuthnot, Vol. II, p. 333; Lawrence, *A Book of Wallpaper*, p. 91.

36   Buckingham House, *Walpole Society* XVI, p. 78. Light Green described by Horace Walpole in 1783; Nostell: *Furniture History*, 1968, p. 17; Lady Holland, *Leinster Letters* I, p. 238; *Lady Mary Coke*, Vol. IV, p. 390; Chambers, John Harris, p. 216b.

37   *Leinster Letters* I, p. 223.

38 Edward Ingram, *Leaves from a Family Tree*, p. 72.
Mrs Delany, Series I, Vol. III, p. 477.

39 Movant, *Country Life*, LXVII, 10 May, 1930, p. 69.

40 Mrs Clayton, *Mrs Delany*, Series I, Vol. I, pp. 289, 305; Houghton, Ripley, *Houghton Hall* (1760); French Colour, Michel Gallet, p. 125; Harewood, *Furniture History*, 1968, pp. 76, 77; Linnell, Helena Hayward, *The Drawings of John Linnell in the Victoria and Albert Museum, Furniture History*, 1969; Plate 165.

41 Duchess of Northumberland's Journal.

42 Chambers, Geoffrey Beard, *Georgian Craftsmen*, p. 92; *Mrs Powys*, p. 146; Letitia Galbraith, *Garrick's Furniture at Hampton. Apollo*, July 1972,

43 Gladys Scott Thomson, *Letters of a Grandmother 1732–35* (1943), p. 76.

44 Marie P. G. Draper, *Marble Hill House & Its Owners* (1970), p. 57.

45 Wanstead, *Mrs Powys*, p. 205; Ditchley, *Walpole Society* XVI, p. 26; Duke of Somerset, Collection Duke of Northumberland; Eastbury, *Mrs Powys*, p. 62; Houghton, *Mrs Powys*, p. 6.

46 *Mrs Delany*, Series I, Vol. II, p. 339; BM Add MSS 41, 133, quoted Geoffrey Beard.

47 Bill at Bowood.

48 See *Papers Read at the RIBA Session 1857–8*.

49 Duchess of Leinster, MS letter. Collection: The Hon Desmond Guinness, Lady Holland, 25 October 1772; Castletown, MSS at Bowood; Lady Sarah Bunting, *Leinster Letters* II, p. 153; *Mrs Delany*, Series II, Vol. II, p. 33.

50 *Jerningham Letters* I, ed. Egerton Castle (1896), p. 28.

51 *Cabinet Maker & Upholsterer's Drawing Book*, p. 379.

52 Peter Thornton, 'The Furnishings of Mersham-le-Hatch', *Apollo*, June 1970, p. 440.

53 *Mrs Powys*, p. 146.

54 Vol. I, plate VII.

55 p. 299.

56 MS letter, Collection: The Hon Desmond Guinness, 2 November 1774.

57 Chippendale at Stourhead, copy of bills at V & A; *Mrs Powys*, p. 352.

58 George Smith, p. XII (1808).

59 Britton, David Watkin, *Thomas Hope* (1968), p. 224; Hope, p. 109.

60 Burghley, see 1815 guidebook; Goodwood, D. Jacques, *Visit to Goodwood*.

61 *The Laws of Harmonious Colouring . . .* (2nd ed. 1829).

Chapter 6

1 Hannah Glass, *The Servants Directory* (1760), see The Housemaid; see also, Samuel & Sarah Adams, *The Complete Servant* (1825), p. 280.

2 *The Housekeeping Book of Susannah Whatman*, ed. Thomas Balston (1956).

3 *Admiral's Widow*, p. 123.

4 M. Grosley, *A Tour of London*, Vol. I (1772), p. 73.

5 *Russells in Bloomsbury*, p. 162.

6 We are grateful to Gervase Jackson-Stops for this quotation.

7 *Celia Fiennes*, pp. 72, 339.

8 Hanover Square, V & A W28–1927.

9 Ware, p. 123.

10 *Mrs Powys*, p. 116.

11 Franklin, Vol. y, p. 382.

12 MSS at Bowood.

13 Vyne, Coleridge, *Chippendale* p. 45.

14 Ware, p. 123.

15 *English Topography* (1891–1905), Vol. XVI, from *Gentleman's Magazine Library*, Vol. XVI, p. 110, ed. by G. L. Gomme.

16 *Apollo*, June 1973, pp. 581–3.

17 George Smith (1812).

18 Collins Baker, p. 150.

19 *Admiral's Widow*, p. 123.

20 Denham, BM. Add MSS 41656. f. 199.

21 John Gloag, *Early English Decorative Detail* (1965).

22 Boulton, Birmingham Assay Office MSS III, p. 424.

23 *Walpole Society* XVI, p. 37.

24 Attingham, 1827 Sale Catalogue; Stourhead, Photostat of bills in V & A Woodwork Department.

25 Nina Fletcher Little, *Floor Coverings in New England before 1850*, (Old Sturbridge Village, Mass. U.S.A. 1967).

Chapter 7

1 William T. O'Dea, *The Social History of Lighting* (1958), p. 3; for 19th century improvements to candle design see Elizabeth Buxton, *The Early Victorians At Home* (1972), p. 99.

2 David Green, p. 168; *The Complete Servant*, p. 280.

3 *Servants Guide* (1830), p. 67.

4 James Pope Hennessy, *Anthony Trollope* (1971), p. 33.

5 James Greig, *The Diaries of A Duchess* (1928), p. 195.

6 Letters, p. 56.

7 *Emily Duchess of Leinster* (1949), p. 128.

8 *Mrs Delany*, Series I, Vol. II, p. 176; Series II, Vol. II, p. 63.

9 Collins Baker, p. 184.

10 Ware (1768), p. 184.

11 Ex. inf. Geoffrey de Bellaigue.

12 Sir Thomas Robinson, HMC 15th Report, Appendix Part VI (1897), p. 85.

13 Pembroke MSS.

14 *Mrs Delany*, Series II, Vol. II, p. 496.

15 MSS at Bowood.

16 *Mrs Delany* Series II, Vol. I, p. 242.

17 Count Kielmansegge, *Diary of a Journal to England in 1761–62* (1902), p. 144.

18 Maria Edgeworth, *Tales of Fashionable Life* I, *Ennui*, Chapter I.

19 Magalotti, p. 376.

20 *Family Background*, p. 70.

21 'Newby Hall' by Hugh Honour, *Connoisseur*, 1954, p. 250; Eaton, *Country Life* CXLIX, 18 February 1971, p. 363.

22 Saltram letters Vol. XVI, p. 183, 14 October 1810. Traces of this kind of lighting were found during the restoration of the Speaker's Parlour and the Palladio Room at Clandon.

23 Sophie Von La Roche, p. 173.

24 *Family Background*, p. 81.

25 Rev. Irwin Eller, *History of Belvoir* (1841), pp. 328, 329.

26 Lady Kildare, *Leinster Letters* I, p. 149; Lady Holland, *Leinster Letters* I, p. 419.

27 Lady Holland, *Leinster Letters* I, p. 357; Bramshill, *Mrs Powys*, p. 116; Grosvenor, Gervas Huxley, *Lady Elizabeth and the Grosvenors* (1965), p. 35.

28 Cullen, copy of MSS in V & A Woodwork Department.

29 Barbara Charlton, *Recollections of a Northumbrian Lady* (1815–1866) pp. 176–8.

30 Francois Misson, p. 37.

31 Wyatt, Drawing in the National Library of Ireland; St-Ford, p. 245.

32 Belvoir, Eller, p. 194.

33 Mark Girouard, *The Victorian Country House* (1971), p. 15.

34 Pococke, *Travels Through England*, Camden Society New Series XLII; Walpole, *Strawberry Hill Accounts*, p. 67.

Chapter 8

1 Sir Henry Wotton, *Elements of Architecture* (1624).

2 *Collected Works* (2nd edition 1729), p. 254.

3 H. Clifford Smith, p. 77; Chippendale, *Apollo*, September 1967, p. 216.

4 *Walpole Society* XXXVIII.

5 *Walpole Society*, Vol. XVI, p. 64, p. 17.

6 Gilpin, Margaret Jourdain, *English Interior Decoration 1500–1830* (1950), p. 63.

7 p. 17.

8 Jonathan Richardson, The *Connoisseur*, 'An Essay on the Whole Art of Criticism As It Relates to Painting, see *Of Originals and Copies*.

9 Atkinson, *Early Georgian*, Fig. 406; Farnborough, *Country Life* CXV, 18 February 1954, p. 430; Saltram, *Country Life* CXXXIX, 2 June 1966, p. 1386; Soane, *Country Life* CLI, 25 May 1972, p. 1307; Melford, *Country Life* LXXXII, 7 August 1937, p. 142.

10 Sheraton, p. 216.

11 *Celia Fiennes*, Chippenham, p. 152; Drayton, *Country Life* CXXXVII, 27 May 1965, p. 1286; Euston, Celia Fiennes p. 150; Grimsthorpe, *Country Life* LV, 19 April 1924, p. 614.

12 *Lord Chesterfield's Letters* II, p. 894.

13 *Handbook*, about p. 55.

14 *Mrs Delany*, Series I, Vol. III, p. 96.

15 *Country Life* CLII 8 February 1973, p. 274.

Chapter 9

1 À la Ronde, *Country Life* LXXXIII, 30 April 1938, p. 448.

2 Aston Hall, *Country Life* CXIV, 20 August 1953, p. 554; Wallington, *Country Life* CXLVII 23 April 1970, p. 922; Newliston, *Country Life* XXXIX, 26 February 1916, p. 275.

3 Milton carpets, *Country Life* CXXIX, 1 June 1961, p. 1271, Fig. 4.

4 Chichley, *Country Life* LXXIX, 23 May 1936, p. 534; Drax, *Age of Mahogany*, Fig. 33.

5 Arbury, *Country Life* CXX, 28 March 1957, p. 601.

6 Liselotte, p. 198.

7 Morritt, *Country Life* CXI, 7 March 1952; Caroline Campbell, *Walpole Society* XVI, p. 14; Gwysany, *Country Life* XCIII, Fig. 8, 21May 1943, p. 927.

8   Duchess of Beaufort, *Lives of the Norths*; Queen Charlotte, *Mrs Delany*, Series II, Vol. III, p. 149.

9   Lady Anne Coventry, *Charlecote and the Lucys*, p. 221.

10 Elizabeth Radcliffe, Albinia Lucy Cust (Mrs Wherry) *Chronicle of Erthig on the Dyke* (1914).

11 Verney, *Age of Walnut*, p. 138; Lady Sunderland, *Mrs Delany*, Series I, Vol. I, p. 212.

12 Louisa Conolly, MS letter, 14 February 1768. Collection: The Hon Desmond Guinness.

13 Duchess of Portland, *Mrs Delany*, Series I, Vol. III, p. 473; Lady Luxborough, p. 16; Lady Hartford, Vol. III, p. 219.

Chapter 10

1   See also *Servants Guide* (1830), p. 131: "Linen takes off the gilding and deadens its brightness; it should therefore never be used for wiping it".

2   Lucy, *Charlecote and the Lucys*, p. 222; Dundas, *Apollo*, September 1967, p. 215; Attingham, 1827 Sale Catalogue.

3   See also *Celia Fiennes*, p. 339: At Ashstead Park she saw several damask rooms "and so neatly kept folded up in clean sheets pinn'd about the beds and hangings".

4   Kensington, *Walpole Society*, Vol. XXXVIII, p. 53; Croome, *Decorative Art From the S. H. Kvess Collection*, p. 20; Inveraray, *Country Life* LXII, 30 July 1927, p. 160, Fig. 9.

5   Sheraton, *Cabinet Dictionary*, p. 336.

6   Woburn, *Family Background*, p. 81.
    Hatfield, *Burlington Magazine*, April 1967, p. 205.

Index of Names

Robert Adam, 26, 27, 32, 43, 45, 46, 63, 66, 67, 82, 92, 109, 120, 168, 175, 180, 181, 185, 188, 198, 207, 214, 215, 235, 236, 241, 246
Mrs Arbuthnot, 25, 202

Lady Grisell Baillie, 199
Mrs Bethell, 17, 18, 20, *4*
Mrs Boscawen, 63, 67, 81, 210, 216
Matthew Boulton, 32, 48, 189, 217, 224, 228
Thomas Bromwich, 26, 30, 137
Lady Sarah Bunbury, 46, 64, 126, 133, 135, 149, 206

John Carwithen, 216
Sir William Chambers, 27, 42, 45, 63, 94, 102, 137, 139, 203, 204, 205, *I*
Duke of Chandos, 25, 68, 102, 159, 199, 215
Lord Chesterfield, 25, 43, 200, 243, 245
Thomas Chippendale, 26, 27, 29, 54, 102, 106, 108, 114, 120, 126, 128, 133, 135, 136, 137, 159, 161, 186, 188, 203, 208, 233, *34, 89, 94, 107, 138, 173*
Lady Mary Coke, 135, 149, 188, 203
Lady Louisa Conolly, 25, 64, 65, 75, 78, 206, 207, 233, 252
J. G. Crace, Crace & Co., 29, 30, 47, 145, 147, *14, 127*
Crompton & Spinnage, 126, 205
James Cullen, 124, 127, 226

Delabrière, 47, 81, *25*
Mrs Delany, 63, 65, 66, 71, 72, 74, 79, 123, 132, 135, 162, 165, 200, 205, 206, 222, 230, 248, 250, 252
6th Duke of Devonshire, 30, 47, 64, 95, 188, 243, *26, 27*
Mr Davies, 25

Eckhardt, 47, 48, 142, 144, *143*
Maria Edgeworth, 30, 67, 74, 75, 76, 79, 223
Princess Elizabeth, daughter of George III, 132, 252, *223*
Elliotts, 124
John Evelyn, 36, 37, 38, 172, 211

Fell & Newton, 115
Celia Fiennes, 38, 85, 122, 129, 130, 133, 171, 190, 211, 242
Benjamin Franklin, 200, 213

George, Prince of Wales and later George IV, 25, 26, 35, 46, 50, 53, 144, 188, 193, 196, 208, 240, *213*
Gillows, 118, 145, *103, 104, 128, 189, XVIII*

Hannah Glass, 210, 254, 255
Lady de Grey, 64, 67, 139
Grosley, 210

Thomas Hardwick, 27, 204, *12*
Randle Holme, 202
Hepplewhite, 50, 157
Lady Hertford, 35, 71, 252
Lady Holdernesse, 133, 135
Lady Holland, formerly Lady Caroline Fox, 35, 45, 64, 133, 136, 203, 206, 225, *23*
Henry Holland, 36, 46, 47, 48, 50, 81, 118, 139, 145, 188, 189, 193, 196, 211, 221, 245
Thomas Hope, 50, 208, *184*
Ince & Mayhew, 159, 160, *156, 158*

Thomas Jefferson, 25

William Kent, 26, 29, 42, 46, 60, 71, 91, 157, 184, 199, 203, 241, *150, 172, XII, XIII, XIV, XXXI, XXXII*
Fanny Kemble, 68

Lapierre, 42, 83, 84, 100, 102, 107, 121, 159, *VII, VIII*
Emily, Duchess of Leinster, formerly Countess of Kildare, 46, 64, 65, 79, 132, 133, 134, 203, 206, 225
John Linnell, 204
Lady Luxborough, 207, 252

Sarah, Duchess of Marlborough, 92, 165, 204, 211, 220, 250
Marot, 26, 29, 41, 83, 86, 88, 100, 103, 115, 122, 129, 159, 233, 256, *20, 63, 64, 81, 82*
Marsh & Tatham, 141
Ralph Montagu, subsequently Lord Montagu and Duke of Montagu, 33, 41, 42, 83, 100, 102, 159
Mrs Montagu, 32, 46, 251
Morant, 29, 47, 204
Morell & Hughes, 29

Samuel Norman, 26, 29, 121, 187
Duchess of Northumberland, 46, 133, 135, 204, 215, 221, *223*

James Paine, 43
Lord Palmerston, 112
J. B. Papworth, 47
Samuel Pepys, 38
Percier & Fontaine, 35, 50, 145
William Porden, 31, 32, 33, 78, 115, 127, 142, 197, 208, *XVIII*
Mrs Lybbe Powys, 26, 65, 67, 134, 135, 139, 149, 204, 205, 207, 208, 211, 225, 248
Pugin, 22, *9*

Repton, 75, 208, 215, 216, *52, 53*
Thomas Roberts, 25, 122
Robson Hale, 124
Sophie Von La Roche, 68, 139, 224
Anthony Ryland, 25

Seddon, 109
Lady Shelburne, 63, 78, 82, 84, 133, 213, 222
Sheraton, 50, 72, 109, 112, 139, 186, 206, 241, 257, *96*
Sheringham, 47
George Smith, 26, 50, 75, 95, 115, 118, 147, 208, 215, *100*
Nathan Smith, 216
Lady Sarah Spencer, 35, 74
Edward Stevens, 27, *11*
James Stuart, 26, 27, 45, 189, 196, 207, *10*
Robert Swann, 26

John Talman, 26, 29

Sir John Vanbrugh, 32, 33, 60, 221
John Vardy, 91, 157, 168, *150*
Vile & Cobb, 102, 123, 213

Horace Walpole, 25, 46, 47, 53, 60, 63, 65, 67, 72, 94, 133, 139, 188, 203, 217, 230, 234, 250
Sir Robert Walpole, 29, 60, 84, 222
Isaac Ware, 42, 43, 66, 71, 211, 213, 222
Josiah Wedgwood, 31, 32, 48, 245
Lady Wharncliffe, 53, 63, 74
Mrs Whatman, 210, 254, 255, 257
B. D. Wyatt, 54
James Wyatt, 27, 109, 133, 193, 227, *13, 196*
Wyatville, 29, 120, 245, 259

Index of Houses

Adare Manor, Co. Limerick, 246, *218*
À la Ronde, Devon, 248, *219, 220*
Alnwick Castle, Northumberland, 30, 207, *XL*
Althorp, Northamptonshire, 47, 66, 74, 124, 241
Apsley House, London, 202
Armley Hall, Yorkshire, 75
Ashburnham Place, Sussex, 95, 96, 145, 156, 165, 215, *76, 78, 79*
Ashtead, Surrey, 77, 133, 211
Aston Hall, Birmingham, 33, 248
Attingham Park, Shrewsbury, 47, 51, 81, 126, 147, 162, 165, 189, 196, 203, 208, 213, 215, 217, 240, 256, *25, 182, III, IV, V*
Audley End, Essex, 25, 33, 78, 133, 206, 214, 224, 230, *16, 199*

Badminton, Gloucestershire, 94, 164, 241, 243, 245
Ballyfin, Co. Leix, 213, *187, 188*
Barnsley Park, Gloucestershire, 51, 197, *31*
Bayfordbury, Hertfordshire, 51
Bedford House, London, 133
Belmont, Kent, 197, *180, 181*
Belton House, Lincolnshire, 67, 85, 147, 219
Belvoir Castle, Leicestershire, 53, 63, 68, 79, 85, 86, 225, 228, *33, 59*
Beningbrough Hall, Yorkshire, 17, 85, 91, 106, *2, 68*
Blair Castle, Perthshire, 85, 183
Blenheim Palace, Oxfordshire, 32, 60, 94, 102, 121, 165, *39*
Blickling Hall, Norfolk, 106, 185, 189, 215, *191, XXXIV, XXXV, XXXVI*
Boughton House, Northamptonshire, 32, 41, 56, 57, 58, 60, 84, 85, 103, 162, 166, 199, 205, 211, 216
Bowood, Wiltshire, 79, 205
Bramshill, Hampshire, 225
Bridewell House, Devon, 109, 209
Bridgewater House, London, *217*
Broadlands, Hampshire, 144
Brocket Hall, Hertfordshire, 133, 138, 150, *136*
Brodsworth Hall, Yorkshire, 200
Buckingham House, later Buckingham Palace, London, 17, 84, 123, 132, 133, 139, 162, 203, 205, 211, 213, 214, 233, *56, 161*

Bulstrode, Buckinghamshire, 63, 67, 68, 71, 79, 215, 222
Burghley House, Lincolnshire, 39, 41, 56, 57, 85, 91, 94, 115, 209, *99*
Burton Agnes, Yorkshire, 130
Burton Constable, Yorkshire, 186, 236

Cairness, Aberdeenshire, 51, 147, *29, 30*
Cannons, Middlesex, 68, 122, 161, 185, 222
Carlton House, London, 26, 35, 47, 48, 68, 81, 112, 118, 139, 142, 196, 208, 240, *28, 46, 213*
Carton, Co. Kildare, 65, 79, 132, 225
Castlecoole, Co. Fermanagh, 79, 95, 118, 169, 228, 254, *75, 105, 224*
Castletown, Co. Kildare, 25, 32, 67, 68, 75, 133, 206, 207, 225, 233, 252
Charlecote, Warwickshire, 22, 103, 188, 256
Chatsworth, Derbyshire, 39, 41, 56, 57, 58, 60, 64, 84, 95, 130, 147, 188, 224, 243, *14, 35, 38, 74*
Chesterfield House, London, 25, 43, 200, *21, 216*
Chippenham Park, Cambridgeshire, 129, 190, 242
Chirk, Denbighshire, 22, *9*
Christchurch Mansion, Suffolk, 139
Clandon Park, Surrey, 71, 78, 85, 89, 96, 105, 107, 114, 115, 120, 122, 124, 126, 137, 138, 155, 159, 165, 173, 181, 182, 183, 185, 189, 200, 201, 203, 205, 207, 213, 243, 245, 250, 256, 259, 261, 262, 265, *83, 106, 108, 142, 143?, 154, 231, 232, XXI, XXII, XXVII, XXIX, XXX*
Claydon, Buckinghamshire, 171, 211, *186*
Compton Place, Sussex, 243
Corsham Court, Wiltshire, 71, 103, 126, 137, 156, 234, 240, 243, *49, 149, 201, 202*
Cossey, Norfolk, 206
Cothele, Cornwall, 53
Cranbury Park, Hampshire, 145, *130*
Croome Court, Worcestershire, 43, 45, 109, 161, 186, 257, *22*
Crowcombe Court, Somerset, 192, 219
Cusworth Hall, Yorkshire, 157, *152*

Dalemain, Cumberland, 85, 86
Dangan, Co. Meath, 66
Daylesford, Gloucestershire, 144
Deepdene, Surrey, 67

Denham, Suffolk, 216
Devonshire House, London, 47, *26, 27, VI*
Ditchley, Oxfordshire, 18, 202, 205, 236, 261
Dodington Park, Gloucestershire, 196, 228
Downton Castle, Shropshire, 196
Drayton House, Northamptonshire, 32, 85, 86, 130, 190, 211, 236, 242, 255, *15, 62*
Drumlanrig Castle, Dumfries, 95, 211, 224, *74*
Dumfries House, Dumfries, 108, 133
Dunster Castle, Somerset, 130
Dyrham Park, Gloucestershire, 38, 60, 85, 91, 106, 107, 122, 130, 166, 183, 192, 226, 229, 232, 256, *19, 91, 92, X, XXXVII, XXXVIII*

Eastbury, Dorset, 205
Easton Grey, Wiltshire, 75
Eaton Hall, Cheshire, 31, 33, 78, 121, 215, 224, 225, *189, XVIII*
Edgeworthstown, Co. Longford, 74
Erthig, Denbighshire, 71, 85, 107, 122, 132, 136, 162, 168, 188, 200, 206, 240, 251, *90, 212, 222*
Euston Hall, Norfolk, 242

Farnborough Hall, Warwickshire, 240, *210*
Farnley Hall, Yorkshire, 68, 241, *44, 45, 214, 215*
Fawley Court, Buckinghamshire, 26, 139, 204, 207
Felbrigg Hall, Norfolk, 122, 126, 133, 204, 213, 240, *208, 209*
Field Place, Sussex, 75, *54*
Firle Place, Sussex, 173, 243
Fonthill Abbey, Wiltshire, 53, 63, 78, 120, 208
Forde Abbey, Dorset, 181, *169*
Frogmore, Windsor, Buckinghamshire, 68, 252, *47, 223*

Garrick's Villa at Hampton, 204
Glemham, Suffolk, 85, 114
Goodwood, Sussex, 51, 134, 159, 196, 209, 251, *155*
Great Hundridge Manor, Buckinghamshire, 192, *176*
Grimsthorpe Castle, Lincolnshire, 17, 224, 242
Grimston Garth, Yorkshire, 115, *98*
Grosvenor House, Park Lane, London, 127, 142, 197, 208
Gwynsaney, Flintshire, 250, *221*

Haarlem, Kop's House, 139, *119, 120, 121*
Hagley Hall, Worcestershire, 45
Ham House, Surrey, 37, 56, 60, 71, 83, 85, 86, 129, 130, 159, 181, 190, 193, 197, 199, 204, 211, 229, 232, 256, *17, 18, 133, 225, II, XX*
Hamilton Palace, Lanarkshire, 58
Hampton Court, Herefordshire, 85, 115
Hampton Court Palace, 57, 58, 69, 85, 91, 92, 102, 103, 131, 137, 155, 166, 199, 224, 257, *226*
Hamstead Marshall, Berkshire, 66
Hanbury Hall, Worcestershire, 205
Harcourt House, London, 172
Hardwick Hall, Derbyshire, 56, 57, 58, 84, 85, 86, 88, 89, 168, *36, VII, VIII*
Harewood, Yorkshire, 26, 108, 109, 112, 126, 188, 204, 235, 241, *94*
Haseley Court, Oxfordshire, 18, 96, 259, 261, *79, 229, 230*
Hatfield House, Hertfordshire, 102, 126, 229, 258
Hawarden Castle, Flintshire, 164, 250
Headfort, Co. Meath, 181
Hesleyside, Northumberland, 226
Heveningham Hall, Suffolk, 67, 109, 188, 203, 206
Highclere, Hampshire, 54
Hill Court, Herefordshire, 190, 192, *174, 175*
Holkham Hall, Norfolk, 45, 60, 63, 65, 66, 71, 78, 85, 91, 108, 131, 136, 139, 150, 160, 201, 202, 222, 234, *41, 70, 132, 157*
Honington Hall, Warickshire 130, *115*
Hopetoun, West Lothian, 94, 124, 127, 133, 137, 157, 202, 226, *72, 110*
Hornby Castle, Yorkshire, 74, 166, *163*
Houghton Hall, Norfolk, 29, 45, 60, 63, 65, 66, 68, 71, 78, 84, 85, 91, 115, 131, 132, 133, 134, 138, 139, 144, 147, 166, 184, 185, 187, 199, 201, 203, 204, 215, 222, 234, 256, *40, 48, 117, 190, XII, XIII, XIV, XVII, XXIV, XXXI, XXXII*

Inveraray Castle, Argyll, 207, 227, 257, *227*

Kedleston Hall, Derbyshire, 26, 45, 60, 63, 66, 71, 78, 94, 126, 157, 160, 166, 168, 202, 204, 207, 227, 234, 235, 236, *10, 41, 42*
Kelmarsh Hall, Northants, 18, *3, 4*
Kensington Palace, London, 122, 131, 183, 184, 199, 234, 257, *172*
Kimbolton Castle, Huntingdonshire, 162, *162*
King's Weston, Bristol, 205
Knole, Kent, 58, 82, 83, 85, 86, 112, 122, 133, 165, 166, 173, *116, 165, IX, XIX*

Lamport Hall, Northamptonshire, 231
Langley Park, Norfolk, *150, 137*
Langleys, Essex, 124
Lansdowne House, London, 51, 82, 222, 229
Levens Hall, Westmorland, 53, *32*
London,
   19 Arlington Street, 106, 128, 161, 186, 200, 203, 233, *173, XV*
   Mrs Fitzherbert's House in Pall Mall, 145

22 Hanover Square, 211, *185*
Lady Holdernesse's House, Park Lane, 133, 135
Lord Townshend's House, Berkeley Square, 108
Longford Castle, Wiltshire, 64, 108, 124, 131, 133, 160, 186, 203, 216, 229, *109*
Longford Hall, Shropshire, 142
Longnor Hall, Shropshire, 211
Luton Hoo, Bedfordshire, 16, 78, 135, 188, 203, 206
Lydiard Tregoz, Wiltshire, 127
Lyme Park, Cheshire, 122, 161, 166, *144*

Marble Hill, Twickenham, 107, 204, 205
Marlborough House, London, 171, 173
Mawley Hall, Shropshire, 211
Melford Hall, Suffolk, 240
Melville House, Fife, 114, 115, 166, *65, 66, 67*
Mersham-le-Hatch, Kent, 26, 100, 126, 133, 206
Milton Manor, Berkshire, 206
Moccas Court, Herefordshire, 142, *123*
Moor Park, Hertfordshire, 45, 187

Narford Hall, Norfolk, 67
Newby Hall, Yorkshire, 45, 67, 224
Norfolk House, London, 43, 187, 200, 256
Northumberland House, London, 33, 200, 216, 235
Nostell Priory, Yorkshire, 26, 78, 94, 133, 135, 136, 137, 150, 203, 235, *135*
Nottingham Castle, 85, 211

Old Battersea House, London, 192, *179*
Ombersley Court, Worcestershire, 78, 141, *122*
Osterley Park, Middlesex, 21, 45, 56, 60, 63, 68, 71, 74, 92, 100, 102, 105, 106, 108, 109, 126, 134, 147, 156, 158, 168, 179, 180, 183, 185, 188, 203, 204, 206, 214, 215, 224, 229, 230, 235, 257, *6, 7, 8, 50, 71, 148, 153, 198*

Painshill, Surrey, 217
Pencarrow, Cornwall, 197, *183, 197*
Penrhyn, Caernarvonshire, 66
Penshurst Place, Kent, 83, 129, 224, *114*
Petworth, Sussex, 41, 43, 203, 245
Portman House, Portman Square, London, 32, 188, 196, *XXXIX*
Powderham Castle, Devon, 169, 206
Powis Castle, Montgomeryshire, 85, 211, *61*

Ramsbury Manor, Wiltshire, 124
Raynham Hall, Norfolk, 67
Redlinch, Somerset, 203
Rousham, Oxfordshire, 236
Rushbrooke Hall, Suffolk, 166, *166*

St. Leonards Hill, Berkshire, 139
Saltram, Devon, 65, 67, 126, 202, 214, 224, 240, *111, 112, 211*
Sezincote, Gloucestershire, 116, 120, 165, *102*
Sheffield Park, Sussex, 136

Shelburne House, London. *See* Lansdowne House
Sheringham, Norfolk, 75, 215, *51*
Shrublands, Suffolk, 145, *129*
Shugborough, Staffordshire, 122, 144, 193, 235, 256, *125*
Slane Castle, Co. Meath, 227, *196*
Soane Museum, London, 197, 208, 240
Southill, Bedfordshire, 47, 51, 81, 116, 142, 150, 241, *101, 124, 134*
Spencer House, London, 45, 206, 207, 235, *24, 55, 203*
Stafford House, London, 54, 126, 188
Stanton Harcourt Parsonage, Oxfordshire, 192, *177*
Stoke Edith, Herefordshire, 85, 88, 192, 248
Stourhead, Wiltshire, 22, 51, 136, 208, 217, 235, 236, 241, *204, 205, 206, 207*
Stowe, Buckinghamshire, 51, 55, 74, 84, 85, 92, 94, 122, 132, 201, 203, 211, 214, 243
Stratfield Saye, Hampshire, 43, 229
Strawberry Hill, Middlesex, 65, 133, 162, *160*
Stretton, Staffordshire, 78
Sudbury Hall, Derbyshire, 21, 181, 188, 210, 224, 259, 261, 265, 266, *170, 171, 233, 234*
Swangrove, Badminton, Gloucestershire, 192, *178*
Syon House, Middlesex, 45, 46, 66, 133, 138, 188, 205, 207, 211, 214, 241

Temple Newsam, Yorkshire, 100
Townley Hall, Co. Louth, 144, *126*
Traquair, Pebbleshire, 213, 250

Uppark, Sussex, 33, 34, 103, 105, 126, 168, 211, *167*

Victoria and Albert Museum, London, 21, 85, 86, 91, 106, 107, 129, 131, 132, 133, 137, 141, 142, 150, 155, 160, 166, 185, 211, 224, *65, 66, 67, 145, 146, 151, 173, 185, XI, XXIII*
The Vyne, Hampshire, 137, 213

Wanstead, Essex, 67, 126
Warwick Castle, 56, 85
Wentworth Castle, Yorkshire, 135
Weston Hall, Warwickshire, 172
Weston Park, Shropshire, 45
West Wycombe, Buckinghamshire, 45, 66, 185, 228, *XXXIII*
White Knights, Berkshire, 208
Wilton House, Wiltshire, 21, 67, 231, 243, *5*
Wimborne House, London, 16, *1*
Windsor Castle, 39, 95, 120, 226
Woburn Abbey, Bedfordshire, 26, 43, 47, 121, 124, 126, 139, 142, 168, 202, 224, 225, 235, 245
Woburn Farm, Surrey, 63, 78
Wolterton Hall, Norfolk, 43, 63, 78
Woodcote Park, Surrey, 43
Worksop Manor, Nottinghamshire, 122, 200
Wrest Park, Bedfordshire, 54

York House, London, 27, *1*

Subject Index

American Influence on English decoration, 15

Apartment, Great Apartment. *See* Uses of Houses, State Rooms

Architects' attitudes to decoration, 26, 27, 29, 42, 43, *10–13, I*

Architectural painting, planning the painting of a room, 180–, *169, 170, 171, 172, III–V, XXVII–XXXII, XXXIV–XXXIX*

Argand Lamps, 224

Attic. *See* Uses of Houses

Beds, 39, 83–, *76, 89, 117, 167, IX*
  Placing of beds, 84, 275, *61*
  Angel or *lit à la duchesse*, 89, *64, VII, VIII*
  Cantonnières, 86
  Mourning beds, 172
  Polonaise beds, 94, *73, 74*
  State beds, 41, 84, 171, 172, *20, 61, 62, 63, 65, 66, 67, 69, 70, 71, 72, 75, 226, 227, X, XII, XIII, XIV*
  See also Bed Carpets, Canopy

Bed carpets, 96, 215, 222, *71, 191*

Bizarre silk. *See* Materials

Blinds, 100, 121, 122, 255

Borders: use of borders for hangings, curtains, upholstery, carpets, 47, 50, 95, 139, 141, 144, 213, *120, 121, 125, 126, 212, XVII, XXIII, XXIV*

Braids, fringes, gimps, tassels, lace, galloon, trimmings, 26, 82, 84, 86, 89, 91, 94, 95, 107, 126, 130, 164–, 250, *66, 67, 68, 75, 147, 152, 163, 164, 165, 166, 167, IX, X, XIII, XXV, XXVI*

Brussels carpet, 96, 215, *78, 79*

Caffoy. *See* Materials

Calimanco. *See* Materials

Canopy, 57, 58, 170, 171, 173, *36, 37, 168*

Cantonnières. *See* Beds

Carpets, 211, 213, *85, 190*
  Fitted, 213
  Planned to room, 213, 214, *189*
  Seasonal use, 210, 215, 216
  See also Brussels carpet

Case Covers, 161, 162, 257, *54, 55, 159, 160, 161, 204, 223*

Case Curtains, 199, 256, *63, 226*

Ceilings, colouring of, 207

Chairs, 148–

Chairs of state, 57, 58, 171, 173

Chandeliers, 171, 172, 224. *See also* Lighting

Changing attitudes to the past, 15, 21, 53, 54, 246, *9, 32, 218*

Chimneyboards, 229, 230, *198, 199*

Cloak Pins, 96, 105, 106, *77, 87*

Colour, 20, 26, 38, 68, 174–
  Black, 170, 209
  Blue, 202, 203, *XXVII*
  Green, 202, 205
  Pea green, 82, 203, 205, 207
  Grey, 204, 205, 207
  Silver, 188, 204
  Stone, 184, 203, 204, 205
  White, 204, 205, 206
  Yellow, 202, 204, *18, II*
  Symbolism of colour, 202
  Fashions in colour and pattern, 20, 200–
  Uniformity of colour, 199–, 206
  Contrasts of colour, 209
  See also Architectural Painting, Colouring of Ceilings, Dead Colour, Uniformity, Paint Manuals, Picture Hanging

Comfort and discomfort, 65, 225, 226

Continued drapery, 116, *28, 100, 102*

Covers, 76, 160–, 256, *53, 54, 162, 225, 227*
  See also Case Covers, Leather Covers

Curtains, 275, *58, 81, 98, 101, 103, 104*
  Tête de Versailles, 109
  Tête Hollandaise, 109
  See also Blinds, Case Curtains, Cloak Pins, Continued Drapery, Drapery Curtain, Draw Curtain, Dress Curtain, Festoon Curtain, Pelmet Cornices, Portières, Reefed Curtains, Valances, Venetian Window

Cushions, Squabs, bolsters, 156–, 158, 159, 161, *148, 153, 155–158*

Damask. *See* Material

Dead colour, 179, 205

Decorator, development of the concept of the, 15–, *1–5*
  20th century firms and decorators, 16, 17, 20

Drapery Curtain, 100, 102, 106, *89*
  Fixed Draperies, 121

Draw Curtain, 100, 105, 109, *95*
  French rod, French draw curtain, 47, 109, *96, 121*

Drawings, architectural, 26, 27, *10–13, I*

Dress Curtain, 121

Drawing Room. *See* Uses of Houses

Dressing Room. *See* Uses of Houses

Dropping the Pattern, 138, 215, *118, 138, 190*

Dry scrubbing, 210, 211, 214, 266

Eating habits, use of dining rooms, hours of meals, 56, 60, 63, 65, 66, 67, 68, 75, *44, 45, 46, 47*

Egyptian style, 51, 146, *29, 30, 31*

Engravings, use of, methods of reproduction, 15, 16, 35, 37, 41, 43, 50, 54, 83, 139, 232, *20, 34, 184*

Feather pictures, 248, 251, *219*

Festoon Curtains, 47, 100, 102, 103, 105, 106, 107, 108, 109, 112, 121, 255, *56, 81–85, 87, 91, 92, 93, 97*

Fillets, 32, 118, 124, 126, 202, 203, 207, *49, 75, 109–113*

Flock Paper, 132, 133, 137, *XXI, XXII*

Flock Linen, Canvas, 137

Floors, 71, 210–
  See also Bed Carpets, Brussels Carpet, Carpets Planned to Room, Dry Scrubbing, Fitted Carpets, Floor Cloth, Inlaid Floors

Floor cloth, 216, 217

France, situation in, 25, 37, 41, 42, 45, 46, 50, 53, 56, 67, 72, 83, 139, 141, 144, 178

France, English trade with, 43, 139, 148, 149, *22*

French Influence, 34, 36, 37, 43, 47, 50, 53, 54, 56, 65, 83, 141, 142, 187, 193, 208, 232, *22, 25, 33, 34, 122*

Fringe. *See* Braids

Furniture Arrangement, 21, 35, 68, 71, 72, 74, 75, 76, 262, *1, 2, 5–8, 10, 20, 26, 28, 36, 44, 46, 47, 49, 50, 52, 53, 54, 63, 70, 81, 195, 203, 204, 214, 218, 223, VI, XV, XVIII*
  See also Eating Habits

Gauffrage. *See* Materials

Gilding, 26, 48, 149, 185–, 208, *XXXIV, XXXV, XXXVI, XXXVII, XXXVIII*
  Colours of Gold, 188, 261

Double gilt, 185, 186
Gilding painted furniture, 131, 186
Gilding pilasters, 184, 189, *172*, *III*,
  XXV, *XXXV*
Hatched gilding, 185, *172*
Oil gilding, 185, 186, *173*
Varnished gilding, 187
Water gilding, 185
Graining, 37, 48, 177, 179, 189–, 208, *176*,
  177, *180*, *181*, *183*
  See also Over-Graining
Great Apartment. *See* State Rooms

Hall. *See* Uses of Houses
Hangings, 71, 122–, *114*, *118*, *120*
  Methods of putting up, 123
  Loose hangings, 147
  Puckered hangings, 145, *128*
  See also Borders, Dropping the Pattern,
    Fillets, Leather Hangings, Paning,
    Tent rooms
Harateen. *See* Materials
Heating, damp, 226
  See also Stoves
Hiring, 173
Housekeeping and care of objects, 161,
  254–, 275, 282
  See also Case Covers, Curtains, Covers

Inlaid floors, 37, 85, 211, *17*, *185–188*

Lacquer rooms, 58, 130
Ladies' Work, 222, 248–
Leather Hangings, 130, *115*
Lighting, 71, 81, 171, 172, 220–224, 281,
  168, *194–197*
Line of Upholstery, 149–, *131*, *132*, *137*,
  138, *142*, *143*, *145–147*
Loose Covers, *162*

Marbling, 37, 48, 179, 189–, 208, *15*, *174–
  178*, *182*, *208*
Materials, 131–
  Bizarre silk, 133, *116*
  Caffoy, 71, 107, 131, 132, 162, 204, *90*
  Calimanco, 133
  Camlet, 131, 132, 136
  Check Materials, 161, 162, *159*, *160*
  Damask, 26, 131, 133
  Worsted damask, 133
  White damask, 107, 201, 206
  Nassau damask, 133
  Norwich damask, 133
  Mixed damask, 133

Gauffrage, 132, 133
Harateen, 131, 136
Lutestring, 108, 121, 131, 135, 207, 208
Mohair, 25, 132, 133, 136
Moquette, 132
Moreen, 131, 136
Plush, 132
Sarsnet, 116, 131
Satin, 38, 82, 121, 135, 136, 204, 208,
  18, *II*
Serge, 136
Taffeta, 65, 95, 108, 131, 134, 135, 199,
  201, *117*
Tammy, 108
Velvet, 71, 91, 131
Cut velvet, 131, 162, *69*, *162*, *XI*
Cotton velvet, 132
Stamped woollen velvet, *XIX*
Wool velvet, 71, 131, *133*
Velours de trecht, 131
Watering, 132, 136, 144, *125*, *126*
Mohair. *See* Material
Moreen. *See* Material
Moiré. *See* Material, Watering
Mourning decorations, 170–, *60*, *168*

Nailing, 71, 126, 150, 151, 157–, *49*, *131*,
  132, *134*, *135*, *147*, *150–152*
Needlework, 248

Over-graining, 190

Paint Manuals, 174, 175
Paint Mediums, 176–, 205
Painting Methods, 177–
Paning or Panelling of Materials, 86, 91,
  128, 129, 142, *62*, *124*
Papier Maché, 32, 126, 127, 207
Patent Materials, 32, 154
Patron, 24, 25
Painted Furniture, 206
Painted Floors, 219, *192*, *193*
Pelmet Cornices, 96, 100, 106, 107, 108,
  114, 115, 116, *94*
Pilasters, 184, 189, *172*
Portières, 107, 122, 129, 133, 172, *20*
Picture Hanging, 128, 202, 231–, *15*, *16*,
  118, *201–218*
  Cords, tassels, bows and decorative
    methods of hanging, 206, 233, *200*
  Literary approach to painting, 245
  Copies, 32, 235, 236, *204*, *205*
  Background colours, 204, 205

Reefed curtains, 100, 106, *88*

Restoration, 15, 21, 178, 202, 259–, *170*,
  171, *229–234*
Rococo, 32, 36, 43, 207
Rustic. *See* Uses of Houses

Saloon. *See* Uses of Houses
Satin. *See* Materials
Scagliola, 37, 48, 193, 196, 208, *17*, *182*,
  XXXIX
Scrapes, 178, 198–205
Shellwork, 248, *220*
Sofa bed, 79, 91, *59*, *70*, *157*
State rooms, rooms of parade. *See* Uses of
  Houses
Stoves, 227, 228, *196*, *197*

Tapestry, Use of, 45, *22*
Tassels. *See* Braids
Tent Rooms, 144, 145, *127–130*
Trimmings. *See* Braids
Tufting and buttoning, 150, 151, 155, 156–,
  131, *139–141*, *145*, *146*, *147*, *149*

Uniformity, 65, 161, 199–, 206, *20*, *161*
Upholsterer, 25, 26, 29, 30, 47, 82, 120,
  149, 258, *60*
Upholstery of a chair
  See Cover, Cushions, Line, Tufting
Uses of Houses, 41, 56–, *39–42*, *51*
  Ante-room, 56
  Attic, 63, 78
  Drawing Room, 56, 71, 74, 75, 78
  Dressing Room, 56, 78, 81, *56–58*
  Family rooms, 60, 78
  Hall, 66, 241
  Living room, 75, *51*, *52*, *53*
  Rustic, 63
  Saloon, 56, 71, *26*, *27*
  State Rooms, 56–, *35*, *36*, *38*, *48*
  See also Beds, Canopy, Eating habits

Valances, 47, 86, 88, 91, 96, 106–108, 115,
  141, *68*, *77*, *82*, *90*, *99*, *105–107*, *121*,
  224, *XVII*
Venetian Window, treatment of it, 120,
  121, *107*
Velvet. *See* Materials
Villa, 42, 48, 60, 64

Wallpaper, 26, 32, 47, 65, 78, 123, 124,
  132, 135, 139, 144, 203, *123*, *125*, *126*,
  212
  Plain papers, *203*, *206*
  See also Flock papers